Frieder Meyer-Krahmer (Ed.)

# Innovation and Sustainable Development

## Lessons for Innovation Policies

With 24 Figures
and 6 Tables

Physica-Verlag
A Springer-Verlag Company

Professor Dr. Frieder Meyer-Krahmer
Fraunhofer Institute for
Systems and Innovation Research (ISI)
Breslauer Str. 48
D-76139 Karlsruhe, Germany

We gratefully acknowledge financial contributions to the workshop and this publication from
Friedrich-Ebert-Stiftung
Federal Ministry for Education, Science, Research and Technology, Bonn
Six Countries Programme. The International Innovation Network

ISBN-13:978-3-7908-1038-7 e-ISBN-13:978-3-642-93639-5
DOI: 10.1007/978-3-642-93639-5

Cataloging-in-Publication Data applied for
Die Deutsche Bibliothek - CIP-Einheitsaufnahme
**Innovation and sustainable development:** lessons for innovation policies;
with 6 tables / Frieder Meyer-Krahmer (ed.). - Heidelberg: Physica-Verl., 1998
(Technology, innovation and policy; 6)



Cover design: Erich Kirchner, Heidelberg
SPIN 10655205 88/2202-5 4 3 2 1 0-Printed on acid-free paper

# Foreword

This book is the result of a workshop of the "Six-Countries-Programme - the Innovation Initiative".

The Six-Countries Programme provides an international network which was established in 1975. Since its foundation this programme has succeeded to gather political decision makers, scientists, industrialists and practitioners in innovation for early discussions of topics which later on often have become political "trajectories". The programme aims at a better understanding of innovation processes, their development and at an assessment of the impact of science and technology on public policies and programmes. As participants do not speak as formal representatives of their institution, an informal and confidential atmosphere is created. Thus, through the discussions and the dissemination of the reports the workshops can serve as a catalyst to stimulate experts in the field to engage in analytical and empirical research work focussing on new perspectives or interrelationships, and to motivate decision makers in governments, companies and organisations to participate in a multi-national learning process.

For this publication of the results of a workshop held within the framework of the Six-Countries-Programme the character of workshop papers has decidedly been kept, so as to show the still very open character of the discussion of this topic and also the gaps, deficiencies and necessities for completion not only in scientific analysis but also in political actions. The workshop character also explains why this publication does not aim at a comprehensive treatment of the topic - that would not have been possible in a one and a half day workshop.

Though from the list of open questions that are being put forward at the end of the introductory chapter it becomes evident, that many important topics have not been solved yet, there was consent among the workshop attestants that the concept of sustainable development should be a guiding principle for future innovation policies.

The bringing together of the communities of experts for sustainable development with those for innovation policy was felt to be of value for this aim because it may lead to combined efforts through a better mutual understanding. This provides a reason to publish these workshop-papers to communicate them to a wider audience. The Six-Countries-Programme has definitely played a decisive role in promoting this important topic.

Frieder Meyer-Krahmer
Director, Fraunhofer Institute for Systems and Innovation Research (ISI)

## Table of Contents

## 3. Policy Issues: Requirements and Consequences



## 4. Annex

# 1. Innovation and Sustainable Development: Introduction

# Innovation and Sustainable Development - Lessons for Innovation Policies? Introduction and Overview

*Uwe Kuntze, Frieder Meyer-Krahmer, Rainer Walz*

## 1. Industrial Innovation and Sustainability - Conflicts and Coherence

When the modern industrial economy emerged the natural environment was considered an unlimited resource by industrial managers and most economists - nowadays we know better: the industrial economy needs fundamental re-thinking. A worldwide polluted environment, shrinking natural resources and ever growing social problems call for radically new concepts for the future industrial society. Since 1987 "sustainable development" became a key notion for visions of a production and consumption system that is able to reduce the use of natural resources and to avoid pollution to the maximum possible extent, blaming the simply growth oriented type of industrial technologies.

There are many definitions of sustainability. We use the term here in the sense of the UN WCED's report "Our common future" (1987): "a development which meets the needs of the present without compromising the ability of future generations to meet their own needs". The concept takes on a global perspective and requires to maintain economic development, to eliminate poverty and deprivation, to conserve the environment and to enhance its resource base simultaneously. Furthermore, the opportunities for the less developed countries shall in the long term approach those of the developed countries.

While the operationalisation of "sustainable development" as a concrete policy goal still has to be achieved, some ingredients without doubt are of common understanding:

- emissions and immissions have to be limited to the carrying capacity of the environment;
- in future, primarily renewable resources should be used;
- the use of renewable resources must not be faster than the renewal rate;
- the total stock of non-renewable resources must not be depleted - technologies will need to use renewable resources or substitutes to replace non-renewable resources as they are used up.

In a different strand of discussion industrialists and politicians in the leading industrial countries call for accelerated "industrial innovations" as a powerful source of economic growth and wealth, and they usually mean by that technological innovations. Most existing governmental innovation policies are claiming to foster the industrial (technological) competitiveness as a main target. There still seem to be hardly any policy approaches that aim explicitly at innovation processes conducive to sustainability, and at technical innovations which would achieve or maintain sustainability. At a first glance the goals of sustainable development and industrial innovations, respectively, seem to be conflicting. Even though since some ten or even twenty years there have been substantial efforts worldwide to raise resource productivity, the achievements since then seem to be far away from the level of ecological sustainability (cf. e.g. RMNO 1992; BUND/Misereor 1996). In many OECD-countries industrial innovations aiming at competitiveness and growth are perceived as more important than such aiming at sustainability. But is this necessarily so or under which conditions can the *two concepts come to a significantly better accordance*? This is the focal question of this book.

Research and technology (R&T) policies and in their consequence industrial/technological innovations cannot by themselves establish a socio-economic system which could guarantee sustainable development but they might substantially contribute to this goal, first because of the need for innovations to solve problems of current unsustainable production methods and consumption patterns and, second, because of the need to develop and diffuse a wide range of environmental technologies.

There is a growing realisation in the business community that high standards of environmental performance are not inconsistent with economic performance. At the same time, government and regulators began to appreciate that industry, while the source of pollution and waste, is also the agent through which cleaner production technologies could be applied and diffused. *Agenda 21*, one of the main outputs of the UNCED in 1992, crystallises many of the strands of emerging thinking about the relationship between governments and industry with respect to environmental performance.

*Agenda 21* proposes two programmes relating to business and industry - one on cleaner production, the other on responsible entrepreneurship. The programme to develop responsible entrepreneurship concentrates on the development of enterprises that are managed in line with the principles of sustainable development and calls for an intensification of R&D for cleaner technologies and a cyclic economy. The latter is the main point of the cleaner production programme which aims to increase the efficiency with which natural resources are utilised, by moving towards processes which generate less waste and increase the recycling and re-use of process wastes. Cleaner production technologies are viewed as being distinct from 'clean-up' processes which are applied end-of-pipe and often simply transfer pollution from one environmental medium to another.

On this background *two views of the possibilities to politically solve the conflict between sustainable development and technological innovation* can be found, a sceptical and an optimistic one. These views differ with respect to their assumptions on political lock-in factors (acceptance and implementation problems) and with respect to the extent of expected effects of resource productivity gains and a competition driven structural change conducive to sustainability.

The *sceptical view* e. g. sounds as follows (OECD 1992, p. 206): "As the 'green' discussion in OECD countries shows, there is only partial community of interest within countries, while the social and political mechanisms for articulating the conflicts are fragile and only slowly becoming institutionalised. Outside the OECD area these mechanisms are even more fragile, partly, perhaps, because the conflicts are greater, but, more importantly, because institutions are weaker." Or Skea (1994, p. 424) criticises: "A cynical view would be that *Agenda 21* contains many laudable aspirations but has little to offer in the way of practical measures."

The *optimistic view* assumes that challenges of sustainability, technological innovation and competitiveness are compatible to a large extent - and therefore does not expect major political obstacles to implement a sustainability policy. E. g. Michael Porter and C. van der Linde (1995, pp. 133-134) argue: "Using resources productively is what makes for competitiveness today. Companies can improve resource productivity by producing existing products more efficiently or by making products that are more valuable to customers - products customers are willing to pay more for. ... Because technology is constantly changing, the new paradigm of global competitiveness requires the ability to innovate rapidly. This new paradigm has profound implications for the debate about environmental policy - about how to approach it, how to regulate, and how strict regulation should be. The new paradigm has brought environmental improvement and competitiveness together."

Countries which pre-emptively set high environmental standards, the optimists argue, can establish strong domestic markets for new technologies which may be used as a springboard for international trade when the standards are taken up elsewhere (concept of first mover advantage). Business in Germany, Japan and California has certainly benefited from this phenomenon. Because Germany adopted recycling standards earlier than most other countries, German companies have first-mover advantages in developing, e. g., less packaging-intensive products, which are both lower in cost and sought after in the marketplace. In the United States, Porter and van der Linde argue, Cummins Engine Company's development of low-emissions diesel engines for such applications as trucks and buses - innovation that U.S. environmental regulations spurred - is allowing it to gain position in international markets where similar needs are growing.

The optimistic view emphasises the role of technology as having enough argumentative power to make concrete policies feasible. The sceptical one is focused on inabilities of the political system and lock-in effects of several subsystems driven by

"Schumpeter dynamics" (Krupp 1992). Implicitly, Western policy favours the optimistic view. Though the importance of environmental goals is recognised, the Maastricht Treaty also indicates that policies to support environmental sustainability must be compatible with the goal of improving the competitiveness of European industry. The basis of these - highly simplified - views are a set of different concepts on innovation and sustainability. Table 1 gives a (selective) overview.

Table 1: Innovation and Sustainability

| **Approach** | **Main Elements** | **Authors** |
|---|---|---|
| Environmental economics | Application of neo-classical theory to environmental problems<br>Concentration on allocation rules, internalisation of external effects | Coase<br>Baumol/Oates<br>Siebert |
| Productivity approach | Resource efficiency | Porter<br>Lovins<br>v.Weizsäcker |
| Schumpeterian approach | Reorientation of trajectories<br>Complex learning processes<br>Institutional change<br>Innovation strategies and qualitative growth | Freeman<br>Krupp |
| Ecological economics | Co-evolution of human preferences, technology, organisation, and ecological conditions<br>Integration of ecological dimensions into economic theory (scale, time dynamics, carrying capacity)<br>Distribution issues: equal living conditions of world's population, intergenerational equity | Daly<br>Costanza<br>Martinez Alier |

Underlying such concepts as well as innovation and environmental policies there are often implicit *assumptions on different future development paths* which seem necessary to be discussed. These assumptions are dealing with:

- Economic development: growth, trade, globalisation and competition;

- Social and demographic assumptions: world population, family structures and policies, availability of resources, patterns of societal organisation;
- Welfare and distribution: migration, international distribution of wealth and income, living opportunities and consumption patterns;
- The political system: adaptivity, flexibility, lock-in effects;
- 'Driving forces': capitalistic exploitation, irreversible processes, evolutionary processes, Schumpeter dynamics, public and private liberties.

Taking into consideration these dimensions of assumptions three different development paths (scenarios) up to the year 2050 and beyond with different conditions and consequences can be distinguished (cf. table 2 which exemplifies this primarily with considerations concerning climate change). These scenarios are highly simplified and should rather illustrate the range of alternatives than being results of a systematic and consistent analysis:

- In the scenario of **Global Crash** (the Darwin path) world population would continue to grow while the slow world wide increase of resource productivity would not be able to compensate population growth. Emissions of $CO_2$ and other greenhouse gases would increase because specific reductions were compensated by an increase of economic activities. The consequences would be climate changes which would lead to the inundation of coastal zones and growing desertification, military conflicts for energy, water, food, etc., high migration movements, and the death of several billions of humans because of hunger, epidemics, and wars. The role of innovation policy for sustainable development could only be characterized as insignificant in this scenario.

- The scenario of **Regionally Limited Crises** with growing North/South inequality is very much characterised by the same features as the Global Crash scenario but for the assumption that there would be limited efforts to increase resource productivity; these efforts, though, would not suffice to avoid climate change and degradation of large parts of the world. A central thesis of this scenario is that the negative consequences would be controlled and regionally limited by a coalition of hegemonial OECD nations. Thus, the industrialised countries would adapt to climate change in their own countries and would increase their interventions to contain the increasing turmoil to the other countries. The death toll therefore would also be limited to the most degraded areas and would reach the number of several hundred millions. The role of innovation policy would consist of initiating technical *and* social solutions to adapt to climate change (e.g. relocation of cities, construction of large dams, ...); furthermore, environmental technologies and solutions to increase resource productivity would be supported. In addition, there were still trust in large scale technological solutions, and innovation policy would be directed to strategies like $CO_2$-dumping in world oceans.

Table 2: Scenarios of Global Development to the Year 2050 and Further

| Global Crash (Darwin path) | Regionally Limited Crises With Growing North/South Inequality | Equality (Humanity path) |
|---|---|---|
| **What could be going to happen?** | | |
| | | *a substantial change of values and consciousness towards equality would be organized by a majority of states |
| * world population will continue to grow | * world population will continue to grow | *world population can be stabilised through birth control and a substantial rise of the welfare level in the less developed countries |
| * no systematic policy to increase resource efficiency | * limited efforts to increase resource productivity, mostly in industrialised countries | *resource productivity will grow to a sustainable level through technical and organisational/ behavioural innovations |
| * world-wide resource productivity growth will not be able to compensate population growth and increase in economic activities | * industrial countries: resource productivity growth compensates increase in economic activities, but no substantial reduction of resource use<br>developing countries: increase in resource use | *substantial changes in life-styles reduce resource use |
| *emisssions of CO2 and other climate gases will increase because reductions are being compensated by an increase of economic activities in almost all countries | *emissions of greenhouse gases will be limited somewhat in Western countries, but increase in developing countries will lead to substantial worldwide increase | *emissions of greenhouse gases will decline substantially in Western countries and will be stabilised in developing countries |

| | | |
|---|---|---|
| **What would be the consequences?** | | |
| | negative consequences will be controlled and regionally limited by a coalition of hegemonial OECD states | |
| * climate changes leading to the inundation of coastal zones and growing desertification | *adaptation measures to climate change in OECD countries | *the inundation of coastal zones and growing desertification can be partially avoided, although it is not clear yet if the processes initiated have already reached a state of irreversibility |
| * military conflicts for resources (energy, water, food, ...) | regionally limited | *interregional and international conflicts can be solved through negotiation |
| * high migration movements | regionally limited | *a moderate level of migration causes more equality in living conditions (knowledge to the South, fresh blood to the North) |
| * death of several billions of humans because of hunger, epidemics, and wars | *death of several hundred millions of humans in degraded areas because of hunger, epidemics, and wars | *the death rate due to hunger and epidemics can be lowered substantially |
| **What is the role of innovation policy for sustainable development?** | | |
| * insignificant, but for military technology | *initiate technical and social solutions to *adapt* to climate change (e.g. relocation of cities, construction of large dams, ...) | *contribute to a very early change of technologies, organisations, behaviour and frame conditions to avoid expected disasters and frictions |
| | *support environmental technologies and solutions to increase resource productivity | *worldwide consensus to direct technological innovation primarily towards an increase in resource efficiency |
| | *emphasis on large scale technological innovations; examples:<br>CO2 dumping in world oceans<br>highly condensed cities | *social and institutional innovations play a key role |

- The **Equality** scenario (humanity path) indicates the consequences of the main assumptions of the advocates of sustainability: equal living conditions and resource consumption opportunities world wide and between generations. In this scenario all actors would follow their global responsibility so that the world population could be stabilised, emissions would be reduced dramatically so that the greenhouse effect would come to a standstill, conflicts would be solved through negotiation, hunger and epidemics would almost completely have vanished, and living conditions in less developed countries would have risen considerably. The main role of innovation policy in this scenario would be to contribute to a very early change of technologies, organisations, behaviour and frame conditions avoiding expected disasters and frictions. Social and institutional innovations would play a key role in this scenario, implying a substantial reduction in the material standard of living in industrialised countries.

It is unavoidable that conclusions on the role of innovation policy, its design and appropriate instruments are highly path-dependent. The papers in this book do not refer explicitly to a specific scenario and do not explicitly outline their respective set of assumptions. Implicitly, though, it becomes clear that most of us regard the "Equality" scenario as being unlikely from today's perspectives and hope that the "Global Crash" scenario can be avoided. As a consequence, a scenario in between the extremes - though not necessarily the one outlined above - turned out to be the common ground in the papers and during the discussions at the workshop.

## 2. Three Paths of Industrial Technological Innovation Towards Environmental Sustainability

At present, a fundamental and widespread dissociation of the consumption of resources from economic growth cannot foreseeably be achieved. Although a change of resource elasticities can definitely be observed over the last decade for some resources and pollutants, nevertheless, the specific efficiency successes are very often more than compensated even by a moderate economic growth (Walz et al. 1992). In addition, it has to be kept in mind that even a reduced pressure on the environment might be much above the carrying capacity, expecially when accumulating and persistent effects are regarded.

Therefore new industrial models for an environmentally acceptable economy are needed which are not only desirable, but also (both for enterprises and consumers) economically attractive, so that they have a chance of being realised. We differentiate three models of this kind:

- more extensive use of environmentally acceptable technologies (end-of-pipe as well integrated) as a traditional model

- the closing of materials cycles
- the integration of product policy and product use.

It has been shown that the more extensive use of environmentally acceptable technologies is resulting in substantial environmental relief and has furthermore brought economic success to the Federal Republic of Germany, which for a number of years was the largest exporter of environmental technologies (now second). Table 3 provides several examples of the environmental benefits from cleaner processes and lower input/output ratios that could result from using information technology to develop real-time sensor devices. In another example Jochem and Hohmeyer (1992) illustrate the argument with data for Germany which shows that German exports of energy saving products increased in the 1980s at twice the rate of all other industrial exports. These successes may be regarded as being due to congruent interests in activities of research efforts, environmental legislation, innovative enterprises and existing acceptance of technology. The basic problem with this model is that, on its own, more extensive use of environmentally acceptable technologies does not produce enough of the probably necessary efficiency gains for an environmentally sustainable economy.

There are already several examples of the closing of materials cycles in production which represent economically interesting options (including utilisation cascades). The present massive efforts towards establishing recycling economics also follow this model; its limits are set largely by the fact that the reconversion of products into raw materials and into secondary materials that are reintroduced into the production process still represents a relatively wide "cycle" whereas for sustainability reasons the cycle should be as narrow as possible which means on as high a level as possible (cf. figure 3 in the contribution of Frieder Meyer-Krahmer in this volume) and with a possible minimum of additional transport demand.

The shift from production responsibility to product responsibility, which is laid down in various waste management or "ecocycle" laws of Six Countries Programme member countries, brings with it a fundamental change in the model of "integrated product policy". In this context, environmentally acceptable management does not simply denote "defensive" protection of the environment (e.g. the observance of regulations) but also brings about an opportunity for enterprises to adopt new innovation and business strategies. This strategic change can be made possible or supported by changes, e.g. in the price system (internalisation of external costs from the consumption of resources), public regulation, voluntary agreements, public procurement programmes and changes in consumer behaviour. It is these entrepreneurial innovation strategies which will really determine the dynamics of the path towards an environmentally acceptable economy under conditions of partially regulated market economies. The conflicts of this model will be primarily determined by the winners and losers emerging from the structural change it initiates.

Table 3: Selected Examples of the Potential Environmental Benefits from R&D Investment in Electronic Sensor Technology

| *Technical Measure* | *Environmental Effects* |
|---|---|
| ***A. Cleaner Processes*** | |
| Reduction of combustion air in rotary cement kilns | 20% reduction of $NO_x$ emissions |
| Improved control techniques for process heat and electricity generation | 10%-20% reduction of $SO_2$ and $NO_2$ emissions |
| Improved control techniques for domestic hot water heaters | 10% reduction of $CO_2$ emissions |
| ***B. Reduction of Input/Output Ratios*** | |
| On-line control of chemical nickel baths in electro-plating by measuring the pH value and nickel content | 2-3 fold increase in the lifetime of the bath |
| On-board control of following distance for vehicles on highways | 2-3 fold increase in vehicle throughput (reduces need for |
| new highway infrastructure) | |
| Automatic dosing of separate detergent ingredients for washing machines | 50% reduction of washing agents, 10% reduction of energy and water use |
| On-line measurement of plastic sheets | 2%-10% reduction in consumption of raw materials |

Source: ISI (Angerer, 1992)

## 3. Technology Policy and Environmental Sustainability

The use of science and technology policies to achieve environmental goals constitutes a new focus for technology policy.* At a first glance, this requires a return to the emphasis in the 1950s and 1960s on public goals that were met through mission-oriented projects (Ergas 1987). However, there is a fundamental difference between older mission-oriented projects, for example nuclear, defence, and aerospace pro-

* The following are results of a series of expert group meetings one of the authors participated in, which were edited by Soete, Arundel (1993).

grammes, and new projects to support environmentally sustainable development. The older projects developed radically new technologies through government intervention that was largely isolated from the rest of the economy, though it frequently affected the structure of related industries and could lead to new spin-off technologies that had wide-spread effects on other sectors. In contrast, modern mission-oriented environmental projects will need to combine many policies, including procurement, in order to have pervasive effects on the entire structure of production and consumption within an economy (see also Lahaye, Llerena 1996; Jaffe et al. 1995; Lévêque 1996).

The pervasive character of new mission-oriented projects to meet environmental goals calls for a systemic approach to policy. This approach results in substantial changes to the mission-oriented projects of the past. Table 4 summarises the key characteristics and differences between the old and new models of mission-oriented projects. It is not difficult to denote the elements of such a policy. When discussing the constituent conditions for realisation at the workshop, the empirical evidence made clear that these conditions are still not fulfilled. Many of these policy characteristics have been discussed since the beginning of the 70s without significant effects on policy practice.

The achievement of the goal of environmentally sustainable development depends on the active participation of a wide range of institutions and firms in the search for new technologies. This requires a network approach to research and procurement to support the rapid diffusion and assimilation of information.

Policy intervention could guide the continual search by industry for innovations towards environmentally beneficial directions and help to create a self-reinforcing process in which additional research for new technical solutions follow environmental pathways. There are four main policy tools for guiding investment and innovation:

(1) Direct regulation through emission and product quality standards and regulated limits for the permissible use of a product.

(2) Economic instruments to attach the externality costs of pollution to the inputs and outputs of production.

(3) Procurement policies to speed up the use or development of environmentally beneficial technologies within private firms.

(4) Policies to influence the types of technologies that are socially and economically feasible. The latter include educational programmes, support for organisations that can influence consumer and producer behaviours, and Constructive Technology Assessment (CTA) to promote a dialogue among the users, producers and social groups which will be affected by a new technology.

Table 4: Characteristics of Old and New "Mission-Oriented" Projects

| *Old: Defence, Nuclear and Aerospace* | *New: Environmental Technologies* |
|---|---|
| The mission is defined in terms of the number of technical achievements with little regard to their economic feasibility | The mission is defined in terms of economically feasible technical solutions to particular environmental problems. |
| • The goals and the direction of technological development are defined in advance by a small group of experts. | • The direction of technical change is influenced by a wide range of actors including government, private firms and consumer groups. |
| • Centralised control within a government administration. | • Decentralised control with a large number of involved agents. |
| • Diffusion of the results outside of the core of participants is of minor importance or actively discouraged. | • Diffusion of the results is a central goal and is actively encouraged. |
| • Limited to a small group of firms that can participate owing to the emphasis on a small number of radical technologies. | • An emphasis on the incrementalist development of both radical and incremental innovations in order to permit a large number of firms to participate. |
| • Self-contained projects with little need for complementary policies and scant attention paid to coherence | • Complementary policies vital for success and close attention paid to coherence with other goals. |

Source: Soete, Arundel (1993, p. 51)

The best combination of each of these policy tools will depend on technology- or group-specific conditions and obstacles. An important goal would be to encourage long-term solutions such as cleaner process technologies or the complete substitution of process chains that substantially reduce the production of waste products at the source.

The rapid diffusion of environmentally beneficial technologies could be enhanced by programmes to increase the number of people that are knowledgeable about an innovation and who can apply it to the needs of the private sector. Procurement, demonstration and technology transfer programmes can help by increasing the number of individuals who know how to use and apply a developing technology.

Because of the large number of technologies and application contexts policy makers lack the information and/or knowledge necessary to determine what types of innovations would best solve given problems. Programmes to develop environmentally benign technologies, therefore, need to ensure that the widest possible range of potentially beneficial technologies is considered for development. Research and procurement programmes should include innovating firms, the potential users of new products and processes, public research institutions, and non-governmental organisations. In addition, government research programmes should include a large number of firms that could potentially benefit from a technology in order to ensure exploration of a wide range of potential applications. This last point is particularly important, given the importance of knowledge and the different and often unique ways in which technologies are utilised by different firms.

These goals could be achieved by the imposition of relatively short development times for each technical advance, severe limits on project sizes, low capital investment levels for each project, and a minimum need for a dedicated infrastructure. These criteria would permit the participation of a wide range of firms and research institutions and would lower costs, thereby allowing parallel research projects in a given area of technology. Both would increase the opportunities for a large number of people to critically evaluate the technology, either through the market or other means, and to use the results of these evaluations to guide further technical developments. Such project criteria, however, primarily lead to technological incrementalism, and the investigation of further reaching technologies or non-technical solutions may even be precluded. Therefore, selection criteria should also include: a substantial reduction of emissions, with possibly lower overall costs (e.g. through process substitution), higher resource productivity and lower end-of-pipe costs.

The goal of environmentally sustainable development requires a wide range of complementary policies to support investment in new environmentally benign technologies and the rapid diffusion of successful applications. The most comprehensive approach to formulate a coherent policy towards environmental sustainability can be found in the various "green plans" (Johnson 1995). Green plans are long-term environmental strategies which replace traditional single-issue policies through a workable plan for environmental prosperity. A successful green plan is comprehensive: it aims at considering all aspects of the environment and is developed through consultation with all relevant actors in society.

The most prominent example, the Dutch National Environmental Policy Plan (NEPP, VROM 1993, cf. also the contribution of Paul E. de Jongh in this volume), is "characterised by a management approach to environmental problems involving:

- adoption of quantified (measurable) targets and time frames;
- the integration of the environment into decision making by all sectors of society;

- clear identification of responsibility for actions;
- creativity in the design and use of policy instruments;
- a commitment to long-term reshaping of social and economic structures;
- recognition of the Netherlands' dependence on international co-operation and action.

The overall goal of the NEPP is sustainability by the year 2010. In order to reach this goal, each of the environmental themes sets quality objectives for this date (or the year 2000) and defines the percentage reduction in key pollutants that will be required to meet them. For example a 'sustainable' level of acidification is defined as requiring a reduction in acid emissions of 70 to 80 per cent on 1985 levels.

The overall theme objectives of the NEPP are broken down further into numerous reduction targets for specified substances and waste streams. Responsibility for achieving these emission reduction targets lies with target groups. Target groups represent the key groups of polluters in Dutch society, for example, the industrial, agricultural and construction sectors. A continuing effort of environmental policy in the Netherlands is to agree on the division of responsibility for achieving specific targets (e. g. $NO_x$ reduction) between target groups and between members of target groups."

One of the elements of this action programme is to use technological innovation and technology policy, too. However: "Technology can never be more than a tool, an instrument among others; and the type of technology that will be developed is very much dependent on the structural and cultural conditions that prevail in society. This is the starting point for a programme that aims to explore the unused potential of technology." (Vergragt, Jansen 1993, p. 136). This Dutch programme on Sustainable Technology Development (DTO, Duurzame Technologische Ontwikkeling) drafted an action plan for technology development under guidance of the long-term vision to achieve sustainability until the middle of the next century. This goal determines "that in a sustainable world the per capita emissions of pollutants and consumption of resources will have to be reduced, generally, to something less than 10 per cent of the present levels practiced in the Western, industrialized world" (DTO 1994). Because such a dramatic goal cannot be achieved through further incremental progress in environmental technologies, the programme recognizes that developments are needed in the three dimensions technology, structure and culture. The first phase of the programme (1990-1994) concentrated on developing an approach to innovations for sustainability. "The result of the STD-programme will not yet be 'sustainable technologies', but 'manuals' that teach the concerned parties how to innovate towards sustainability" (DTO 1994).

While new opportunities and indeed whole new paradigms could be opened up by technology, technological trajectories will be shaped by the decisions which determine future costs of production and patterns of economic activity. To the extent that environmental concerns take a central place in policymaking, environmentally driven technologies (affecting innovation, diffusion, and technological paradigms) may shift industrial structures and competitive advantages, both nationally and internationally. At the same time, there is widespread evidence of market failure with existing price signals: much environmental investment would be profitable but is not undertaken, for reasons that seem to involve market structures, corporate cultures and investment time horizons, given present price signals and rates of reward to environment friendly measures by firms.

Technology policy can become an increasingly important instrument in attaining environmental objectives. More cross-sectoral, multi-disciplinary approaches are called for. Consistent strategies for funding research on technologies to improve industrial and other sectors' (e.g. transport) performance and environmental quality need to be expanded, and co-operative research programmes among countries should be promoted. Funding research and development is, however, not sufficient. The appropriate mix of regulatory and market incentives that spur firms and consumers in environmentally desirable directions must be identified. This will require both shifts in political priorities and more research on how to target the incentives to obtain the desired results. However, a careful policy analysis has to include policy dilemmata (e.g. lock-in-effects, symbolic policy) and the logic of political decision making to identify feasibility conditions and implementation obstacles more systematically than this has been done in the past.

## 4. Contradictions, Inconsistencies and Open Questions: the Outset of the Discussion

In a selective and simplifying way one can observe the following contradictions and inconsistencies in the field of innovation and sustainability:

(1) The term innovation was defined originally in a very broad sense integrating technical, behavioural, organisational and institutional change (Schumpeter). In the meantime, the 'modern' terminology is highly limited. Innovation is used mostly in terms of technical innovation neglecting a broad range of economic, social and political contexts (nevertheless it is apparent that social innovation is as important (or more) as technical innovation). The situation is totally different in the field of sustainability. The various chapters of *Agenda 21*, the common basis for political discussions on sustainable development, rather contain a broad list of relevant problems than a precise definition. The search for indicators of sustainable development has produced a number of totally different approaches (Walz et al. 1995). The indicator list of the Com-

mission for Sustainable Development (CSD), perhaps closest to a consensus, contains much more than hundred, partially extremely broad and complex indicators covering economic, social, environmental, and institutional aspects. On the other hand, economists have taken another path transforming sustainable development into an academic debate on the substitution between natural and man-made capital (weak or strong sustainability). Thus, the concept of sustainable development is still extremely broad and vague. That means on the level of terminology both concepts are far from being compatible in terms of conceptional thinking, precision and consistency.

(2) Technology policy is focused mostly on R&D, hard- or software. Sustainability requests an approach which is far beyond R&D and technology and includes economic and institutional change, new economic and social incentive structures, government regulation etc. Technology and innovation policy in such a perspective needs an intersectoral (cross-sectional) approach. But in many countries technology policy is an element of a vertical fragmented policy system and stands in significant contradiction to such a systemic and integrative approach.

(3) On the other hand, in many countries environmental policy cares primarily for short-term environmental problems only which translate into additional votes. The sustainability concept has so far not been translated into an operational environmental policy frame. Furthermore, the incentives for technology development affected by environmental policy are still not clearly defined. Insofar, environmental policy ignores conditions and processes of innovations. Environmental Economics in its pure form cannot serve as a base for policymaking either: it is based on simplified assumptions and neglects both the institutional and political setting and the uncertainty, complexity, and irreversibility of (global) environmental problems.

(4) Radical ecologists demand for a highly moral code of conduct (such as equal distribution of living opportunities in the world) and very often do not consider the consequences of social and world economic interdependencies. Wishful thinking dominates realistic visions. Ecological Economics challenges traditional economics but is still far from both establishing a new paradigm of economic thinking and being applicable for policy making (yet).

The main lessons which can be drawn from these contradictions and inconsistencies are that an innovation policy for sustainability is far from being conceptionalised adequately. A systemic approach is needed which integrates change of behaviour, structural change, regulations, incentives and technologies. Technology (and innovation) policy for sustainability has to overcome the inherent limitations of technology policy developing a comprehensive approach of a broad range of different policies (technology, price system, attitudes and behaviour, incentives, regulations etc.), different subsystems and actors (public, semi-public bodies, firms, banks, research institutes etc.) on different levels (regional, national, international). This creates a series of policy dilemmata. Consequently, the workshop was not simply to look for improved approaches to the protection of the natural environment, and it was not mainly to deal with new tools of "environmental management" of industrial companies. The aims of this workshop were more ambitious: it should provide room for *fundamental considerations* and debates of the relationship between innovation and sustainability which implies also that *conflicting positions* were put forward, including a discussion of the role of political regulation and legislation as a medium for sustainability-oriented innovations.

## 5. The Contributions to this Book

When we prepared this workshop, our main assumptions on innovation and sustainable development were the following (they are only indicated here because they are mostly self-explaining):

- In the last decade, the ecological situation in many areas became worse, though also improvements can be found.
- In many countries, environmental policies did not push sustainable development as much as the Rio and Berlin conferences promised.
- Industrial innovation is a necessary but not sufficient condition for sustainable development.
- From these findings it follows that the need for industrial innovations has rather risen. But industrial innovation is conducive to sustainable development only to a limited extent. Under the present economic conditions innovation is primarily seen to be an engine of growth and productivity. In this context, industrial innovation is mostly short-term oriented. Therefore, severe contradictions between innovation and sustainable development exist.

Therefore, we resume that the present practice of industrial innovation still stands in significant contradiction to sustainable development. It is an (or the) important dynamic engine for economic development. How can it be adapted to sustainability and under which conditions is this possible? This was the main leading question of the workshop and this book.

The concept of sustainable development basically takes on a global perspective. For the *Six Countries workshop*, however, it was proposed to concentrate on the perspectives of industrialised countries so that the discussion would not become too wide. Therefore, the workshop was structured around three blocks of papers and discussions:

(1) The concept of environmental sustainability and its consequences for production and consumption

(2) Guiding principles for sustainable industrial innovations and practical examples

(3) Policy issues: requirements and consequences.

The papers included in this volume discuss various aspects of this set of questions.

In his paper "Can a Market Economy Produce Industrial Innovations that Lead to Environmental Sustainability?" ***Paul Ekins*** argues along the assumptions that industrial innovations are necessary to achieve environmental sustainability, that a market economy can produce enough innovations for this aim and that this will not happen automatically within the current system so that much of the paper explores some possible answers to the question: What kinds of policies and intervention in the market economy are required? While this probably represents the mainstream set of assumptions, they are not entirely uncontroversial.

"If industrial innovation is required to move towards environmental sustainability, and it is also the root source of economic growth, the question then arises as to what kind of innovation will achieve each of these very different objectives, and how it might be stimulated, and whether innovations for environmental sustainability are likely to be compatible or inconsistent with those for economic growth and vice versa." *Paul Ekins* concludes that in itself, innovation need not be of particular benefit to the environment. There are plenty of new products and technologies which cause environmental damage, while the economic growth to which innovation gives rise can also pull more energy and materials through the economic system to the detriment of the environment.

According to *Ekins*, markets should be directed, however, "by appropriate policies to encourage moves towards sustainable development, preferably by the use of the price mechanism. However, price changes need to be both gradual and anticipated if they are to avoid economic disruption. Firms must be given the time, and perhaps financial support, to develop a new generation of low environmental impact products and technologies."

*Ekins* mentions other policy instruments which can and should be used to reinforce the unremitting signals from the price mechanism, e.g. corporate environmental accounting, environmental management systems, regulations and voluntary agreements. He presents "some evidence that shows that such instruments need not cause costs to a firm. Sometimes, by encouraging innovation, they can lead to cost-savings which improve corporate performance. However, the evidence suggests that, contrary to assumptions in the past, innovation can enable firms to move towards environmental sustainability at low, if not negative, cost. For consumers, the main reinforcement to price signals will be from the provision of information which brings about attitude changes towards environmental destruction, and enables consumers to express new environmental concerns through their purchasing habits."

***Frieder Meyer-Krahmer*** presents in his paper "Industrial Innovation Strategies - Towards an Environmentally Sustainable Industrial Economy" three guiding principles of environmental policy for an environmentally sustainable economy:

- increased use of environmentally friendly technology as traditional principle
- closing of industrial material cycles
- holistic product policies and product utilisation.

He demonstrates that the increased use of environmentally friendly technology has resulted in considerable advantages for the environment but will not produce the degree of efficiency which is probably required for an environmentally sustainable economy. Though the closing of material cycles makes economic sense (the present gigantic efforts to set up a recycling economy also follow this model), its limitations are that the reconversion from goods into raw materials and secondary materials which can be re-utilised in the production process still represents a relatively wide "cycle" (which means losses in resource efficiency). The transition from production responsibility to product liability causes a basic change in the direction to the guiding principle "holistic product policy", which can be regarded as symptomatic for an environmentally sustainable industry.

These guiding principles, however, are not only desirable from a point of view of environmental policy, but are also attractive for the participants in economic activities (enterprises and consumers alike) under market economy conditions. Therefore, they have good chances to be realised and will mean a really substantial change for the better in our environmental conditions.

Assuming market economy conditions also for a sustainability scenario, the guiding principles described above will only have a chance of being realised if they meet economic profitability criteria and do not deteriorate the competitiveness of enterprises. In fact, such impulses arise from the implementation of rules that will increasingly force enterprises in Germany as well as in other industrial states, at the beginning of the 21st century, to take over not only the external costs of their production but also the external costs of their products. As a consequence of the anticipated obligation to take back their products after use, they will be increasingly confronted with the necessity to optimize the utilisation and life period of these same products which means to establish holistic product policies.

*Frieder Meyer-Krahmer* argues that a longer active life for products has considerable impacts on the economic structural change, the way to deal with the existing stock of goods (stock management), as well as on research and development.

Impulses for this shift in strategy may be changes in the price system (internalisation of external costs of resource utilisation), state regulations, voluntary self-regulation and changes in consumer behaviour. In his view, such entrepreneurial innovation strategies will determine the essential dynamics of the way towards environmentally sustainable economics under market economy conditions.

"The Firm's Perspective of Industrial Innovation Strategies towards an Environmentally Sustainable Industrial Economy" was presented by ***Jacqueline Cramer.*** She argues, if one wants to make greater eco-efficient strides in environmental areas, there are two things needed to do: 1. Stimulate research into function-oriented innovations and, 2. Support practical initiatives which lead to far-reaching modernisation of the current production techniques.

Implementation of these initiatives in practice necessitates not only technical but also economic, socio-organisational and broad social change processes. The more radical the environmental innovation, the *higher the risk* and the *more complex* such change processes prove to be. It involves a complex process of weighing up interests and negotiating between the participating groups in the process chain or in society so that a choice can be made that is acceptable to all parties.

"It is clear therefore that needs have to coincide both within the company and outside it if far-reaching environmental improvements are to take place. This is why we cannot just expect large numbers of companies to take initiatives of this sort off their own bat. There are some front runners which do after all play an essential role in the acceleration of change processes. Encouragement of the front runners is certainly not exclusively a task for the government but also for consumer bodies and environmental groups as well as the financial world."

***Walter R. Stahel*** in his paper "Business Strategies for a Sustainable Society" sets out from the observation that there are indications that the industrial economy is no longer efficiently catering for our needs: (a) the part of goods that go directly from production to disposal has reached 30% in some sectors; (b) the number of goods that are disposed of is comparable to the number of goods sold, for many products, indicating a substitution of wealth rather than an increase in wealth; (c) technological progress is still focused on production, not on utilization; (d) for many goods, increases in efficiency through system break-down are comparable to increases in efficiency through product innovation (e.g. safety through traffic jams v. air bags). As a counter-image he sketches a service economy as being "fundamentally different from the industrial economy in that its main objective is to maintain or increase total wealth and welfare, i.e. the monetary and non-monetary assets of society, over long periods of time. Its focal point is the optimization of utilization, i.e. of the performance and the results achieved with goods, rather than the goods themselves. In the case of the mandatory or voluntary take-back of goods, the new economic objective for industry now becomes to maximize profits through the re-use of components and goods, instead of the old minimization of costs in recycling and disposal of goods.

Wealth management, new corporate and industrial design strategies, and different economic policies can lead to a higher sustainability as well as an increased international competitiveness due to a substantially higher resource productivity." Some of the key issues of an industrial policy for sustainability he summarizes as follows:

(1) introduce the factor 'time' into the legislation governing the economy

(2) increase the self-responsibility of economic actors
- through a product responsibility 'from cradle to the next cradle',
- by replacing mandatory technical standards by mandatory free market safety-nets, thus introducing the insurability of risks as the main criterion for an economic choice between technological options,
- by eliminating subsidies and incentives for economies of scale which often hide diseconomies of risk

(3) introduce self-correcting taxation loops in the economy: tax resource consumption and waste instead of labour, thus rewarding all sufficiency and efficiency solutions (and eliminating the discrimination of 'voluntary work', 'moonlighting' and 'non-productive work' at the same time).

Presenting Examples from Sweden, ***Lars J. Nilsson*** provides "Experiences from Energy Markets" for the topic "Services instead of Products". The overall objective of energy systems is to provide energy services, at affordable cost and without socially unacceptable side effects. More efficient use of fuels and electricity is a key strategy in a transition to more sustainable energy systems. The challenge to society is finding ways of accelerating the development of energy efficient technologies and in particular their market introduction and widespread use. Historically, end-use energy efficiency and other value-added services has not been a high priority with many consumers and suppliers of fuels and electricity. Governments and publicly owned utilities have attempted to improve the situation through taxes, regulation, Demand-Side-Management (DSM) programmes, R&D support, and other policy measures. Improving efficiency in the end-use of energy is one of the least expensive ways of improving the situation with respect to energy related environmental and other problems. A saved kWh does not, in most cases, contribute to, for example, climatic change or increased reliance on imported fuels.

Electricity markets, and to some extent gas markets, are subject to reform in many countries. He shows, increased competition in electricity markets does not remove any of the traditional barriers to energy efficiency. However, policy measures to promote energy efficiency in deregulated markets must be adapted to the new situation. Governments must learn to influence the market forces and thereby contribute to transforming the market for energy efficiency. There are some indications from

Sweden that the electricity market reform has induced utilities to become more customer and service oriented. Deregulated energy markets, in combination with appropriate government intervention and increasing environmental awareness among consumers, may prove to be better suited than monopoly markets to achieve many of the goals set up by society for the development of energy systems.

Turning explicitly to ***policy issues***, there were contributions from two colleagues who are directly involved in policy making themselves. Paul E. de Jongh has played a key role in the design of the world's first "Green Plan", the Dutch NEPP, whereas Erkki Ormala as the Secretary General of the Science and Technology Policy Council of Finland is responsible for directing research and technology policies towards the aims which were politically decided, e.g. sustainable development. The third contribution to this topic by Uwe Kuntze takes an analytical-descripitive point of view from outside on to research and technology policies and sustainable development. That it is included into this publication only as an annex is due to the fact that it was not originally initiated as a contribution to the workshop, though it ideally fits into the subjects discussed.

***Paul E. de Jongh*** describes "The Policy Concept behind the Dutch National Environmental Policy Plans" and highlights the role that the preparation process for the World Conference on Environment and Development in Rio de Janairo 1992, played. Concerning the role of industrial innovation for sustainable development, *Paul de Jongh* stresses the role of the involvment of target-groups in the implementation of the NEPP; the NEPP also indicated that covenants might be a good way of implementing the plan. For the representatives of industry, the commitment to the implementation of the NEPP was related to direct involvement in the implementation strategies, because the main reason for cooperation from their side was to "buy certainty" (of at least to reduce uncertainty) about government's actions.

At the other hand, doubts remain until results are shown. Environmental groups and members of Parliament were very skeptical in the beginning of the process. The covenants do not replace the licensing procedures, but are managements tools on top of the "normal" licensing. As the Environmental Management Act asks for update of licenses every four to five year, and as the covenants are worked out by corporations in corporate and facility improvement plans, these plans fit in the licensing procedures for updating. Joint monitoring is an important element in the overall process of implementation.

Essential for the Dutch approach is the focus on environmental problems and the physical solutions (measures to be taken), the costs of solutions, and not on policy instruments as such. Policy instruments are seen as to be adapted according to the type of target-group, to the stage of implementation of policies, and to the restrictions in national and international political contexts. Also essential is the focus on integration of measures in relation to stakeholders interests; the continuity of the stakeholders business is never questioned, only the way this continuity is achieved is in discussion.

In the consensus building process scientific information is of crucial importance. Scientific information should be as politically and ideologically neutral as possible (focussing on causes and effects, including economic effects of proposed measures) and as much based on consensus in the scientific community as possible. Scientific information always consists of an amount of uncertainty; this should not be hidden away for policy makers, but should play an explicit role in the design of policies. The constant monitoring of costs, emissions and environmental qualities is a way to deal with uncertainties; contingency plans are another way to answer uncertainties in a sensible way.

It was recognized in the Netherlands that every player in the area of environmental policy-development had his of her own function in this development. Although environmental groups always will argue for stricter and quicker solutions for environmental problems, they are not adversaries in the political process. The direct contact between promoters and adversaries can be an important management tool to change adversaries into stakeholders.

***Erkki Ormala*** in his paper "The Role of RTD Policy and the Adequate Policy Mix - Comprehensive Policy Approaches and Problems of Implementation" is very operational on the policy issues which aim at catalysing policies to support innovation *and* sustainable development. He explores that new concepts such as the systems model of innovation, national systems of innovation, the distribution power of innovation systems etc. together with a better understanding of knowledge i.e. the distinction between tacit and codified knowledge expanded the scope of RTD policies in the 1990's. Networking and absorptive capacity of firms became important issues in the RTD policies. A new concept of innovation policy was developed to complement the traditional RTD policy. This development led to the adoption of new types of national programmes, which were aimed at enhancing networking, knowledge circulation and innovation.

He argues, that RTD and innovation policies and environmental policies are highly interrelated through a number of links at various levels. Innovation policy can make significant contributions to sustainable development and environmental policy shapes in many different ways the conditions for innovation. A major effort is required to improve the interaction between RTD and innovation policies and environmental policies.

"Without clear market demand new technologies will not be developed nor disseminated. Thus the natural next step for government environmental policies would be to develop by means of appropriate interventions a strong demand for new clean technologies and relevant innovation. This would also involve a close interaction with the RTD and innovation policies.

RTD and innovation policies, while having their main emphases on knowledge creation and diffusion are intrinsically facilitating sustainable development by creating new technologies and providing mechanisms for their diffusion and absorption. On the other hand, it is reasonable to accept that not all technological development must directly contribute to sustainable development. A balance between environmental objectives and the other objectives of innovation policy must be found. To enhance such a development, environmental regulations should be developed from technology-based regulations and end-of-pipe solutions towards more performance-based regulations and comprehensive systems solutions. Regulations should also encourage completely new solutions and innovation rather than modifications of existing technologies. The regulatory framework should also be sufficiently predictable and stable."

The contribution of ***Uwe Kuntze*** "Research and Technology Policies and Sustainable Development - The Situation in the USA, Japan, Sweden and The Netherlands" in the annex states that the sometimes almost inflationary use of the term sustainable development does not always go along with a real alteration of the policy, leave alone that the policy exhausts the approach in full. Above all an intensification of the earlier followed research and technology policy lines can be noted, particularly in the fields of:

- development of 'environmentally friendly' energy forms (including nuclear energy) and increase of the energy efficiency
- development of additive and rehabilitating and integrated environmental technologies.

In fact, the paradigm of sustainable development concerns the much more comprehensive approach of social and economic development within the framework of global and inter-generational equity at simultaneous conservation of nature. A reduction of this paradigm to ecological criteria or protection of resources would fall much too short. To make producers and consumers prepare for this the research and technology policies have to act considering longer-term perspectives: technical solutions for future problems will increasingly become more complex and therefore will require a considerable temporal precourse since they have to be embedded in *optimised systemic solutions.*

Considering the inclusion of these elements of sustainable development in the research and technology policies of the USA, Japan, Sweden and The Netherlands, *Uwe Kuntze* summarises the following:

- Apart from the acquisition of basic ecological knowledge ("eco-systems research"), the development of technical solutions to avoid, reduce and rehabilitate damages to the environment has been a central field of the research and technology policies of the countries dealt with for two decades or more. Developments for an integrated environmental technology have mostly been intensified or started in the beginning of the 1990s.

- The increase of the resource efficiency (including energy) in diverse facets has also been part of the standard repertoire of the research and technology policies for some time because it is often combined with economic advantages. But it can only be characterised as an element of sustainable research and technology policies when it is combined with defined sustainability targets, like in Sweden or the Netherlands.
- The approach to substitute non-renewable materials is only prominent in the energy sector where particularly a replacement for fossil fuels is searched for in all countries but not in other fields of technology.
- The research of social, economic and political conditions which cause environmental problems and determine their solutions, and the general social framework of the transition to a sustainable way of life and economy seems to be especially recognised in the Netherlands with their approach to the analysis of the fields of social needs within the framework of the programme *Sustainable Technology Development.*
- The global dimension of the paradigm of sustainable development, too, is mentioned in all programmatic documents, even if in some cases obviously only with marginal activities resp. exploited in view of resulting marketing opportunities.
- The definition of sustainability targets as a criterion for the support of research and development projects cannot be found in the strategic policy documents.
- Quantitative reduction targets with a defined time frame are used particularly in Sweden and the Netherlands, and in the Netherlands they are derived from an operationalised definition of the paradigm of sustainable development.

## 6. Conclusions

The papers and invited contributions from discussants spurred a vivid discussion of these topics during the workshop and made it clear that the bringing together of the communities of experts for sustainable development with those for innovation policy really provided a fruitful ground for a broad exchange of approaches for new, mutually fertilising views towards the interrelationsships between (industrial) innovation and sustainable development. Looking at the contributions to the workshop in the light of the main question: "How can innovation dynamics be used in favour of sustainable development?" the following main conclusions can be drawn in a condensed and simplified manner:

(1) Concept of innovation: Innovation which is more suitable to sustainable development has to be conceptionalised much broader than the primarily used term of technological innovation suggests. Technology is only one part of the relevant set of parameters. Institutions (actors), behaviour, organisation and strategies and other driving forces have to be included. A broad consensus exists on the need for a systemic and holistic approach. In fact that means: back to the roots of Schumpeterian thinking.

(2) Direction of innovation: For innovation to support sustainable development, a *re-orientation* of innovation is necessary: a re-orientation towards efficiency in natural resources, new industrial concepts, services, product use etc. and towards the solution of problems of the society such as energy, food, climate, health and the provision of jobs. Some evidence exists that this re-orientation is compatible to a certain extent with current changes of industrial and service companies. But it is obvious that a broad re-orientation of the economy requires also a severe change of outside pressures and frame conditions. Innovation as a driving force for growth and consumption still stands in contradiction to innovation suitable for sustainable development. An approach to improve the linkage between environmental sustainability and industrial innovation should not start from a harmonized view but has to accept that these conflicts exist. This is relevant not only for analysis but also for policy conceptualisation.

(3) Time perspective: Industrial innovations often have long incubation times with respect to their consequences. Likewise, a change in concepts and directions of industrial innovations require long adaptation times to avoid a crash of the socio-economic structures. Public as well as private actors have to reflect changes in time perspectives for their respective policies.

(4) Role of enterprises: Enterprises could be far more proactive. Changes in markets and competition are already occurring as has been shown with numerous examples. This proves that there are chances for new strategies to reach business aims (such as market share, profits, differentiation to competitors). This creates a large room of creativity and new solutions. Especially in the 1990s in many industrialised countries strategies suited to environmental sustainability offer new opportunities via resource efficiency, the change from sales of products to sales of product use and the acquisition of first mover advantages.

(5) The role of regions: Industrial innovation suitable to environmental sustainability requires a close interaction between all relevant actors such as producers, users, intermediaries, public authorities. Therefore, regions are an important space for such intensified interactions and gain additional responsibilities for offering a platform for them. Because of the global dimension of sustainable development and the factual globalisation of economic activities it cannot be expected that a regionalised approach to environmental sustainability can suffice to solve the problem. Furthermore, there are still no findings about if

and how the advantages of globalisation may be preserved with regionalised concepts of sustainability.

(6) Uncertainties are increasing: Innovation paths become less predictable because of increased complexity. Sustainable development is far from being precisely operationalised. The impacts of the discussed concepts (such as proactive role of enterprises, outside pressures, etc.) are rather unclear. The steps taken were unanimously judged to be steps into the right direction, but by far no solution yet. Insofar, uncertainty is high in which scenario of the future world development (section 1 of this introduction) the world really is moving: One part of the participants had a deep scepticism whether it would be possible to avoid the "global crash" scenario.
Such uncertainties refer to the longer-term cause/effect relationships (e.g. climate change) but also to longer-term effects of newly introduced substitutes for hazardous products. An adequate reaction calls for systemic, longer-term technology assessment exercises (in a wider sense, i.e. including the assessment of regulative activities).

(7) Innovation policy: Some empirical evidence – as well as sociological and political sciences theories – lead to the conclusion that the old policy model is dead: the concept of the government role as a powerful authority of control, setting rules and guidance. The new concept of the government role could be appropriately described as the management of processes of bargaining, negotiating and social contracting between different relevant actors which behave according to their aims, power and available action parameters. Here is a need to study in depth the far-reaching issue of the structure of policy-making systems, i.e. the coherence and compatibility of political administration, the conditions of policy making as well as interaction and process management in view of the dynamics of innovation and sustainable development - this might well be a deserving topic for the Six Countries Programme.

This new concept of the government role, together with the specificities of sustainable development leads to partially new characteristics of innovation policy:

- Because of the horizontal nature of environmental questions, innovation policy has to build on horizontal as well as on vertical structures.
- Application of the full range of instruments (RTD policies, re-regulation, economic incentives, information, institutional changes, competition, coordination/integration with other sector policies, international cooperation, etc). In short: a comprehensive policy approach.
- Initiation and management of change processes to reach a social contract. Communication is essential (like for change processes in industry) and requires a professional management of the process in addition to driving forces.

- New or renewed fields of innovation policy, especially the renewal of the demand-side approach, which contains procurement, information labelling, performance specification and concertation of user groups (to support front runners). Furthermore, a close connection with policies for social and cultural change towards environmental sustainability is necessary.
- Consideration of feasibility conditions: Excellent concepts without having chances of implementation are an indication that the policy-making process and the consultation of actors is not sufficiently clarified. Among the relevant aspects are negotiation networks (regional, national, international) and the balance of power between losers and winners.
- Large systems tend to be inflexible and difficult to re-direct, which is one of the reasons for the present state of unsustainability. Measures and actions taken to achieve environmental sustainability should therefore aim at creating highly flexible conditions. Irreversibilities must be avoided so that no positive developments would be hampered and no negative effects be installed with a long-term perspective.

The reality of innovation policy is often different from this new concept of the government role. Nevertheless, in several countries successful initiatives exist in environmental policy to realise this new concept in one way or the other. Innovation policy can learn from environmental policy in this respect.

(8) Open questions

During the workshop the focus of the discussion was primarily on issues of industrial innovation related to environmental sustainability. A large set of questions around the sustainable development issue therefore were deliberately excluded. The workshop also excluded important polluting sectors (such as agriculture, traffic, tourism) which are not a part of the industrial system in a narrow sense. Also those areas of sustainable development were excluded to which innovation cannot contribute. Among the remaining topics, the following main questions were left open:

- How can the constituent demand of sustainable development for intra- and inter-generational equity be operationalised?
- How can positive employment effects be achieved? Up to now we do not know enough about this topic and discussions are based more on hopes and fears than on valid results.
- How to provide for economic dynamism?
- A change of lifestyles is probably necessary - how can this be achieved without severe social and economic frictions?
- More generally: how to design the appropriate change management?

Though from this list of questions it becomes evident that many important topics have not been solved yet, there was consent that the concept of sustainable de velopment should be a guiding principle for innovation policy.

## References

Angerer, G. (1992): The Role of Electronics in Environmental Technology and its Impacts on the Environment, Paper presented to the international conference ECO WORLD '92, Washington D.C.

BUND/Misereor (eds.) (1996): Zukunftsfähiges Deutschland. Ein Beitrag zu einer global nachhaltigen Entwicklung. Studie des Wuppertal Instituts für Klima, Umwelt, Energie, Basel/Boston/Berlin (Birkhäuser)

DTO (Programmabureau Interdepartementaal Onderzoekprogramma Duurzame Technologische Ontwikkeling) (1994): Looking Back from the Future. Dutch Governmental Programme for Sustainable Technology Development (STD), Delft

Ergas, H. (1987): Does technology policy matter?, in: Guile, B., Brooks, H. (eds.): Technology and Global Competition, National Academy Press, Washington

Freeman, C. (1992): The economics of hope, Pinter, London

Jaffe, A., Peterson, S., Portney, P. & Stavins, R. (1995): 'Environmental Regulation and the Competitiveness of US Manufacturing: What does the Evidence Tell Us?', Journal of Economic Literature, Vol. XXXIII (March), pp. 132-163

Jochem, E., Hohmeyer, O. (1992): The economics of near-term reductions in green-house gases, in: Mintzler, Irving (eds.): Confronting climate change. Risks, implications and responses, Cambridge University Press

Johnson, Huey D. (1995): Green plans. Greenprint for sustainability, Lincoln, London (University of Nebraska Press)

Krupp, Helmar (1992): Energy Politics and Schumpeter Dynamics. Tokyo, Springer,

Lahaye, Nathalie; Llerena, Daniel (1996): Technology and Sustainability: An Organisational and Institutional Change, in: Faucheux, Sylvie et al. (eds): Models of Sustainable Development, Cheltenham (Elgar Publishers)

Lévêque, F. (1996): Environmental Policy in Europe: Industry, Competition and the Policy Process, Edward Elgar, Cheltenham, UK

Meyer-Krahmer, Frieder (1995): Industrielle Leitbilder, in: Levi, H. W.; Danzer, B. (eds.): Umweltverträgliches Wirtschaften. Von der Utopie zum operativen Ziel. Eine Publikation der Karl Heinz Beckurts-Stiftung, Stuttgart

OECD (1992): Technology and the Economy. The Key Relationships. TEP. The Technology/Economy Programme, Paris

Porter, Michael E.; van der Linde, Claas (1995): Green and Competitive - Ending the Stalemate, in: Harvard Business Review

RMNO (Dutch Advisory Council for Research on Nature and Environment) (1992): The Ecocapacity as a Challenge to Technological Development, Rijswijk (Publication RMNO No. 74a)

Skea, Jim (1994): Environmental issues and innovation, in: Dodgson, M.; Rothwell, R. (eds.): The Handbook of Industrial Innovation, Edward Elgar

Soete, L.; Arundel, A. (1993): An Integrated Approach to European Innovation and Technology Diffusion Policy. A Maastricht Memorandum. Publication no. EUR 15090 EN of the Commission of the European Communities, Luxembourg

Vergragt, Philip J.; Jansen, Leo (1993): Sustainable technological development: the making of a Dutch long-term oriented technology programme, in: Project Appraisal, vol. 8, no. 3

VROM (The Netherlands Ministry of Housing Physical Planning and the Environment): National Planning for Sustainable Development. The Netherlands Experience (1993). Internet: www.rri.org/neppsumm.htm, 16.2.1996

Walz et al. (1995): Walz, R.; Ostertag, K.; Block, N.: Synopsis of Selected Indicator Systems for Sustainable Development, Karlsruhe (ISI)

Walz et al. (1992): Walz, R.; Gruber, E.; Hiessl, H.; Reiß, T.: Neue Technologien und Ressourcenschonung, Karlsruhe (ISI)

WCED - World Commission on Environment and Development (1987): Our Common Future (The Brundtland-Report), Oxford

Weizsäcker, E. U. von; Lovins, A. B.; Lovins, L. H. (1995): Faktor Vier. Doppelter Wohlstand - halbierter Naturverbrauch. Der neue Bericht an den Club of Rome, München (Droemer Knaur)

# Can a Market Economy Produce Industrial Innovations that Lead to Environmental Sustainability?

*Paul Ekins*

## 1. Introduction

The subject of the session from which this paper takes it title has several levels of meaning, some explicit, some implied. Logically there is a prior question to that in the title, namely: are industrial innovations *required* if environmental sustainability is to be achieved? If 'yes', then the question in the title becomes relevant, and its answer is obviously, but not very interestingly, also 'yes'. There are very many industrial innovations in market economies that reduce environmental burdens and therefore may be said to 'lead to environmental sustainability'. This answer immediately begs further, more interesting questions, such as:

- Can a market economy produce enough industrial innovations to *achieve* environmental sustainability?
- If 'yes', will this happen more or less automatically as markets evolve in conditions of environmental deterioration, or will it need to be stimulated by government policy and intervention?
- If the latter, what kinds of policies and interventions are likely to be required? A decision-diagram showing these questions and their implications is shown in figure 1.

This workshop appears to be based on the assumption that industrial innovations are necessary to achieve environmental sustainability. This paper makes the further assumptions down the decision diagram indicated by the path Y2, N3, so that much of the paper explores some possible answers to the question in Box 4. While this probably represents the mainstream set of assumptions, they are not entirely uncontroversial.

With regard to N1, this is not a tenable view if it is accepted that the current position is one of environmental unsustainability and if innovation is defined as below. N2 leads to a counsel of despair, given that no viable broad alternative to a market economy currently seems to exist. On the contrary, the trend towards global marketisation is continuing to accelerate. Y3 is sometimes the interpretation that is given to the widely discussed phenomenon of the environmental Kuznets curve (EKC), whereby the graph of pollution plotted against income has an inverted-U shape. Elsewhere I have shown that the evidence for such a relationship is far from conclusive (Ekins 1997). Moreover, even where it holds, it is more the outcome of environmental policy than the untrammelled operation of markets. Nor is Y3 the correct characterisation of 'free market environmentalism' (FME; see, for example, Anderson & Leal 1991), as might be imagined. Free market environmentalists advocate the tackling of environmental problems by making environmental resources subject to private property rights. However, given current property rights, FME involves a huge amount of government action in the definition and redefinition, allocation and redistribution, and enforcement of environmental property rights. Given that all government regulation can be regarded in some sense as a redefinition of property rights, it is clear that FME is actually a particular answer to the question in Box 4.

Figure 1: A Decision Diagram Leading from Innovation to Policy

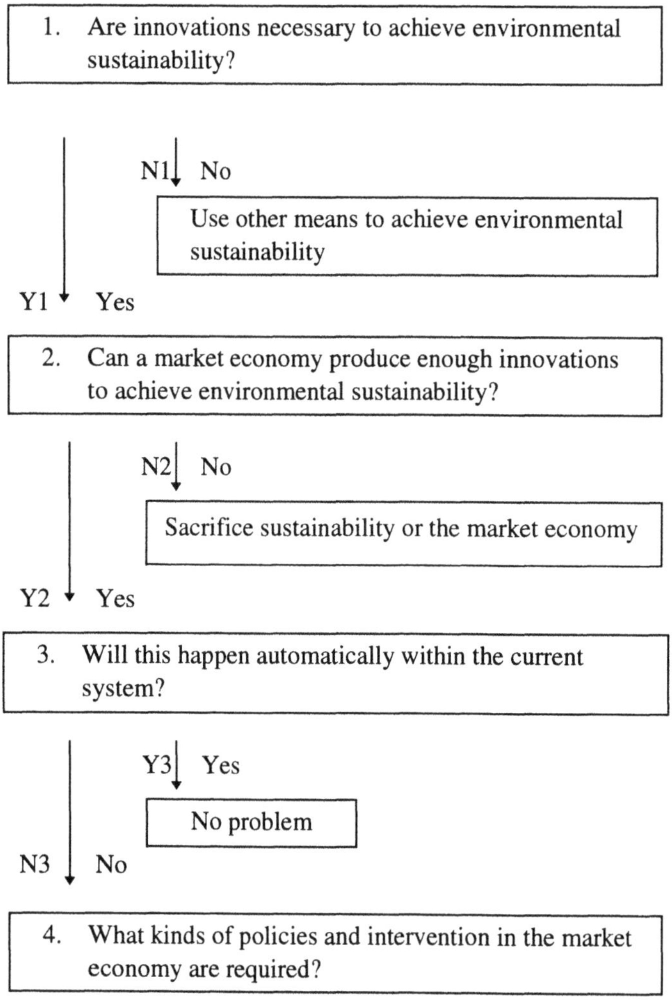

With regard to the definition of innovation, Wallace (1995, p. 11) has written: "Innovation can encompass any change in technology, production processes or organisational and managerial structure and techniques." Box 4 in figure 1 asks what kind of environmental policy will bring about environmentally improving innovations, but in fact there is much more at stake than this.

Innovation is increasingly becoming regarded not only as a prerequisite of substantial moves towards environmental sustainability, but also as the principal source of wealth creation. According to Wallace (pp. 1,5): "Innovation is the one constant factor in wealth creation." and "The history of economic development tells us that innovation is the key to sustained development." The burgeoning literature on endogenous economic growth is largely derived from a perception of industrial innovation as "the engine of growth" (see, for example, Grossman & Helpman 1994, p. 24). If industrial innovation is required to move towards environmental sustainability, and it is also the root source of economic growth, the question then arises as to what kind of innovation will achieve each of these very different objectives, and how it might be stimulated, and whether innovations for environmental sustainability are likely to be compatible or inconsistent with those for economic growth and vice versa. Answering this question requires a clear conceptualisation of both the process of wealth creation and the concept of environmental sustainability, leading to understanding as to why the economy is currently producing environmental unsustainability, so that the characteristics of innovations which will both resolve environmental problems and create wealth may be identified.

## 2. A Conceptual Model of Wealth Creation and Environmental Sustainability

The process of wealth creation is most commonly characterised as one in which different kinds of asset, or capital, are brought together in production to produce goods and services. It is evident from any consideration of real-life production that one of the most fundamental stocks of capital is that provided by nature, here called ecological or natural capital. It is the role of this kind of capital that is emphasised in the model that follows, so that the natural environment 's role in and contribution to business activity and the economy may be better understood.

Figure 2 portrays four kinds of capital stock: ecological (or natural) capital, human capital, social and organisational capital, and manufactured capital. Each of these stocks produces a flow of 'services' from the environment (E), from human capital (L), from social/organisational capital (S), and from physical capital (K), services which serve as inputs into the productive process, along with 'intermediate inputs', M, which are previous outputs from the economy which are used as inputs in a subsequent process.

Manufactured capital comprises material goods - tools, machines, buildings, infrastructure - which contribute to the production process but do not become embodied in the output and, usually, are 'consumed' in a period of time longer than a year. Intermediate goods, in contrast, either are embodied in produced goods (e.g. metals, plastics, components) or are immediately consumed in the production process (e.g. fuels). Human capital comprises all individuals' capacities for work; while social and organisational capital comprises the networks and organisations through which the contributions of individuals are mobilised and co-ordinated.

Figure 2: Stocks, Flows and Welfare in the Process of Production

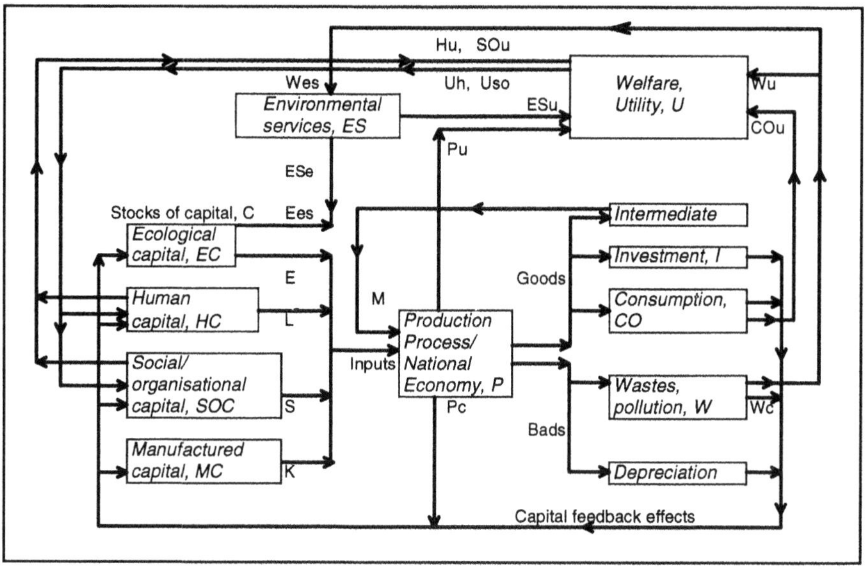


Note: In the flow descriptors, the upper case letters denote the source of the flow, lower case letters denote the destination. Those relating to the various capital stocks have the C omitted for simplicity.

Ecological capital is a complex category which performs three distinct types of environmental function (Pearce & Turner, 1990 pp. 35ff.), two of which are directly relevant to the production process. The first is the provision of resources for production (E), the raw materials that become food, fuels, metals, timber etc. The second is the absorption of wastes (W) from production, both from the production process and from the disposal of consumption goods. Where these wastes add to or improve the stock of ecological capital (e.g. through recycling or fertilisation of soil by livestock), they can be regarded as investment in such capital. More frequently, where they destroy, pollute or erode, with consequent negative impacts on the ecological, human or manufactured capital stocks, they can be regarded as agents of negative investment, depreciation or capital consumption. Either way, the wastes contribute to the capital feedback effects identified in figure 2.

The outputs of the economic process can, in the first instance, be categorised as 'Goods' and 'Bads'. The Goods are the desired outputs of the process, as well as any positive externalities (incidental effects) that may be associated with it. These Goods can be divided in turn into consumption, investment and intermediate goods and services. The Bads are the negative effects of the production process, including capital depreciation and polluting wastes and other negative externalities, which contribute to environmental destruction, negative effects on human health etc. Insofar as they have an effect on the capital stocks, the Bads can be regarded as negative investment.

The necessity for a matter/energy balance on either side of the production process means that all matter and energy that feature as inputs must also emerge as outputs, either embodied in the Goods or among the Bads. On disposal of the former, therefore, all these former inputs are returned to the environment, to the stock of ecological capital, where they may have a positive, negative or neutral effect.

Human welfare, or utility as economists call it, is generated at many points of the overall process of wealth creation. It is derived from consumption (COu); it can be generated through work satisfaction (Pu); it is derived from social and organisational structures (SOu); it is a function of human capital itself (Hu); and, most importantly for this paper, it is affected by the quality of the natural environment (ESu), and by the nature and level of wastes (Wu).

Wastes and pollution from the production process and consumption affect utility directly (Wu, e.g. litter, noise) and through their mainly negative feedback into the stocks of environmental, human and manufactured capital. These feedbacks, Wc, can reduce the productivity of environmental resources (e.g. through pollution) and affect the ecological capital that produces environmental services (e.g. by engendering climate change or damaging the ozone layer); they can damage human capital by engendering ill health; and they can corrode buildings (manufactured capital). They can also affect environmental services directly (Wes, e.g. by reducing the appreciation of natural beauty).

Figure 2 emphasises feedback effects. One that has not yet been mentioned is the joint relationship between the stock of ecological capital (EC) and the environmental services (ES) deriving from it. In a stable ecosystem, EC and ES will tend to be symbiotically balanced.

This model clearly identifies the contribution of the environment to wealth creation. However, sustaining this contribution requires the adequate maintenance of the ecological capital which produces it. This is the heart of the concept of environmental sustainability that is becoming the organising principle of much environmental policy.

The basic meaning of sustainability is the capacity for continuance more or less indefinitely into the future. It is now clear that, in aggregate, current human ways of life do not possess that capacity, either because they are destroying the environmental conditions necessary for their continuance, or because their environmental effects will cause unacceptable social disruption and damage to human health. The environmental effects in question include climate change, ozone depletion, acidification, toxic pollution, the depletion of renewable resources (e.g. forests, soils, fisheries, water) and of non-renewable resources (e.g. fossil fuels) and the extinction of species.

A way of life is a complex bundle of values, objectives, institutions and activities, with ethical, environmental, economic and social dimensions. While current concern about unsustainability largely has an ecological basis, it is clear that human situations or ways of life can be unsustainable for social and economic reasons as well. The pertinent questions are: for the environment, can its contribution to human welfare and to the human economy be sustained? for the economy, can today's level of wealth-creation be sustained? and for society, can social cohesion and important social institutions be sustained? In what follows the focus is on the environmental-economic dimensions of sustainability.

Economic sustainability is most commonly interpreted as a condition of non-declining economic welfare projected into the future. As has been seen, economic welfare derives from, *inter alia*, income and from the environment, which performs various functions, some of which contribute to production, and therefore income, others of which contribute to welfare directly. Income is generated by stocks of capital, including manufactured, human and natural capital. Natural capital also performs the welfare-creating environmental functions. Non-declining economic welfare requires, *ceteris paribus*, that the stock of capital be maintained (Pezzey 1992, pp. 14ff.)

There is then the issue as to whether it is the total stock of capital that must be maintained, with substitution allowed between various parts of it, or whether certain components of capital, particularly natural capital, are non-substitutable, i.e. they contribute to welfare in a unique way that cannot be replicated by another capital component. Turner (1993, pp. 9-15) identifies four different kinds of sustainability, ranging from very weak, which assumes complete substitutability, to very strong, which assumes no substitutability so that all natural capital must be conserved. The assumption of the former is implicit in the so-called 'Hartwick rule' (Hartwick 1977), namely that, provided that the resource rents from the exploitation of exhaustible resources are invested in manufactured capital, per capita consumption can remain constant indefinitely over time. Very strong sustainability has been called "absurdly strong sustainability" (Daly 1995, p. 49) in order to dismiss it from practical consideration. Turner's more interesting intermediate categories are:

- Weak environmental sustainability, which derives from a perception that welfare is not normally dependent on a specific form of capital and can be maintained by substituting manufactured for natural capital, though with exceptions.

- Strong sustainability, which derives from a different perception that the substitutability of manufactured for natural capital is seriously limited by such environmental characteristics as irreversibility, uncertainty and the existence of 'critical' components of natural capital, which make a unique contribution to welfare. An even greater importance is placed on natural capital by those who regard it in many instances as a complement to manufactured capital (Daly 1992, pp. 27ff.).

The point at issue is which perception most validly describes reality. Resolving this point should be an empirical rather than a theoretical or ideological matter. However, if weak sustainability is assumed *a priori*, it is impossible to show *ex post* whether the assumption was justified or not, for the following reason.

The assumption underlying weak sustainability is that there is no essential difference between different forms of capital, or between the kinds of welfare which they generate. This enables, theoretically at least, all types of capital and the services and welfare generated by them to be expressed in the same monetary unit. In practice, there may be insuperable difficulties in performing the necessary monetisation and aggregation across the range of issues involved, but the theoretical position is clear and strenuous efforts are being made to make it operational. But the numbers that emerge from these efforts can only show whether or not weak sustainability has been achieved, i.e. whether overall welfare has been maintained. They cannot shed any light on the question as to whether the assumption of commensurable and substitutable capitals was justified in the first place. In assuming away any differences at the start, there is no way of establishing later on whether such differences were important.

The strong sustainability assumption does not suffer from this severe defect in scientific methodology. In keeping natural capital distinct from other kinds of capital, it can examine natural capital's particular contribution to welfare, distinguishing between its contribution to production (through resource-provision and waste-absorption) and its services that generate welfare directly. The examination may reveal that in some cases the welfare derived from natural capital is fully commensurable with other welfare from production and can be expressed in monetary form, so that in these cases substitutability with other forms of productive capital exists, and the weak sustainability condition of a non-declining aggregate capital stock is sufficient to maintain welfare. In other cases the outcome of the examination may be different. The important point is that, starting from a strong sustainability assumption of non-substitutability in general, it is possible to shift to a weak sustainability position where that is shown to be appropriate. But starting from a weak sustainability assumption permits no such insights to enable exceptions to be identified. In terms of scientific methodology, strong sustainability is therefore greatly to be preferred as the *a priori* position.

There are other theoretical reasons for choosing the strong sustainability assumption, in addition to the practical reason of the sheer difficulty of carrying out the necessary weak sustainability calculations for complex environmental effects. Victor (1991, pp.

210-211) notes that there is a recognition in economics going back to Marshall that manufactured capital is fundamentally different from environmental resources. The former is human-made and reproducible in the quantities desired, the latter is the "free gift of nature" and in many categories is in fixed or limited supply. The destruction of manufactured capital is very rarely irreversible (this would only occur if the human capital, or knowledge, that created the manufactured capital had also been lost), whereas irreversibility, with such effects as species extinction, climate change, or even the combustion of fossil fuels, is common in the consumption of natural capital. Moreover, to the extent that manufactured capital requires natural capital for its production, it can never be a complete substitute for resources.

Victor et al. (1994, p. 107) identify the elements of natural capital that are essential for life as we know it as water, air, minerals, energy, space and genetic materials, to which might be added the stratospheric ozone layer and the relationships and interactions between these elements that sustain ecosystems and the biosphere. Some substitution of these essential elements by manufactured and human capital can be envisaged, but their wholesale substitutability, as assumed by weak sustainability, appears improbable, certainly with present knowledge and technologies. In fact, if the process of industrialisation is viewed as the application of human, social and manufactured capital to natural capital to transform it into more human and manufactured capital, then it is possible to view current environmental problems as evidence that such substitutability is not complete. If our current development is unsustainable, it is because it is depleting some critical, non-substitutable components of the capital base on which it depends.

In figure 2, the key contribution of the environment to the human economy and to human life in general is perceived to be through the operation of a wide range of 'environmental functions'. This concept was first employed in economic analysis by Hueting (1980) and has been extensively developed by de Groot (1992). De Groot defines environmental functions as "the capacity of natural processes and components to provide goods and services that satisfy human needs" (de Groot 1992 p. 7). These "natural processes and components" can in turn be identified as the stocks of and flows from natural capital (though de Groot does not use the term), which features as ecological capital in figure 2 and in various definitions of sustainability and sustainable development (see for example Pezzey 1992, pp. 55ff.). De Groot identifies thirty-seven environmental functions, which he classifies under four headings: regulation, carrier, production and information (ibid., p. 15).

Figure 2 and the subsequent discussion used another method of grouping these functions, under three headings:

A. Provision of resources for human activity
B. Absorption of wastes from human activity
C. Provision of environmental services independently of or interdependently with human activity.

These two classifications are not contradictory. The resource functions in the second typology correspond broadly to the production functions of the first, but also include some carrier functions. The waste absorption functions are included among the regulation functions; and the provision of services includes the information functions and some regulation and carrier functions.

*Environmental sustainability is therefore here defined as the maintenance of important environmental functions.* The advantage of defining it in this way, rather than as the maintenance of natural capital *per se*, is that such a definition makes explicit the requirements of manufactured or human capital and technical change if they are to be full substitutes for natural capital. Manufactured capital is a substitute for natural capital if it performs the same environmental functions as the natural capital. It is clear that this is more likely to be the case when the natural capital performs a single resource function (e.g. as an energy source) than when it is multifunctional in diverse ways (e.g. a rainforest). Similarly technical change can only be said to compensate for natural resource loss when, through the new technology, a reduced quantity of natural resources can perform the same environmental functions. To the extent that manufactured capital and technical change do not fully perform the environmental functions of the natural capital they replace, then substitutability between them has not been complete and there has been a trade-off between them.

There will be cases when such a trade-off appears justified; environmental sustainability is not here perceived to require the maintenance of *all* environmental functions. But the loss of natural capital to date, combined with ignorance about the importance of what remains, together with threshold effects and irreversibilities that make unwelcome changes impossible both to predict and undo, argue for caution. As Perrings et al. (1995, p. 22) observe: "Ecosystems typically continue to function in the short-term even as resilience declines. Indeed, they often signal loss of resilience only at the point at which external shocks at previously sustainable levels flip these systems into some other basis of attraction and so some other regime of behaviour."

Given the uncertainties involved in matters of sustainability, and the possibility of irreversibility, and of the incidence of very large costs, once environmental functions have been lost, the question of risk is crucial, not least because risk, through insurance premia, for example, incurs present real, as well as hypothetical future, costs. This simultaneous coincidence of uncertainty, irreversibility and possible large costs has long been recognised as an important consideration for environmental policy. Ciriacy-Wantrup (1952)'s classic work prefigured many of the current concerns of sustainability with his development of the concept of 'the safe minimum standard'.

First Ciriacy-Wantrup (1952, pp. 38ff.) identified the existence of 'critical zones' for many, especially renewable, resources, where such a zone "means a more or less clearly defined range of rates (of flow of the resource) below which a decrease in flow cannot be reversed *economically* under presently foreseeable conditions. Frequently such irreversibility is not only economic but also technological" (ibid., p. 39) and, one may add with regard to extinguished species, biological. In the terminology being employed here, this means that the loss of environmental functions may be irreversible. The 'critical zone' concept is strikingly similar to that of the 'critical load' which is employed in modern environmental policy.

Then Ciriacy-Wantrup (ibid., p. 88) identifies the possibility of "immoderate losses" arising from environmental degradation, with respect to which: "One important objective of conservation decisions is to avoid *immoderate* possible losses - although of small probability - by accepting the possibility of moderate ones - although the latter are more probable." A decision rule which would achieve this is the 'minimax' criterion, which involves minimising maximum possible losses. The application of this criterion to resources characterised by critical zones leads Ciriacy-Wantrup (ibid., Chapter 18, pp. 251ff.) to recommend the 'safe minimum standard' (SMS) as an objective of conservation (what today would be called environmental) policy: "A safe minimum standard of conservation is achieved by avoiding the critical zone - that is, those physical conditions, brought about by human action, which would make it uneconomical to halt and reverse depletion."

Bishop (1993, p. 72) brings the SMS approach into the context of current environmental discourse by relating it to sustainability: "To achieve sustainability policies should be considered that constrain the day to day operations of the economy in ways that enhance the natural resource endowments of future generations, but with an eye towards the economic implications of specific steps to implement such policies." Here the safe minimum standard has been converted into a sustainability standard. In the terms previously discussed, those activities that entail the possibility of irreversible effects and immoderate costs are now identified as environmentally unsustainable.

What counts as an 'unsustainable effect' rather than a sustainable economic cost is a matter of judgement which can only partially be resolved by science. Ethics and the attitude to risk also play a significant role here. It is important that the basis of judgement is articulated clearly, especially as to who is responsible for the effects and who is bearing their costs, and differentiating the contributions played by science, ethics and risk acceptance or aversion.

Detailed sustainability standards will need to be formulated for all the important environmental functions that are perceived to be at risk from human activities, but some general principles for these standards can be posited with regard to the generic functions of resource use, waste absorption and life support. Daly (1991, pp. 44-45) has suggested four principles of sustainable development:

(1) Limit the human scale (throughput) to that which is within the earth's carrying capacity.

(2) Ensure that technological progress is efficiency-increasing rather than throughput-increasing.

(3) For renewable resources harvesting rates should not exceed regeneration rates (sustained yield); waste emissions should not exceed the assimilative capacities of the receiving environment.

(4) Non-renewable resources should be exploited no faster than the rate of creation of renewable substitutes.

These principles are among the rules that Turner (1993, pp. 20-21) has formulated "for the sustainable utilisation of the capital stock", the others of which are: correction of market and intervention failures; steering of technical change not only to increase resource-using efficiency but also to promote renewable substitutes for non-renewable resources; taking a precautionary approach to the uncertainties involved.

Of these rules, the correction of failures and the steering of technical change are more do to with achieving sustainability than defining standards for it; and in view of the complexity of applying the concept of carrying capacity to human activities, it seems desirable to express it more specifically in terms of those environmental problems that appear most pressing. Such considerations enable the Daly/Turner rules to be reformulated into a set of sustainability conditions:

(1) Destabilisation of global environmental features such as climate patterns or the ozone layer must be prevented. Most important in this category are the maintenance of biodiversity (see below), the prevention of climate change, by the stabilisation of the atmospheric concentration of greenhouse gases, and safeguarding the ozone layer by ceasing the emission of ozone-depleting substances.

(2) Important ecosystems and ecological features must be absolutely protected to maintain biological diversity. Importance in this context comes from a recognition not only of the perhaps as yet unappreciated use value of individual species, but also of the fact that biodiversity underpins the productivity and resilience of ecosystems. Resilience, defined as "the magnitude of the disturbance that can be absorbed before the system changes its structure by changing the variables and processes that control its behaviour" (Folke et al. 1994, p. 6) depends on the functional diversity of the system. This depends in turn, in complex ways, not just on the diversity of species but on their mix and population and the relations between the ecosystems that contain them. "Biodiversity conservation, ecological sustainability and economic sustainability are inexorably linked; uncontrolled and irreversible biodiversity loss ruptures this link and puts the sustainability of our basic economic-environmental systems at risk." (Barbier et al. 1994, p. 41)

(3) The renewal of renewable resources must be fostered through the maintenance of soil fertility, hydrobiological cycles and necessary vegetative cover and the

rigorous enforcement of sustainable harvesting. The latter implies basing harvesting rates on the most conservative estimates of stock levels, for such resources as fish; ensuring that replanting becomes an essential part of such activities as forestry; and using technologies for cultivation and harvest that do not degrade the relevant ecosystem, and deplete neither the soil nor genetic diversity;

(4) Depletion of non-renewable resources should seek to balance the maintenance of a minimum life-expectancy of the resource with the development of substitutes for it. On reaching the minimum life-expectancy, its maintenance would mean that consumption of the resource would have to be matched by new discoveries of it. To help finance research for alternatives and the eventual transition to renewable substitutes, all depletion of non-renewable resources should entail a contribution to a capital fund. Designing for resource-efficiency and durability can ensure that the practice of repair, reconditioning, re-use and recycling (the 'four R's') approach the limits of their environmental efficiency.

(5) Emissions into air, soil and water must not exceed their critical load, that is the capability of the receiving media to disperse, absorb, neutralise and recycle them, nor may they lead to life-damaging concentrations of toxins. Synergies between pollutants can make critical loads very much more difficult to determine. Such uncertainties should result in a precautionary approach in the adoption of safe minimum standards.

(6) Landscapes of special human or ecological significance, because of their rarity, aesthetic quality or cultural or spiritual associations, should be preserved.

(7) Risks of life-damaging events from human activity must be kept at very low levels. Technologies which threaten long-lasting ecosystem damage at whatever level of risk, should be foregone.

Of these seven sustainability principles, 3, 4 and, to some extent, 2 seek to sustain resource functions. 5 seeks to sustain waste-absorption functions; 1 and 2 seek to sustain life-supporting environmental services; 6 is concerned with other environmental services of special human value; and 7 acknowledges the great uncertainties associated with environmental change and the threshold effects and irreversibilities mentioned above. The principles are clearly an application of the SMS approach, but they seek to reinterpret it explicitly in the context of ensuring the sustainable use of important environmental functions. Following the SMS tradition, none of the principles are absolutely sacrosanct, but the presumption underlying them is that their observance and promotion will be violated only when they entail intolerable costs. In some cases the principles may be in conflict. For example, excessive fossil fuel use violates principle 1 on global warming, while that of nuclear power violates principle 7 on environmental risk. In this case acceptance of the sustainability principles suggests that the efficiency of energy use should be maximised, and safe renewable energy sources should be developed (as per principle 4), while, in the interim, $CO_2$ emissions from fossil fuels should be minimised (e.g. by switching to low carbon fuels) and the safety of nuclear power should be a prime concern. In this way, the principles give clear guidance how to approach today's principal perceived environmental problems. They may need to be supplemented as new environmental problems become apparent.

The principles are also reflected in a number of international treaties, conventions and principles, including the Montreal Protocol to phase out ozone-depleting substances (1 above), the Convention on International Trade in Endangered Species and the establishment of World Biosphere Reserves to maintain biodiversity (2 above), the Second Sulphur Protocol to limit $SO_2$ emissions (5 above), and the Precautionary Principle, endorsed by the United Nations Conference on Environment and Development in *Agenda 21*, to limit environmental risk-taking (5 and 7 above).

Interpreting the SMS approach as the setting of sustainability standards to ensure the sustainable use of important environmental functions offers a practical methodology to address those environmental problems where uncertainty, irreversibility or possible large costs make the use of benefit-cost analysis problematic. The methodology was applied in the formulation of the Second Sulphur Protocol. It was applied by the German Advisory Council on Global Change to recommend the necessary level of $CO_2$ reduction to the First Conference of the Parties on Climate Change in Berlin (WBGU 1995). Hueting et al. (1992, Appendix 2, pp. 44-52) have also used the methodology to indicate how sustainability standards can be derived for seventeen different environmental problems.

## 3. Addressing Unsustainability through Innovation

The root causes of the environmental problems to which the sustainability standards above relate are the *quantity* of some forms of energy and materials that flow through the economy (which may be termed the economy's material throughput), and the *quality* of some of the releases into the environment to which this gives rise. From the first law of thermodynamics, the law of conservation of matter and energy, it is clear that all the resources which enter the economy are conserved in some form. From the second law of thermodynamics, the law of entropy, it is clear that these resources ultimately end up as wastes, i.e. matter that is in a more dispersed, less organised state than the resources from which the wastes were derived.

No amount of innovation, or any other response to environmental problems, can negate the entropy law, but it can reduce the quantity of energy and materials that is used to produce a unit of economic output, and it can seek to keep materials in useful circulation, by judicious repair, reconditioning, re-use and recycling, for longer periods before they become wastes. Clearly the 4Rs need energy to drive them, but this could be human energy (e.g. extra labour in sorting or washing), so that the activities do not require extra energy inputs, or solar energy, which is environmentally more benign than the use of fossil fuels, or simply less energy than would be required for fresh production.

There are three possible mechanisms which cause the four types of capital in figure 2 to come together and produce output: the market, the state and reciprocity (where this entails the voluntary production of goods and services because of kinship, community, culture and tradition). All these mechanisms are important in real-life economies, and all may be expected to play a role in reducing environmental impacts. However, the focus of this paper is on the market mechanism.

The market is a social institution based on exchange. Producers buy from each other and consumers buy from producers. If the flow of matter and energy that constitutes the physical basis of these exchanges must be reduced in quantity and changed in quality, this will require a change in behaviour from either producers or consumers or both. Such a change is an 'innovation' in production or consumption. Because of the importance of institutions in the operation of markets, it is likely that institutional innovations will also be required. The remainder of this paper will discuss these three kinds of innovation in turn, with most emphasis being given to innovation in production. It is often hoped that thereby environmental improvements may be gained without losses in competitiveness, an issue which will be explored in some detail. First, however, it may be noted that, unsurprisingly, an important element throughout will be the role of the market's fundamental means of coordination, price.

## Changing Prices for Sustainability

In markets goods flow from producers to other producers or consumers because willing sellers and willing buyers find their prices of exchange mutually acceptable. A relative and absolute change in these prices will be likely to alter both the quantity and composition of the flow. In particular, an increase in the relative price of some goods will tend to reduce their consumption compared with the rest. This is the basic rationale behind environmental taxation which seeks the systematic increase in the prices of those resources the use of which entails external costs, including contribution to environmental unsustainability. Producers and consumers are likely to respond to the price increases by using fewer of the resources. Consumers will switch to other goods which contain fewer taxed resources. Producers will both switch to producing these other goods, and try to find ways to produce the same goods with fewer, or less heavily taxed other, resources. This change in price through a tax- or charge-oriented environmental policy has the potential to produce profound innovations in both production and consumption, some of which are discussed below. It also represents a marked innovation in environmental policy itself.

The OECD's first review of the use of environmental economic instruments, including environmental taxation, in member countries (OECD 1989) identified about 150 instruments in use in 1987, or 100 if subsidies, purely administrative charges and liability are excluded (OECD 1994, p. 22). However, the significance of these instruments was not very great. Only about a third may have had some incentive impact and the OECD (1994) review concluded: "Basically, then, in 1987 environmental policies in the OECD Member countries were command-and-control policies with some financial and economic add-ons." (p. 177)

By 1994 the number of instruments had increased by over 50%, with the most growth in product charges and deposit-refund systems. Moreover, four countries had conducted a limited green tax reform (Denmark, the Netherlands, Norway and Sweden), five countries had introduced carbon or carbon-energy taxes (the above plus Finland), eight had set up official task-forces or commissions to explore further opportunities for such reform, or for implementing environmental taxes in general, and a further six had announced an intention to make an increased use of economic instruments in environmental policy (OECD 1994, p. 188). It is clear that, at the national level in OECD countries, economic instruments in general, and environmental taxes in particular, are commanding greater attention than they were eight or nine years ago. Given that the desire for policy integration and a broader mix of environmental policy instruments are now well established elements of environmental policy, one may expect this attention to continue to increase. The implications of this for innovation in production and consumption are addressed below.

## 4. Innovation in Production

Figure 3 gives a schematic illustration of the transformation of matter/energy into products and thence wastes. Environmental impacts are associated with the extraction of matter/energy and the emissions of wastes that result from each stage.

It is a truism to say that, in order to know the environmental impact of a business, the flows of matter/energy as a result of its activities must be measured. Increasingly, for those impacts recognised as environmentally serious, there is a legal requirement for them to be measured. However, such requirements currently fall far short of what would be necessary for businesses to construct mass/energy balances (i.e. tables of material and energy inputs and outputs) for their operations, far less account for the environmental implications of their products' use and disposal. Yet if the impact of business on the environment is to be understood and effectively managed, it is difficult to see how the development of such an information system can be avoided.

Figure 3: Inputs of Matter and Energy into the Life-Cycle of a Product

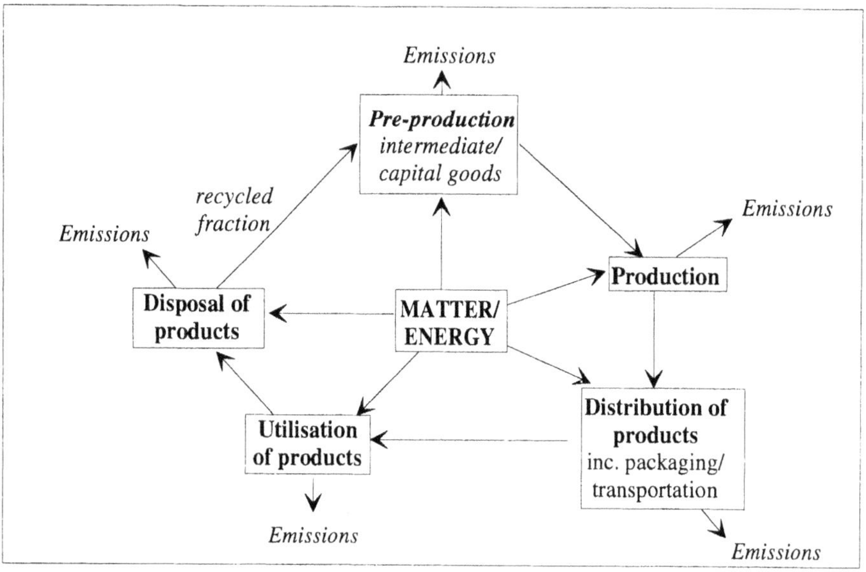


## Corporate Environmental Accounting and Reporting

The desirability of measuring corporate environmental throughput, over and above what is legally required, is increasingly being recognised by companies as a necessary precondition of effective environmental management and is being reflected in the growth of voluntary corporate environmental reporting. By 1993 over 100 companies had published environmental reports on a voluntary basis (Elkington & Robins 1993, p. 5), with the number rapidly growing, partly at least as a result of encouragement from business associations (including the International Chamber of Commerce and Confederation of British Industry), business-environment networks (such as the World Business Council for Sustainable Development), and the European Commission, with its voluntary Environmental Management and Auditing System (EMAS). While many of the early corporate environmental reports were largely descriptive and textual, there is a clear trend towards quantification in the assessment of environmental impacts.

It is interesting to compare these new efforts at environmental reporting, considering where they might lead, with the systems of financial accounting that have been adopted for the management of business and the economy. Business accounts are entirely analogous to mass balances. Money flowing into a business is balanced by money flowing out and a change in the value of net assets. Economy-wide, the national accounts are explicitly constructed on an input-output basis, so that interactions between industries can be identified, as well as the producers and composition of final demand. Attempts to construct integrated environmental-economic accounting at the national level (see, for example, UN 1993) use the same techniques for environmental resources. If moving towards environmental sustainability really is an important, perhaps even over-riding, imperative, then it seems likely that companies will need to account to society at large for their use of the environment with as much rigour as they do to their shareholders for the use of their money. Certainly this was the view expressed in DTTI et al. (1993), who identified the final stage in corporate environmental reporting as one "based on the extensive use of quantitative methods such as life cycle assessments and mass balances" (DTTI et al. 1993, p. 9)

Once the physical flows to and from the environment have been calculated, it becomes possible to consider a business's performance in relation to sustainability. Initially the information enables the business to set targets for environmental improvement, which both DTTI et al. (1993, pp. 60-61) and Gray et al. (1993, p. 73) perceive as important stages in the development of corporate environmental reporting. Ultimately, if sustainability is the objective, the targets for improvement must comply with standards of sustainability. Gray et al. (1993, p. 273) consider that a sustainable organisation is one which leaves the biosphere no worse off at the end of the accounting period than it was at the beginning. It is important to recognise that such a zero-pollution criterion is not the same as zero emissions, because of the environment's ability to absorb and neutralise a certain quantity of waste, but it is a demanding criterion nevertheless.

Gray et al. (1993) have also proposed that the notional expenditure required for the firm to make good any biospheric damage caused during the accounting period, which they call the 'sustainable cost', be identified in the company accounts as a measure of the firm's contribution to natural capital depreciation, analogously to the figures for depreciation of other assets. While a challenging task in practice, this valuation of the 'maintenance cost' is also the technique recommended in UN 1993 as a means of linking the physical with the monetary accounts at the national level. For the firm it offers the intriguing prospect of being able, by deducting the sustainable cost from the operating profit, to arrive at a 'sustainable profit' figure which takes account of the environmental degradation caused by the company's activities.

In addition to identifying, and accounting for, their environmental impacts, it seems as important that businesses identify and correctly account their actual environmental expenditure, whether this is for abatement, source reduction, monitoring or regulatory compliance. This is because, unless firms know how much they are paying to prevent or monitor environmental damage, they will not feel the correct incentive to move towards products and processes that are inherently less environmentally damaging - and which could save them money. Ditz et al. (1995) report on nine case studies which were carried out on five large and four medium-sized firms, to see whether their environmental expenditures were correctly reported in their management accounts. In each case they found that they were not, and that, because environmental expenditures were sometimes subsumed under non-environmental headings, real environmental expenditures were substantially larger than they appeared in the accounts, financially justifying environmental improvement measures which before had not appeared economic.

Such revised accounting procedures have been called Total Cost Assessment (TCA, Jackson 1993, pp. 200ff.). Table 1 shows one application of TCA to an investment that converted a solvent/heavy metal to an aqueous/heavy metal-free coating at a paper coating company.

Table 1: Financial Data for a Project Comparing Conventional Company Analysis with a Total Cost Assessment (TCA)

| | Company analysis | TCA | Difference |
|---|---|---|---|
| Total capital costs | $623,809 | $653,809 | 6% |
| Annual savings (BIT)[1] | $118,112 | $216,874 | 84% |
| Net present value, years 1-10 | ($98,829) | $232,817 | 336% |
| Net present value, years 1-15 | $13,932 | $428,040 | 2972% |
| IRR, years 1-10 | 12% | 24% | 12% |
| IRR, years 1-15 | 16% | 27% | 11% |
| Simple payback (years) | 5.3 | 3.0 | -43% |

[1] Before interest and taxes

Source: Jackson 1993, p. 203

The company analysis column shows how the company's conventional accounting system assessed the project's costs and benefits. The TCA column includes costs and benefits that were accounted in the company analysis under headings which obscured their relation to the project. These hidden, or indirect, costs and benefits included costs of waste management, utilities (energy, water, sewerage), pollution control/solvent recovery and regulatory compliance. It can be seen that the project under TCA was substantially more profitable than with the conventional company analysis.

## Corporate Environmental Management

For companies that aspire to move towards environmental sustainability, environmental accounting and reporting are only two of several necessary management initiatives. Others include the adoption of a corporate environmental policy, of an environmental strategy and action plan to give it effect, and appropriate communication of environmental outcomes, both internally and externally. The whole environmental management process needs to be integrated as in figure 4 (Source: Gray et al. 1993, p. 91).

Figure 4: Stages in the Pursuit of Environmental Excellence

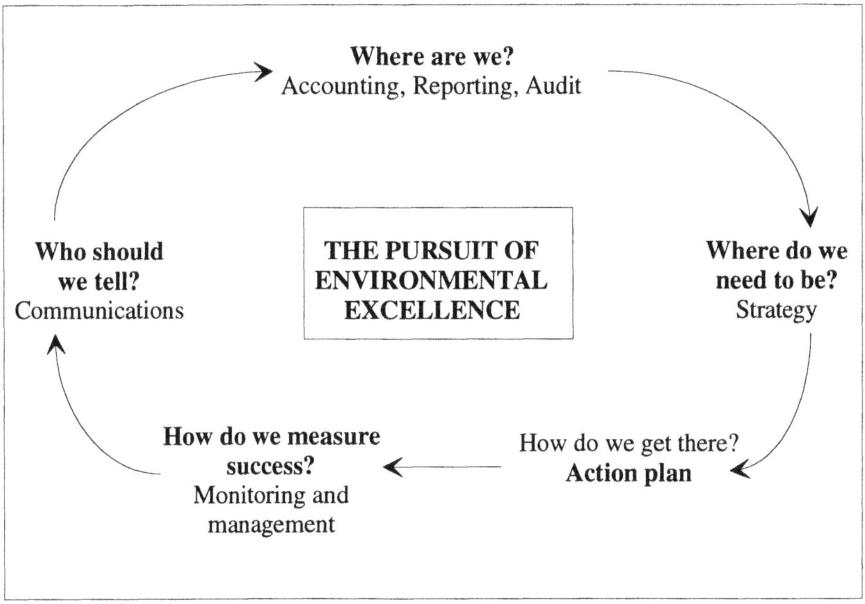


Source: Gray et al. 1993, p. 91

It may be imagined that the development and implementation of such an environmental management system, seeking to meet targets of continual environmental improvement, with a view ultimately of enabling the economy as a whole to comply with strong sustainability standards, would be expensive and damaging to competitiveness. This can be true. However, there is now substantial evidence that this need not be the case.

The natural resources that are used in economic processes normally have to be purchased. The discharge of wastes during or at the end of a process represents a failure to use productively all the purchased inputs. The waste resource is also wasted money. Moreover, disposal of the waste will often have to be paid for. Waste management costs, while vital once wastes have been generated, are also a waste of money in that they add nothing to the service delivered by a product. Finally, where the processes or products involved are potentially toxic or otherwise hazardous, they will be subject to regulations and controls, compliance with which may also be costly. Therefore environmental management systems can actually result in net savings and improve competitiveness, if they lead to changes in company practices which save money in excess of the cost of implementing the management systems.

Smart 1992 (p. 3) gives five reasons why it can benefit corporations to move 'beyond compliance' with regulations in their environmental performance:

- Preventing pollution at source can save money in materials and in end-of-pipe remediation.
- Voluntary action in the present can minimise future risks and liabilities and make costly retrofits unnecessary.
- Companies staying ahead of regulations can have a competitive edge over those struggling to keep up.
- New 'green' products and processes can increase consumer appeal and open up new business opportunities.
- An environmentally progressive reputation can improve recruitment, employee morale, investor support, acceptance by the host community and management's self-respect.

Smart gives many examples of firms which have benefited financially for these reasons from voluntary environmental management initiatives:

- Between 1975 and 1992 the 3M Corporation saved more than $530 million from all the projects in its 3P (Pollution Prevention Pays) programme (Smart 1992, p. 13).
- Feeling exposed because of its status as highest reporter of listed substances in the Toxic Release Inventory of the US Environmental Protection Agency, Dupont's CEO reports that the company embarked on an ambitious emissions reduction programme. "The result is a total air emission reduction of 80 percent within one year. Our investment of just over $250,000 results in annual savings of $400,000 - instead of a $2-million investment for an incinerator that would have cost an additional $1 million annually to maintain and operate." (Smart 1992, p. 191)
- Under its Tank Integrity Program, Chevron replaced all its old underground petrol tanks with double-walled fibreglass tanks although this was not strictly required. However, a Chevron Vice-President notes: "Making right contamination from a leaking tank could cost the company $250,000 or more. If such a liability could be prevented with an expenditure of $25,000 to $50,000, then it's well worth it." (Smart 1992, p. 103)
- Pacific Gas and Electric adopted a programme on Customer Energy Efficiency, which involved it investing in the more efficient use of energy by its customers, and sharing in the resulting financial savings. Its 1991 measures under this programme reduced emissions of nitrogen oxides by 445 tons, of sulphur oxides by 120 tons and of carbon dioxide by 340,000 tons, and earned the company $45.1 million before taxes.

The Smart (1992) 'beyond compliance' studies were of US corporations, but very similar results were reported in a recent study of UK business: "The main benefits reported from investment in cleaner production systems were cost savings through improved waste management, improved public image for the company and staff motivation, cost savings through better energy management, improved process efficiency, and increased profitability. Substantial savings could be made though energy management systems and relatively simple 'housekeeping' modifications to production processes. Longer term gains in competitiveness were expected by many firms, mainly large corporations with sophisticated strategies for environmental management." (Christie et al. 1995 p. xi)

**Responses to Environmental Regulation and Taxation**

The companies whose experiences of environmental management have been briefly reviewed above have shown how far it is possible to improve environmental performance alongside conventional business goals through voluntary commitment. Their actions are equivalent to the voluntary internalisation of costs which before were escaping their management systems and reducing the welfare of others. The case studies show the extent to which these companies have been able to turn such internalisation to their competitive advantage in order to remain profitable in an economic context which currently permits the externalisation of costs to continue.

However, there is little prospect that the necessary transformation to 'clean business' can be achieved through voluntary action alone. Companies like those above are in a small minority in business as a whole. Most do not proceed voluntarily down the route of environmental improvement. Indeed, Christie et al. (1995, p. 216) report a widespread view among the environmentally leading companies they surveyed that "diffusion (of cleaner production systems) so far was patchy and disappointing given the imperative of the transition towards sustainable development, and the fact that cleaner production techniques hold out the prospect of integration of business goals with environmental protection and of major new opportunities for product and process innovation." The diffusion is slow and patchy due to organisational and market failures, especially in the small business sector. But it also seems likely that, in competitive markets, if the option of externalising costs is available, the baseline for business profitability will be set by taking advantage of that option. Only exceptional companies will be able to maintain profitability where others routinely externalise costs. The purpose of government intervention in such a situation is to change the competitive rules, enforcing the internalisation of environmental costs, so that the firms which achieve it most efficiently have a competitive advantage rather than the reverse.

This is not the place for a detailed exposition of the possible ways government may seek cost internalisation. Jackson (1993, pp. 301ff.) lists regulatory programmes, economic instruments, the provision of training and information, including eco-labelling systems, voluntary agreements with industrial sectors (usually backed up by the threat of regulation), the imposition of liability for environmental damage and insistence on full disclosure. Government can also seek to use its power as a major purchaser by applying environmental conditionalities to its contracts.

Both Jackson (1993, pp. 301ff.) and Christie et al. (1995, p. 218) are in agreement that regulations are the most important factor in the promotion by government of clean or cleaner production. It is also generally desired by firms that are committed to proactive environmental management themselves. In Christie et al.'s survey of environmental leaders, "Very few user-company respondents wanted to see voluntary approaches in place of legislation: they wished to see environmental requirements apply to all firms in order to avoid the problem of free-riding" (Christie et al. 1995, p. 218). Other firms tend to be nervous about stringent regulations, believing them to impose costs and damage business competitiveness. Such fears are transmitted to politicians, who worry in their turn about closures, corporate relocation and unemployment.

There is in fact very little evidence that environmental regulations to date have harmed competitiveness in any way. Not only is there the experience cited earlier of the firms who had gone beyond regulatory requirements and improved their competitive position. In addition a number of studies have sought but failed to find significant evidence of economic disadvantage from environmental regulation. Surveying these studies, the OECD reports: "The trade and investment impacts which have been measured empirically are almost negligible." (OECD 1996, p. 45) Jaffe et al. (1995, p. 157)'s recent review concludes that "studies attempting to measure the effect of environmental regulation on net exports, overall trade flows, and plant-location decisions have produced estimates that are either small, statistically insignificant or not robust to tests of model specification." Curiously, despite these results, they persist in believing that "the long-run social costs of environmental regulation may be significant" (ibid., p. 157) and that regulation imposes "large direct and indirect costs" (ibid., p. 159), when their review of the relevant studies seems to have shown just the opposite. De Andraca & McCready (1994, p. 70) of the Business Council for Sustainable Development dismiss fears that environmental regulation can damage an economy: "Concerns about pollution havens, free riders or an exodus of capital and jobs from countries with tough standards are unsubstantiated." They emphasise in contrast the competitive benefits to be gained by innovation and eco-efficiency induced by stringent regulations and high prices of environmental resources.

Porter has explored in detail the factors that seem to contribute to competitive advantage. He is in no doubt about the potential benefits for competitiveness of corporations pushing themselves, or being pushed by regulations, towards improved environmental performance: "Stringent standards for product performance, product safety, and environmental impact contribute to creating and upgrading competitive advantage. They pressure firms to upgrade quality, upgrade technology and provide features in areas of important customer (and social) concern. ...Particularly beneficial are stringent regulations that *anticipate* standards that will spread internationally. These give a nation's firms a head start in developing products and services that will be valued elsewhere. Social concerns such as the environment are increasingly differentiating factors in advanced markets, and regulation influences the response of a nation's firms to them. ... Firms, like governments, are often prone to see the short-term cost of dealing with tough standards and not their longer-term benefits in terms of innovation. Firms point to foreign firms having a cost advantage. Such thinking is based on an incomplete view of how competitive advantage is created and sustained. Selling poorly performing, unsafe, or environmentally damaging products is not a route to real competitive advantage in sophisticated industries and industry segments, especially in a world where environmental sensitivity and concern are rising in all advanced nations." (Porter 1990, pp. 647-648)

There is now enough case-study evidence to confirm that environmental regulations can stimulate cost-saving innovation, while not implying that they will always do so. Similarly the evidence does not support a view that environmental regulations cause competitive disadvantage. A cautious conclusion, therefore, is that environmental regulations have a broadly neutral, if not positive, economic effect overall. However, there is widespread agreement among economists and policy analysts that they are a less efficient way of achieving many environmental goals than the use of economic instruments, such as environmental taxes and charges, tradable permits and other means of direct financial incentives for environmental improvement. There are several reasons for their greater efficiency:

- They equalise the marginal cost of abatement across polluters, so that all the cheapest options for abatement are implemented first.
- They can be as effective for diffuse sources of pollution, which are difficult to regulate, as for point sources.
- By becoming incorporated into the prices of products, environmental taxes in particular give incentives to consumers as well as producers to shift away from environmentally intensive consumption.
- Because environmental taxes are payable on all a particular use of the environment (unlike regulations which permit its free use once the regulatory requirements have been met), they give an incentive for continual environmental improvement at all levels of use.
- By raising revenue, environmental taxes provide the means to give earmarked subsidies, where appropriate, to achieve environmental improvements beyond those arising from the price effect, or to reduce distortionary taxes elsewhere. Where these are labour taxes, greater employment may result.

The increasing use of environmental taxes and charges has been noted above. Despite their theoretical advantages such instruments tend not to be popular with businesses, which continue to fear their impact on competitiveness. Such taxes also have the effect of causing businesses to pay for all their use of the taxed environmental resource, whereas with regulation their use up to the regulated limit tends to be free of charge. Businesses therefore tend to prefer negotiated, sometimes called voluntary, agreements to reduce their environmental impacts. Such agreements have become an important element of environmental policy in several countries (e.g. Netherlands, Germany, Japan). They are entered into with governments, who agree to preserve a stable policy climate during the duration of the agreement, provided that the relevant business or businesses fulfil(s) agreed environmental conditions. Sanctions in the event of non-fulfilment may or may not be part of the agreement, which is in any case usually negotiated under an implied threat of regulation or environmental taxation if the agreement fails to be concluded. Businesses do not only tend to like these agreements because of the flexibility such agreements give them in the attainment of environmental goals. Lévêque (1996, p. 28) has found that during the negotiation process the environmental goal of the agreement tends to be progressively weakened.

The differing nature and advantages of different policy instruments mean that environmental policy needs to be carefully designed to maximise the chances that firms will respond to it innovatively rather than defensively. Porter & van der Linde (1995, p. 110) give three conditions for the design of environmental policy to encourage innovation: the adoption of clear goals, with a flexibility which allows firms to attain them in their most cost-effective way; the encouragement of continuous improvement through the use in policy of economic incentives, voluntary agreements and the dissemination of information; and better co-ordination of environmental regulation, between industry and regulators and between regulators themselves at different levels (local, national, supra-national). Wallace (1995, pp. 250, 266), on the basis of his case-study of six European countries, regards the last condition as the most important of all: "The choice of instrument will frequently have less of an influence on the prospects for harnessing innovation than the political climate of industry-regulator relationships and the nature of day-to-day industry-regulator interactions. ... Stable long-term policies and effective dialogue can create a culture which rewards proactive, responsible firms and reduces the risk of investing in innovative solutions."

# 5. Innovations in Consumption and Institutions

## Consumption

In order to encourage changes in consumer behaviour towards environmental sustainability, a similar range of policy instruments is available as for producers:

(1) Economic incentives
Environmental taxes encourage consumers to switch away from environmen-

tally intensive products, while deposit refunds encourage them to facilitate re-use and recycling. Environmental taxes on consumption have no effects on competitiveness, in contrast to production, where such effects (real or imagined) have proved a major constraint on their implementation. On the other hand, care must be taken that the imposition of environmental taxes on consumers is not regressive (relatively more burdensome on the poor than on the rich). Also, institutional constraints and market failures can sometimes reduce the responsiveness of consumers to price incentives. This issue is discussed further below.

(2) Regulation
Sometimes, as with producers, environmentally destructive consumer behaviour is restricted by legislation. Examples include restrictions on coal-burning in cities (to improve urban air quality); obligations on car owners to maintain their vehicles adequately (to reduce exhaust emissions); bans on the hunting of wild animals or the ownership of endangered species; duties on households to separate for recycling certain fractions of their waste-stream, and so on. For consumers who are thus constrained, such prohibitions or obligations represent costs, or a loss of welfare, whether or not they actually entail expenditure. Of course, the presumption behind the regulation is that social welfare overall is enhanced by the regulation. To the extent that consumer preferences change, through education or changes in social values, such that they no longer wish to pollute the air, or they become to keen to recycle, the loss of welfare from the obligation or prohibition may be reduced, and the expenditure may actually come to be viewed in a positive light. For example, a change in attitude may come to regard a catalytic converter, for example, as a valued consumer good, which adds to individual welfare, rather than an externally imposed cost. Such changes are the consumer equivalent of the innovation in production which enables a firm to reduce its environmental impact and its costs.

(3) Provision of Information: Ecolabels
If changes in attitude reduce the costs to consumers of changing their behaviour, then information which facilitates such attitude-change becomes an important source of wealth-enhancing innovation. Clearly consumer attitudes are partly shaped by social events, awareness and fashion, which may generate broad shifts in consumption, and it is important that such shifts are informed and motivated by general environmental awareness as much as possible. However, to bring about particular changes in consumption requires the provision of product-specific information, which presents its own problems. Environmental information is complex, but product information, whether provided by a manufacturer or an independent source, and whether in advertisements or with the products, needs to be simple to retain consumer attention. The perception that environmental concern may affect spending behaviour has led to a the adoption of a wide range of slogans and symbols by both manufacturers and official bodies, intended to transmit an 'environmentally friendly' mes-

sage. There is some evidence, in the UK at least, that consumers have been confused by this plethora of sometimes misleading information (NCC 1996, p. 53), resulting in a decline in their green purchasing commitment. However, an ecolabel that is trusted by consumers remains an immensely important innovative device, with the potential of simultaneously bringing about environmental improvement, increasing consumer welfare and sending signals of environmental concern to producers through a single purchase. The slow progress in the development of the European ecolabel is causing a regrettable delay in the realisation of these benefits.

In many ways the archetypal policy approach to environmentally damaging consumer goods remains the treatment of cigarettes. A regularly increasing tax (in the UK at least) provides an unequivocal price signal that this is a demerit good. The health warning on the packet serves as an unambiguous 'ecolabel'. This message is periodically backed up by national, publicly-funded advertising. The result has been a pronounced decline in the use of a highly addictive product and a change in social attitudes towards smoking, away from regarding it as a sign of sophistication and modernity, towards a perception that it is private vice to be pitied and a social nuisance to be strictly controlled in public. There are few signs of a similar attitude emerging towards, say, the motor car (to take one example of a product that is highly damaging environmentally), but it is possible to detect even here a shift towards social disapproval in some quarters, and apology from some users. However, there are currently no proposals that motor cars should be forced to display a prominent health warning. Perhaps that will come.

## Institutions

An emphasis on the importance of institutions in economic life, with regard to both production and consumption, is one of the major strands in economic literature, produced by one of the major schools in the discipline. Institutions are not just organisations. They are the structures of rules, habits and routines that guide daily life, including market transactions, in practically every respect. As far as innovation is concerned, institutions may exert a positive or negative influence. Negatively their reliance on habits and routines may cause them to miss opportunities and act inappropriately when circumstances change. Positively, the routinisation of everyday detail can enable institutions to focus on new situations and act swiftly and effectively. It is the institutional nature of the firm that causes it to overlook profit-making improvements to its environmental efficiency, examples of which were given above. But it is also the institutional nature of the firm that enables it to respond quickly once these possibilities have been brought to its attention. Herein lies the importance of the price mechanism in achieving environmental innovation in firms, because all firms have their attention on costs. Once a previously external environmental cost becomes perceived as a cost increase, through the imposition of an environmental tax or charge, it engages with all the firm's well-established routines of cost-reduction. The negative aspect of firms' institutional nature is overcome, because all firms are conscious of costs, and the positive aspect is fully exploited because cost-reduction is one of the major goals towards which all of firms' routines are directed. Turning environmental costs into business costs is an absolutely sure way of ensuring that they will be attended to.

On the consumer side, Hodgson (1988, p. 129) presents evidence that consumers too are to a large extent creatures of habit, which suggests that environmentally positive changes in consumer behaviour may not be easy to achieve. Although price increases of consumer goods may cause consumers to re-assess their habits, it is unlikely that this mechanism will be as effective as with firms, because consumption is not as competitive an activity as production. That is to say that although goods clearly do compete on price in a consumer's mind, except for the poor there is not normally the same need as for firms to focus as single-mindedly on cost. This underlines the importance of combining price increases with environmental awareness raising and easily assimilated information about products if patterns of consumer behaviour are to be substantially altered.

Finally there is also evidence that the structure of some institutions can itself militate against environmental efficiency and improvement. A well-known example is the so-called landlord-tenant problem, in which neither party has the incentive to invest in energy efficiency, because the former does not benefit from the energy savings derived (unless the rent can be increased), and the latter may not have security of tenure for the required payback period, or, perhaps, the right to make alterations to the premises. Such problems occur, as Jackson (1996, p. 108) notes, "whenever there is a separation of responsibility for costs from the enjoyment of benefits". Another problem also noted by Jackson (1996, pp. 108, 132) is that energy utilities derive their profitability from supplying energy, rather than conserving it, even when the marginal cost of conservation is less than the marginal cost of supply. In such a situation it would be in the interest of both the utility and its client to invest in conservation in the client's home, rather than expand supply, provided that the price of the saved energy could be charged to the client at between the marginal cost of conservation and that of the now unnecessary supply. However, to achieve this often requires a radical revision of energy pricing arrangements. The positive results of such institutional innovation with regard to Pacific Gas and Electric is described above.

Another institutional innovation in the operation of markets with great potential for environmental improvement is the assignment to producers of the responsibility for the take-back and disposal (usually with minimum recycling requirements) of their products. Effectively this amounts to a radical shift away from the purchase and ownership of products by consumers towards the purchase of the services to be derived from them. The 1991 German Packaging Ordinance was the first full-scale application of this idea, but experienced problems arising from a lack of commercial professionalism and a failure to prepare markets for the quantities of recyclable material conserved (see Wallace 1995, p. 74). For more complex products, such as vehicles and personal computers, which are both being investigated in this connection, a take-back provision would provide substantial encouragement for design and recovery for recycling. Where applicable, the costs of the research and development for the necessary product reformulation could be offset with payments of some part of what it currently costs public agencies to dispose of such products.

## 6. Conclusion

Innovation is the very stuff of markets and gives to capitalism its uniquely dynamic quality among economic systems. Producers are always looking for opportunities to innovate, in order to cut costs and to develop new products which will cause consumers to innovate (i.e. change their consumption patterns). In itself, innovation need not be of particular benefit to the environment. There are plenty of new products and technologies which cause environmental damage, while the economic growth to which innovation gives rise can also pull more energy and materials through the economic system to the detriment of the environment.

However, markets' restless search for innovation can be harnessed by appropriate policy to encourage moves towards sustainable development. The most important component of such a policy is probably the use of the price mechanism, the basic means of co-ordination of markets. Firms are uniquely attentive to prices in both absolute and relative terms, and they give important signals too to consumers. However, price changes need to be both gradual and anticipated if they are to avoid economic disruption, such as the premature scrapping of capital, and encourage innovation rather than retrenchment. Innovation takes time and cannot be produced to order. Firms must be given the time, and perhaps financial support, to develop a new generation of low environmental impact products and technologies.

There are numerous other policy instruments which can and should be used to reinforce the unremitting signals from the price mechanism. This paper has mentioned corporate environmental accounting, environmental management systems, regulations and voluntary agreements. It has presented some evidence that shows that such instruments need not cause costs to a firm. Sometimes, by encouraging innovation, they can lead to cost-savings which improve corporate performance. Again this is not an inevitable rule, and 'technology forcing' for its own sake would not appear to be a sound policy. However, the evidence suggests that, contrary to assumptions in the past, innovation can enable firms to move towards environmental sustainability at low, if not negative, cost.

For consumers, the main reinforcement to price signals will be from the provision of information which brings about attitude changes towards environmental destruction, and enables consumers to express new environmental concerns through their purchasing habits. Institutional changes may also help win-win gains in environmental efficiency to be realised. Such changes can reduce, or completely remove, consumers' perceived loss of welfare from less environmentally damaging consumption patterns.

Returning to the question at the beginning of this paper, it is not yet clear whether innovation will yield enough environmental benefits for environmntal sustainability to be reached not only without reducing consumption but in a context of continually increasing incomes. It is also not clear whether, even in rich countries, if the choice really is between increasing incomes and environmental sustainability, consumers will choose the latter. Certainly the market's prodigious capability to induce innovation, and the various policy instruments to channel that capability towards environmental improvement, gives society its best chance of not having to make that choice.

## References

Anderson, T. & Leal, D. (1991): Free Market Environmentalism, Westview Press, San Francisco/Oxford

Barbier, E.B., Burgess, J. & Folke, C. (1994): Paradise Lost? The Ecological Economics of Biodiversity, Earthscan, London

Bishop, R. (1993): 'Economic Efficiency, Sustainability and Biodiversity', Ambio, Vol.22 No.2-3 (May), pp. 69-73

Christie. I., Rolfe, H. & Legard, R. (1995): Cleaner Production in Industry: Integrating Business Goals and Environmental Management, Policy Studies Institute, London

Ciriacy-Wantrup, S.V. (1952): Resource Conservation: Economics and Policies, University of California Press, Berkeley

Daly, H.E. (1991): 'Elements of Environmental Macroeconomics', *in* Costanza, R. Ed.: Ecological Economics: The Science and Management of Sustainability, Columbia University Press, New York

Daly, H.E. (1992): 'From Empty World to Full World Economics', *in* Goodland, R., Daly, H.E. & Serafy, S. El (Eds.): Population, Technology and Lifestyle: the Transition to Sustainability, Island Press, Washington DC

Daly, H.E. (1995): 'On Wilfrid Beckerman's Critique of Sustainable Development', Environmental Values, Vol.4 (1995), pp. 49-55

De Andraca, R. & McCready, K. (1994): Internalizing Environmental Costs to Promote Eco-Efficiency, Business Council for Sustainable Development, Geneva

De Groot, R.S. (1992): Functions of Nature, Wolters-Noordhoff, Groningen, Netherlands

Ditz, D., Ranganathan, J. & Banks, R.D. (1995): Green Ledgers: Case Studies in Corporate Environmental Accounting, World Resources Institute, Washington D.C.

DTTI (Deloitte Touche Tohmatsu International), IISD (International Institute for Sustainable Development) & SustainAbility (1993) Coming Clean: Corporate Environmental Reporting, DTTI, London

EC (European Commission), (1992): Towards Sustainability: a European Community Programme of Policy and Action in Relation to the Environment and Sustainable Development, Volume 2, European Commission, Brussels

Ekins, P. (1997): 'The Kuznets Curve for the Environment and Economic Growth: Examining the Evidence', *in* Environment and Planning A, Vol. 29, pp. 805-830

Elkington, J. & Robins, N. (1993): 'The Corporate Environmental Report', Discussion Paper, New Economics Foundation, London

Folke, C., Holling, C.S. & Perrings, C. (1994): 'Biodiversity, Ecosystems and Human Welfare', Beijer Discussion Paper Series No.49, Beijer International Institute of Ecological Economics, Stockholm

Gray, R., Bebbington, J. & Walters, D. (1993): Accounting for the Environment, Paul Chapman Publishing, London

Grossman, G.M. & Helpman, E. (1994): 'Endogenous Innovation in the Theory of Growth', Journal of Economic Perspectives, Vol.8 No.1, pp. 23-44

Hartwick, J. (1977): 'Intergenerational Equity and the Investing of Rents from Exhaustible Resources', American Economic Review, Vol.67 No.5, pp. 972-974

Hodgson, G. (1988): Economics and Institutions, Polity Press, Cambridge

Hueting, R. (1980): New Scarcity and Economic Growth, North Holland, Amsterdam (Dutch edition first published 1974)

Hueting, R., Bosch, P. & de Boer, B. (1992): Methodology for the Calculation of Sustainable National Income, Statistical Essay M44, Netherlands Central Bureau of Statistics, Voorburg/Heerlen

Jackson, T. Ed. (1993): Clean Production Strategies: Developing Preventive Environmental Management in the Industrial Economy, Lewis Publishers, Boca Raton (FL)/London

Jackson, T. (1996): Material Concerns: Pollution, Profit and the Quality of Life, Routledge, London

Jaffe, A., Peterson, S., Portney, P. & Stavins, R. (1995): 'Environmental Regulation and the Competitiveness of US Manufacturing: What Does the Evidence Tell Us?', Journal of Economic Literature, Vol. XXXIII (March), pp. 132-163

Lévêque, F. (1996): Environmental Policy in Europe: Industry, Competition and the Policy Process, Edward Elgar, Cheltenham, UK

NCC (National Consumer Council) (1996): Green Claims: a Consumer Investigation into Marketing Claims about the Environment, National Consumer Council, London

OECD (1989): Economic Instruments for Environmental Protection, OECD, Paris

OECD (1994): Managing the Environment: the Role of Economic Instruments, OECD, Paris

OECD (1996): Implementation Strategies for Environmental Taxes, OECD, Paris

Pearce, D. & Turner, R.K. (1990): Economics of Natural Resources and the Environment, Harvester Wheatsheaf, Hemel Hempstead, Herts., UK

Perrings, C., Turner, R.K & Folke, C. (1995): 'Ecological Economics: the Study of Interdependent Economic and Ecological Systems', Beijer Discussion Paper Series No.55, Beijer International Institute of Ecological Economics, Stockholm

Pezzey, J. (1992): Sustainable Development Concepts: an Economic Analysis, World Bank Environment Paper No.2, World Bank, Washington DC.

Porter, M. (1990): The Competitive Advantage of Nations, Free Press (Macmillan), New York

Porter, M. & Van Der Linde, C. (1995): 'Toward a New Conception of the Environment-Competitiveness Relationship', Journal of Economic Perspectives, Vol.9 No.4, Fall, pp. 97-118

Smart, B. Ed. (1992): Beyond Compliance: a New Industry View of the Environment, World Resources Institute, Washington D.C.

Turner, R.K. (1993): 'Sustainability: Principles and Practice', *in* Turner, R.K. (Ed.): Sustainable Environmental Economics and Management: Principles and Practice, Belhaven Press, New York/London, pp. 3-36

UN (United Nations) (1993): Integrated Environmental and Economic Accounting, Interim Version, UN Statistical Office, New York

Victor, P.A. (1991): 'Indicators of Sustainable Development: Some Lessons from Capital Theory', Ecological Economics, Vol.4 (1991), pp. 191-213

Victor, P., Hanna, E. & Kubursi, A. (1994): 'How Strong is Weak Sustainability?', paper presented to the conference 'Models of Sustainable Development', Paris, March, in Conference Papers, Vol.1, pp. 93-114

Wallace, D. (1995): Environmental Policy and Industrial Innovation, Royal Institute for International Affairs/Earthscan, London

WBGU (German Advisory Council on Global Change) (1995): 'Scenario for the Derivation of Global $CO_2$ Reduction Targets and Implementation Strategies', WBGU, Bremerhaven

# 2. Guiding Prinicples for Sustainable Industrial Innovations

# Industrial Innovation Strategies - Towards an Environmentally Sustainable Industrial Economy

*Frieder Meyer-Krahmer*

## 1. Introduction and Overview

This contribution sets out from the assumption that policies in our states will try to develop actions and relations between actors in such a way that the second scenario of global development, as described in the introduction of this book, will be aimed at: i.e. a development with growing North/South inequality and regionally limited crises would be the background for innovations and innovation policy. The industrial innovation strategies discussed in this paper would aim at supporting this path towards an ecologically sustainable economy though it does not seem to be clear yet, if these strategies would suffice to reach the goal.

Considering this pattern of development and the role of industrial techno-organisational innovation, this paper begins with the presentation of three guiding principles of environmental policy for an environmentally sustainable economy:

- increased use of environmentally friendly technology as traditional principle
- closing of industrial material cycles
- holistic product policies and product utilisation.

It will be demonstrated that the increased use of environmentally friendly technology has resulted in considerable advantages for the environment. The basic problem of this guiding principle is that the increased use of environmentally friendly technology alone does not produce the degree of efficiency which is probably required for an environmentally sustainable economy.

There are already a great number of examples of closed-loop material cycles in industrial production, which also make interesting economic sense (including cascaded re-use). The present gigantic efforts to set up a recycling economy also follow this model; its limitations however are that the reconversion from goods into raw materials and secondary materials which can be re-utilised in the production process still represents a relatively wide "cycle" (which means losses in resource efficiency).

The transition from production responsibility to product liability causes a basic change in the direction to the guiding principle "holistic product policy", which can be regarded as symptomatic for an environmentally sustainable industry.

These guiding principles, however, are not only desirable from a point of view of environmental policy, but are also attractive for the participants in economic activities (enterprises and consumers alike) under market economy conditions. Therefore, they have good chances to be realised and will mean a really substantial change for the better in our environmental conditions. This can be seen in the shift in the perspectives in the industrial attitude towards environmental technology. Initially regarded principally as cost-increasing investments, environmental technologies have brought the Federal Republic of Germany, as the second largest exporter worldwide, considerable economic success meantime. The cost-saving potentials of resource-conserving management have been implemented in part in many branches of the economy.

This shift in perspective will continue, as is to be expected in an evolutionary economic system. Environmentally sustainable economics means in this case not only "defensive" environmental protection (e.g. compliance with regulations), but makes possible new innovation and business strategies for enterprises. Impulses for this shift in strategy may be changes in the price system (internalisation of external costs of resource utilisation), state regulations, voluntary self-regulation and changes in consumer behaviour. In my view, such entrepreneurial innovation strategies will determine the essential dynamics of the way towards environmentally sustainable economics under market economy conditions. To illustrate this view, innovation strategies to intensify product utilisation and to prolong the life cycle will be treated in detail, their consequences as regards production, product characteristics and market strategies presented. Examples from daily practice will illustrate their successful realisation.

## 2. A Necessary Change of Perspective in the Industrial Attitude Towards Environmental Technology

In Germany we have been discussing the environment, pollution, and the possibility of coming to grips with this problem since the 1960s. It was a highly controversial and wide-spread discussion in which politics promised e.g. "blue skies over the Ruhr" and demanded the application of protective and clean-up techniques to attain this end. Economics and economic policy discussed above all the question of resulting costs and the disadvantages for German competitiveness, whereas even early studies on this subject pointed to positive impacts for employment (Sprenger 1979). Only few enterprises recognised a *potential for new business areas* in the *state-created market.* Only a few understood the imperative need to save energy and material, which had been growing noticeably since the early 1970s, with the oil crisis, and the evidence from studies such as "Limits to Growth" (Meadows et al. 1972) and "Global 2000" (1980), as a potential for saving costs. On the contrary, technologies for environmental protection were mainly judged to entail cost-increasing investments. Since the second half of the 1980s, however, the *growing private demand* for environmentally compatible products began to shape consumer markets, which in turn influenced the industrial markets (see figure 1).

Figure 1: Changes in Perspective in the Industrial Attitude towards Environmental Technology: The Case of Germany

- 1960s and 1970s
  - cost-intensive investments
- 1980s
  - cost-saving potentials of resource-conserving production
  - beginnings of market development:
    recycling and waste disposal industry
- 1990s
  - change from production to product responsibility
  - orientation towards customer needs

The *cost-saving potentials* of resource-conserving production are recognised in the meantime in many industrial branches and have also been realised in part. As regards environmental relief, however, the limits of end-of-pipe technologies have become obvious, so that in the meantime - also with government support for research and development projects (cf., e.g.: BMFT: Produktionsintegrierter Umweltschutz, 1994; US Government: National Environmental Technology Strategy, 1995) - a concentration on the development of integrated technologies has developed. In addition, a new market is beginning to crystallize, nourished through increasing costs and limited waste disposal capacities. In common with state initiatives to encourage recycling they contribute to the formation of a new sector, waste disposal management. Not least because of the concentration of environmental policy on waste disposal, the waste disposal industry is one of the branches with the highest growth rates. The German Federal Association of Disposal Management Enterprises (BDE) quotes the total sum for waste disposal services in Germany in 1992 as DM 20 billion. It assumes that this market will grow by 20-30% annually in the years to come. Powerful enterprises have recognised the growth possibilities in the waste disposal market and have entered the market in a big way, especially large energy-supplying companies but also big businesses from the building sector.

The German exports of goods for environmental protection show that the increased use of environment-friendly technology can mean commercial success, too: Germany was the worldwide biggest exporter of environmental protection technologies between 1989 and 1992, and was second largest exporter in 1993 with a share of 18.5% of the world market (BMBF 1996). According to the figures of NIW and ISI (NIW/ISI 1994; cf. also their remarks on the difficulty of statistical demarcation of this sector), exports amounted in 1992 to approx. DM 38 billion. Goods to protect the environment in the widest sense thus made up approx. 6% of German exports in 1992. The demand for technologies to protect the environment also creates jobs. It is not surprising, therefore, when serious estimates of the impact of environment protection on the job market point to a positive balance. At present roughly 956,000 jobs in Germany can be classified as involving environmental protection activities (DIW 1993; DIW, Ifo, IWH, RWI 1996). The number is expected to increase continously within the next years.

The change in perspective is continuing. In future the main task will not be to dispose of waste in as environmentally friendly a manner as possible (and to recycle), but to prevent waste being generated at all (or reduced to small amounts). This means not only environmental efficiency in production, but above all in the products. This change in perspective will be greatly accelerated by the further cost increases for waste disposal and the use of environment capacities which are to be expected and the resulting demand from the market.

The change in perspective also shows that an increase in net profits can be achieved by cutting the costs for waste disposal. Here the need is for new products and services. Ways to this end, which can be explored besides material recycling, are the extension of product and component life cycles, or the intensified utilisation of products and components. Both strategies lead to higher profits because the customer is offered multiple uses, a reduction of material and energy costs and simultaneously less waste disposal costs by slowing down material throughput.

This is supported by the results of recent ISI enquiries with the Delphi technique on the realisation timetable for important technical/scientific environmental innovations (cf. BMFT 1993). From these data pointers to future market developments can be deduced. For innovations relevant to the environment expected to be realised between 1998 and 2015 it appeared that aspects of communal waste disposal are judged to have (absolute) priority timewise, which finally means the introduction of economical methods of recycling domestic waste. The future of domestic waste sorting lies with machinery, which is expected to be available from 2008. The beginning of the next century will herald the use of biologically degradable packaging material on a large scale.

The other priority subject timewise is the problem of global climate change. Here, a better understanding of processes in the ozone layer, then the clarification of the impacts of the destruction of tropical rainforests on climate and the weather, the influence of the greenhouse effect on worldwide agricultural production, the influence of the growing desertification on the climate are expected. Because for many of the problems of climate change the understanding of the phenomena and the complex cause-effect-relationships still has to be developed, the proposal of concrete innovations in this technology foresight exercise were rather scarce. Among these, however, are the utilisation of substitute substances for CFC and halons before the end of the century and the reduction by 20% worldwide of the present carbon dioxide levels by the year 2009. At the end of the timescale in the area of ecotechnology are rather Utopian technical visions like e.g. the absorption of carbon dioxide in oceans and through the use of coral riffs or the development of a technique to use fossile fuels while preserving the balance of nature (see the examples in figure 2).

# 3. New Industrial Guiding Principles

The guiding principles of environmental policy are not strictly divided: often different expressions are used for the same or similar objects, besides, there are floating boundaries between the guiding principles, and overlapping occurs. Without raising a claim to completeness, the technology-oriented guiding principles (for the following cf. Böhm/Walz 1994) will be described and their scope and limitations commented upon. These guiding principles do not mutually exclude, but complement each other.

### Increased Use of Environmentally Friendly Technology

This guiding principle is the continuation of the environmental policies pursued until now. The basic idea consists in reducing the environmental damage in the future through the increased use of environmentally friendly technologies (cf. Angerer et al. 1991, Enquête-Kommission - Commission of Inquiry - 1990, Prognos/ISI 1991). This guiding principle encompasses (cf. Böhm/Walz 1994) not only cleaner technologies, but also additive technologies, because emissions and waste cannot be completely avoided, despite greatly improved production and manufacturing processes. The development is proceeding in the direction of more efficient, i.e. especially effective, reliable and cheap additive technologies, which are more specifically tailored to the combination with integrated measures.

The focus of technological developments, however, lies indubitably on integrated production processes ("clean[er] technologies"), in which pollutant emissions and waste are avoided or considerably reduced right from the start. The trend to substitute environmentally protective processes for traditional ones will form an integral

Figure 2: Some Future Environmental Technologies

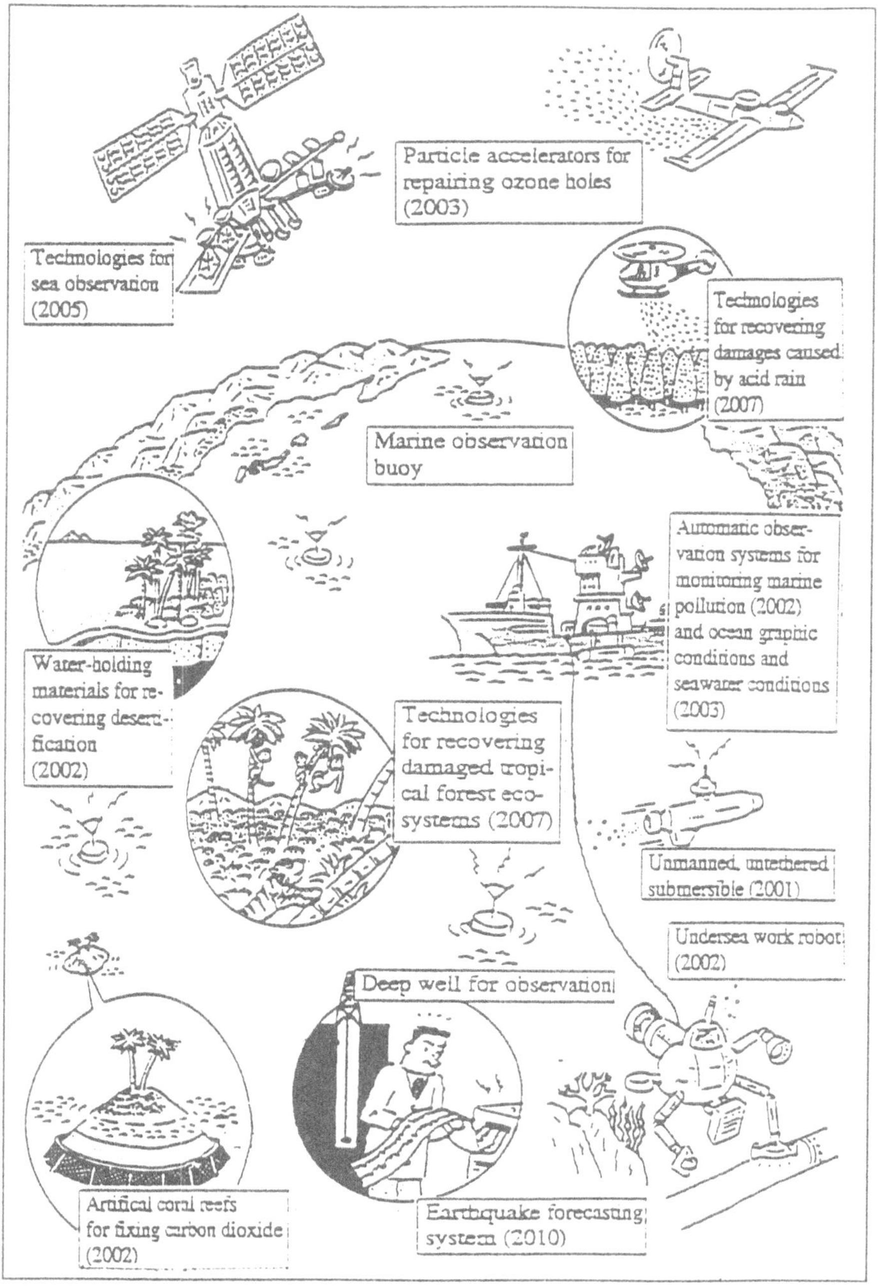


Source: NISTEP 1992

part of new developments in future, whereby the solutions can be very specific to the individual problem or branch. However, some cross-sectoral attempts to improve traditional processes have also been made (Böhm/Walz 1994):

- changes in raw materials, intermediary products or process materials;
- substitution of complete processes by improvements/substitutions in individual steps, process technologies, machines;
- optimisation of process operation and control with the aid of modern measurement, control and adjustment techniques;
- technical alterations in operating processes.

## Closing of Industrial Material Cycles

In the production process, the guiding principle for closing the material loops of industrial streams aims to work up any residues arising from production, and to filter emissions from process materials, and to re-use them in the production process (cf. Böhm/Walz 1994 for the following). Such process materials are emitted from the process on the one hand, on the other hand they are impure or alter their characteristics in time, so that they must be exchanged, leading to production backlog. By means of additional adjustments/steps in the production process these materials could be separated off, cleaned up or regenerated and be available for use again. Due to the great increase in costs for waste disposal, the recuperation of emissions or residues often makes economic sense. The ideal of a *closed-loop system* without emissions and total recycling can only be realised in rare cases, as the cleaning or regeneration of process materials usually also produces waste matter; its quantity, however, is small by comparison with the recycled amount.

The *re-use system in cascade form* refers to the utilisation of production residues in subsequent processes either in the same production process or in other branches. The cascade re-use system does not completely fill the requirement of the closed-loop system for material streams, but can still lead to significant reductions in material flows. The expression "cascade" hints to the fact that each step in the cascade takes place at a somewhat lower quality or energy level than in the preceding step. It should only be selected if a closed-loop cannot be realised for technical reasons or because of high costs (from the individual enterprise's viewpoint).

A variety of closed-loop and cascade re-use systems in production processes which are interesting from the economic side are already being used. The reduced water requirements in industry have resulted to a large extent from the recycling of cooling or waste water in the same or in other processes in the sense of a closed-loop or cascade re-use, with up to 14 recycling steps. There are examples of genuine closed-loop systems to be found in the chemical industry, too (cf. Wiesner 1990), and for the use of cascade recuperation (the coupled production in the chemical industry is regarded as a classical example of this). Further examples of closed-loop systems can be seen in the recycling of solvents in lacquer and in cleaning facilities, recycling methods in electroplating, and the regeneration of industrially used catalytic converters. The crucial impulse to adopt closed-loop systems and cascade recuperation are cost savings and the increased economic efficiency of the method (caused by alterations in the price system, the internalisation of external costs, and increasing shortages).

Besides the use of closed-loop systems in production, waste disposal policy intends to close the loop of material flows by feeding back used *products* into the production process. The aim is to increase the re-use of "waste". The beginnings can be seen in several products at present, e.g. packaging material, electronic scrap, batteries, automobiles. At present, waste disposal and recycling are the foci on which industry's innovation endeavours are especially concentrated. This guiding principle is thus aiming at the reconversion of goods into raw materials and secondary materials and feedback into production.

**Holistic Product Policies**

The shift from production responsibility to product liability (as it is also formulated in § 22 of the German Ecocycle Law) is causing a fundamental change in the guiding principles of industrial activities. Starting point is the recognition that not only the production processes but even more so the resulting products use up a major part of the available resources and cause considerable emissions into the atmosphere (e.g. solvents), into surface water bodies and in ground water (e.g. detergents, pesticides), and critical forms of waste. Core demand of this guiding principle for industrial activity is therefore to watch out for ecological compatibility even during product development. Several strategies are possible here. An ecological design can start off with the material content of the products (non-use of pollutants) or aim to extend the product life and usage, and the re-use and recycling capacity of the products. In order to effect a real saving of resources, product design must not be regarded in a void, but the entire life cycle of the product, from the materials and intermediary goods via production and utilisation to its ultimate disposal, must be taken into consideration. The top instrument to realise this guiding principle is the transition from a linear production/consumation/waste progression to a cradle-to-grave strategy of *utilisation cycles.* As far as production technology is concerned, this means the closing of material flow cycles on as high a level as possible (see figure 3).

The demand for ecologically sustainable products requires diverse new technological provisions. So all manufacturing technology must be optimised, not only with a view to production, but also as regards waste disposal, in order to facilitate e.g. the re-use and recycling of individual components. Further requirements result, such as

Figure 3: Technical Strategies for Closing the Material Loop for Products

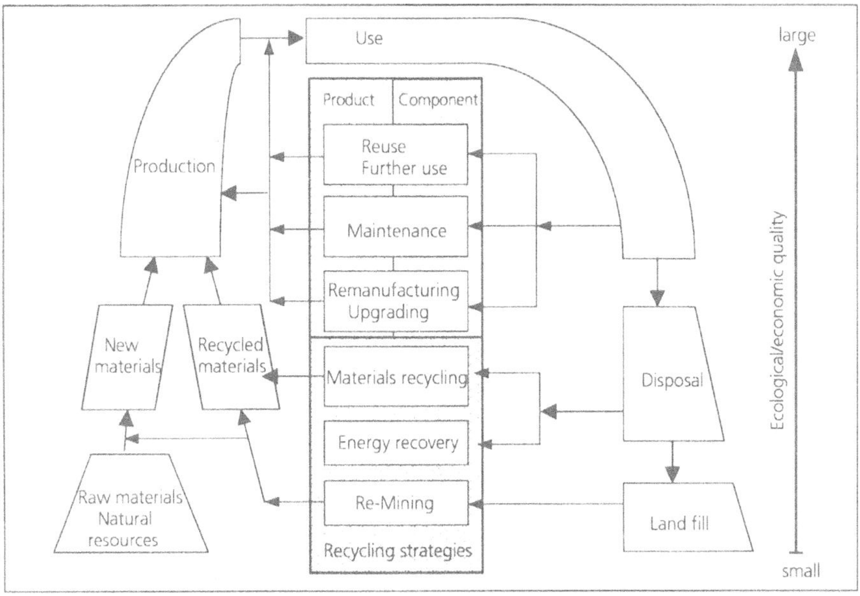


cutting down on the number of different materials, identifying materials in order to simplify sorting, designing constructions easy to disassemble, and easily released connecting systems. Following technological requirements are derived from the aim of extending product life: constructions easy to repair, check and maintain; modular production concepts, in order to provide for modernisation and upgrading of durable goods; constructive solutions and protective measures to minimise wear and tear and corrosion; re-use of component parts as exchange goods (cf. VDI 1993). Ecologically sustainable economic management means in this case not just "defensive" environment protection (e.g. compliance with regulations), but pre-supposes new innovation strategies on the part of enterprises (Lenox 1996). In my opinion these enterpreneurial innovation strategies will determine the essential dynamics of the way towards an ecocycle economy and thus towards a future-oriented market economy.

## 4. Management of Ecocycle Product Strategy: Design and Utilisation

Assuming market economy conditions also for a sustainability scenario, the guiding principles described above will only have a chance of being realised if they meet economic profitability criteria and do not deteriorate the competitiveness of enterprises. In fact, such impulses arise from the implementation of rules that will increasingly force enterprises in Germany as well as in other industrial states, at the beginning of the 21st century, to take over not only the external costs of their production but also the external costs of their products. As a consequence of the anticipated obligation to take back their products after use, they will be increasingly confronted with the necessity to optimize the utilisation and life period of these same products which means to establish holistic product policies. This trend has already led to the present day situation, where services that prolong product life (repairs, reconditioning) as well as leasing are increasingly an important profit source, as compared with the manufacture of products. Also, the establishment of "after-sales" markets in several countries (for example in the USA) is an indicator of such a development.

Generally speaking, the *following strategies* can be distinguished for *designing an improvement of the utilisation and life span of products* (adapted from Stahel 1991):

- products designed to last longer,
- increased use of maintenance and repair,
- the upgrading of products in use through modernisation,
- the re-use of components from used products in manufacturing new products, as well as
- service strategies (sales of utilisation instead of sales of products; divided, joint or multiple use; selling the service "function guarantee" instead of selling substitute products).

The changes in perspective contained in such strategies open up new market possibilities through introducing new consumer durables to the market, or through introducing new modes of usage for such goods (e.g. by selling the function instead of the product itself). The benefits expected from usage will finally determine how the product is actually acquired (buying, rental, leasing, user coops, use on public offer), as well as the most suitable product design. Thus the strategy "sales of results (practical use) instead of goods" means that the economic emphasis of the enterprises is shifted from manufacturing (production) to product management, that is from production companies to operating and leasing companies ("fleet management"). This is accompanied by a far-reaching manufacturer's liability, which requires the constructors to design products of great reliability, tolerance of misoperation, protection against unauthorized or improper use, which also inevitably means an extended life cycle for the goods. A holistic product policy also demands a substantial change in the requirements of continuous incorporation of technical change into the products.

Thus very differing concepts, through all stages from manufacturing to disposal, lead to more long-lasting products, whereby the strategies can start from the product, component or materials level (figure 4). Several paths are open to exploitation:

Figure 4: Strategies for Products, Components and Materials

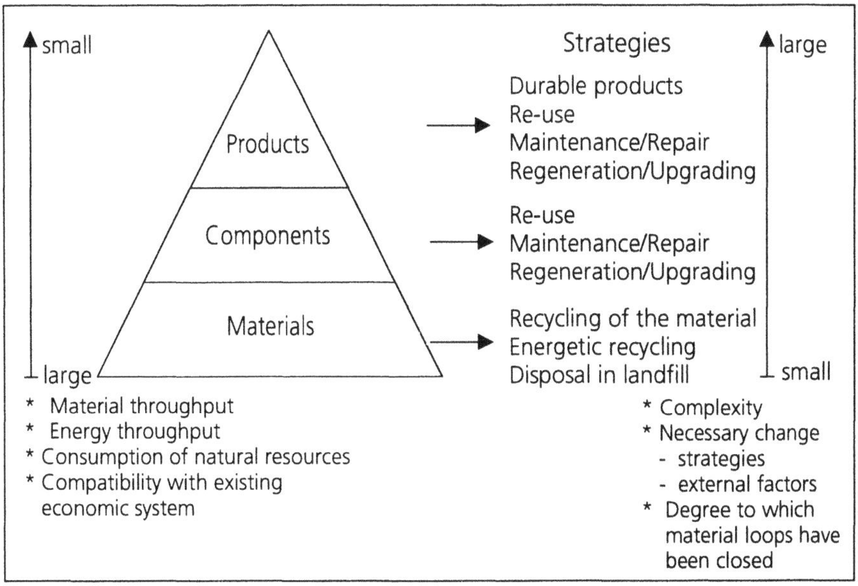


from modular construction with the exchange of single, compatible components, long-lasting durable goods, prolonging the useful life through re-use (recycling), repair, and re-conditioning and the technological upgrading of products. But new marketing strategies are necessary, also with a view to the suppliers and consumers (figure 5).

On the supplier side the increased introduction of "more intelligent" products (multi-purpose products) seems appropriate, while the consumer can develop a "more intelligent" expression for utilisation which gives precedence to joint using of (suitable) products (shared or multiple use) over individual use. Furthermore, alterations to improve resource productivity are possible at the interface between product suppliers and users/consumers. The basis for this is a definition of prosperity which does not regard the possession of products (and the associated selling of products) as the source of affluence, but rather the utilisation of products (and the selling of product utilisation). These approaches lead to a more intensive utilisation of products and to an extension of the product life and so contribute to conserving resources.

A longer active life for products has considerable impacts on the economic structural change, the way to deal with the existing stock of goods (stock management), as well as on research and development, for example (see figure 6):

- Components and products that can be flexibly repaired and adapted to future requirements and technologies, open systems with a high degree of interchange-

Figure 5: Integrated Strategies for the Vendor/Customer

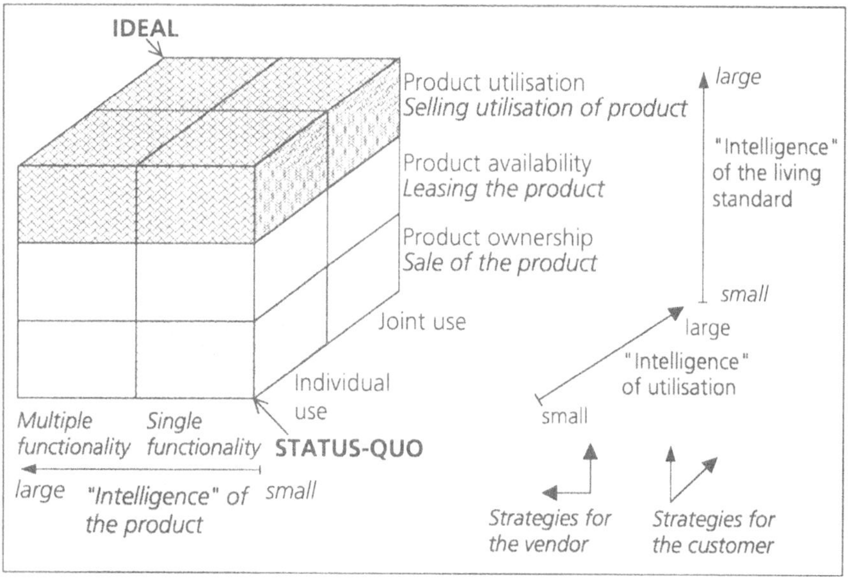


ability, in order to continually integrate technical advances into existing systems (without having to exchange a complete system, thus slowing down progress), should be developed. "Life cycle engineering" is called for in product development, in order to close the loop of material flows.

- Substitution of central manufacturing plants by decentral workshops staffed by specialist craftsmen (servicing, maintenance, technological upgrading).
- Increasing significance of the insurance business through the growing importance of product liability.
- Shift from a production-oriented industrial society to a utilisation-oriented industrial service society.

Completely novel entrepreneurial strategies can be realised with this approach. They contain a variety of objectives such as cost-saving, quality improvement, new business fields, as well as combined product/service offers, and are at the same time compatible with the aim of an ecologically sustainable economy. There are already markets and companies which pursue these strategies. Examples are to be found in the aviation industry, manufacturers of photocopiers, drink vending machines and component manufacturers (see e.g. Stahel 1994, ISI 1995 for examples). This behaviour can be partly explained by special characteristics of the market (such as costly capital goods, strong market power of buyers, high safety precaution measures,

Figure 6: Effects and Prerequisites of/for Ecocycle Product Policy

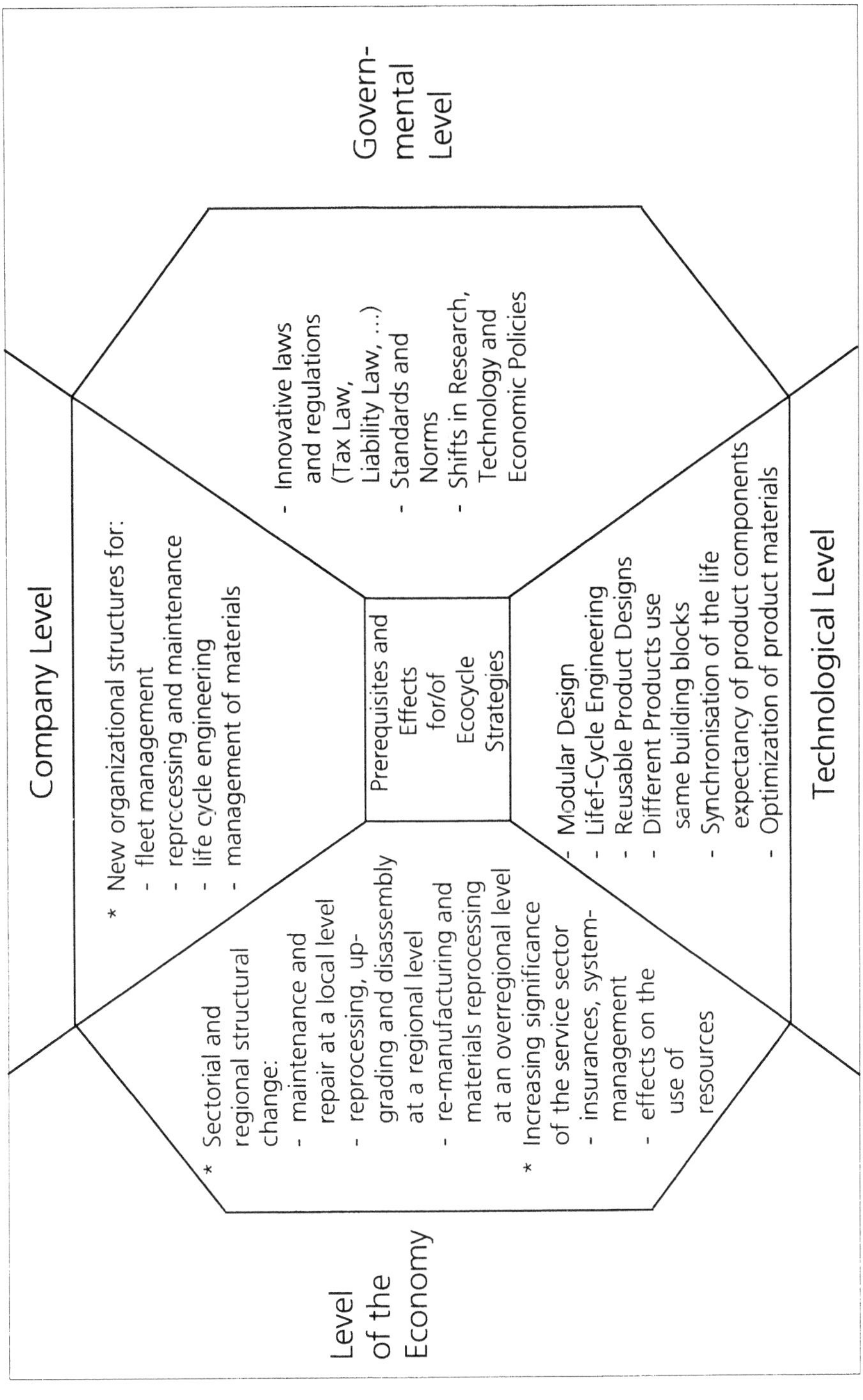

high market transparency (in the case of the aviation industry), but also by company-specific strategic approaches. Individual enterprises have developed and implemented solutions for specific problems of product durability and use-intensification, often in a historical process. These solutions are often in the fields of re-manufacturing processes, i.e. dismantling, cleaning, and re-assembly, or of service and hire concepts. Other aspects of product life cycles have seldom been considered up to now. Also, research into the subject under which conditions such innovation strategies are technically viable, business-wise profitable as well as economically and ecologically desirable is very much in its infancy.

The speed with which such innovation strategies are adopted depends not least on the changes in the political framework conditions, the shifts in consumer preferences and also the "mental structural change" in the enterprises. In any case these innovation strategies will bring about a radical sectoral structural change, the consequences of which the companies will have to consider in advance. Von Glass (1993) studied the impacts on raw material suppliers, manufacturers/component suppliers, dealers/workshops and scrap car merchants of the "cascade car". The long life of the cascade car because of the (re-newed) components leads to a slump in the business activities of the raw material suppliers and the scrap car merchants, because of the conservation of resources. For the car manufacturers, dealers and component suppliers the sinking potential in new cars is more than compensated for by the new business areas with the cars of the second utilisation cycle. The car recycling companies also suffer from the drop in the number of cars taken off the road, i.e. less scrap cars. A re-orientation in the growing repair branch offers substitution possibilities. This example shows that the speed of dissemination of such innovation strategies is substantially influenced by the power of the winners and losers. Here lies the real line of conflict determining the speed with which these guiding principles assert themselves. This battle is not joined between left/right, ecological/non-ecological, employer/employee, but runs right through the economy, society and politics.

## References

Angerer, G./Hiessl, H. (1991): Umweltschutz durch Umweltelektronik - Anwendungen, Chancen, Forschungs- und Entwicklungsbedarf, Berlin/Offenbach

BMBF: Bundesministerium für Bildung, Wissenschaft, Forschung und Technologie (Hrsg.) (1996): Zur technologischen Leistungsfähigkeit Deutschlands, Bonn

BMFT: Bundesministerium für Forschung und Technologie (Hrsg.) (1993): Deutscher Delphi-Bericht zur Entwicklung von Wissenschaft und Technik (Studie des Fraunhofer-Instituts für Systemtechnik und Innovationsforschung (ISI) im Auftrag des BMFT), Bonn

BMFT: Bundesministerium für Forschung und Technologie (Hrsg.) (1994): Produktionsintegrierter Umweltschutz, Förderkonzept des BMFT, Bonn

Boehringer Mannheim (1990): Symposium Umweltschutz durch Biotechnik, Penzberg

Böhm, E./Walz, R. (1994): Neue Zielsetzungen der Umweltpolitik und deren Konsequenzen für den künftigen Technologiebedarf, *in:* Jahrbuch Arbeit und Technik

DIW (Deutsches Institut für Wirtschaftsforschung) (1993): Beschäftigungswirkungen des Umweltschutzes. Erich Schmidt Verlag, Berlin

DIW, Ifo, IWH, RWI (1996): Aktualisierte Berechnung der umweltschutzinduzierten Beschäftigung in Deutschland, in der Reihe Umweltpolitik des BMU, Bonn

Enquête-Kommission "Vorsorge zum Schutz der Erdatmosphäre" (1990): Schutz der Erde, 3. Bericht der Enquête-Kommission "Vorsorge zum Schutz der Erdatmosphäre", Bundestagsdrucksache 11/8030, Bonn

Grupp, H. (1995): Der Delphi-Report: Innovationen für unsere Zukunft, Deutsche Verlags-Anstalt Stuttgart

Hohmeyer, O./Walz, R. u. a. (1992): Methodenstudie zur Emittentenstruktur in der Bundesrepublik Deutschland. Verknüpfung von Wirtschaftsstruktur und Umweltbelastungsdaten, Studie des FhG-ISI im Auftrag des Umweltbundesamtes, Karlsruhe

Infratest Industria (1990): Auswirkungen von Umweltschutzmaßnahmen auf die Wettbewerbsfähigkeit umweltkostenintensiver Produktionen der Deutschen Wirtschaft, Eigenverlag, München

ISI - Fraunhofer-Institut für Systemtechnik und Innovationsforschung (Hrsg.) (1995): Industrielle Konzepte der Nutzungsintensivierung und Lebensdauerverlängerung von Produkten, Ergebnisse eines Workshops, Karlsruhe

Kunz, P. (1992): Umwelt-Bioverfahrenstechnik, Vieweg-Verlag, Braunschweig/ Wiesbaden

Lenox, Michael (1996): Reverse Logistics and Industrial Ecology: Innovation and Design in the Recovery Allocation Decision, MIT Working Paper, Cambridge

Meadows, Dennis L./Meadows, Donella (1972): The Limits to Growth, Universe Books, New York

NISTEP 1992: The Fifth Technology Forecast Survey - Future Technology in Japan, National Institute of Science and Technology Policy (NISTEP), Tokyo 1992

NIW/ISI: Niedersächsisches Institut für Wirtschaftsforschung (NIW), Fraunhofer-Institut für Systemtechnik und Innovationsforschung (ISI) (1994): Innovationspotential und Hochtechnologie - technologische Position Deutschlands im internationalen Wettbewerb, Schriftenreihe des Fraunhofer-Instituts für Systemtechnik und Innovationsforschung (ISI), Band 8, Physica-Verlag, Heidelberg

Prognos/ISI (1991): Konsistenzprüfung einer denkbaren zukünftigen Wasserstoffwirtschaft, Kurzfassung, FhG-ISI-B-44-91, Basel/Karlsruhe

Reiß, T. (1990): Perspektiven der Biotechnologie, Köln

RWI (1991): Umweltschutz, Strukturwandel und Wirtschaftswachstum, Essen

Sprenger, R.-U. (1979): Beschäftigungseffekte der Umweltpolitik, unter Mitarbeit von G. Britschkat, Schriftenreihe des Ifo-Instituts für Wirtschaftsforschung, Nr. 101, Duncker & Humblot, Berlin - München

Stahel, W. R. (1991): Langlebigkeit und Materialrecycling - Strategien zur Vermeidung von Abfällen im Bereich der Produkte, Essen

Stahel, W. R. (1994): Produkt-Design und Ressourcen-Effizienz, *in:* Zoche, P. (Hrsg.): Herausforderungen für die Informationstechnik. Schriftenreihe des Fraunhofer-Instituts für Systemtechnik und Innovationsforschung (ISI), Band 7, Physica-Verlag, Heidelberg

(US-) Council on Environmental Quality and the (US-) Foreign Department (ed.) (1980): The Global 2000 Report to the President, Washington, U.S. Government Printing Office

US Government (1995): Bridge to a Sustainable Future, Washington D.C. 1995, (containing the National Environmental Technology Strategy)

VDI (1993): Konstruieren recyclinggerechter technischer Produkte - Grundlagen und Gestaltungsregeln, VDI-Richtlinie 2243, Düsseldorf

von Glass, Th. (1993): Einzel- und volkswirtschaftliche Auswirkungen einer ressourcenschonenden Produktgestaltung. Manuskript, ISI/Universität Karlsruhe, Karlsruhe

Walz, R. unter Mitarbeit von Gruber, E., Hiessl, H., Reiß, T. (1992): Neue Technologien und Ressourcenschonung, Fraunhofer-Institut für Systemtechnik und Innovationsforschung (ISI), Karlsruhe

Wiesner, J. (Bearb.) (1990): Produktionsintegrierter Umweltschutz in der Chemischen Industrie - Verpflichtung und Praxisbeispiele, DECHEMA, Frankfurt

# The Firm's Perspective of Industrial Innovation Strategies Towards an Environmentally Sustainable Industrial Economy

*Jacqueline Cramer*

## 1. The New Challenge

The need to achieve sustainable development represents an enormous challenge for society. It means that within the space of a few decades we will have to learn how to use energy and raw materials much more efficiently. According to some estimates, within the next 50 years the burden on the environment will, on average, have to be reduced to one tenth of the current levels in highly industrialized, Western countries (this means an increase in eco-efficiency by a factor of ten) (Weterings, Opschoor 1992). As a first step into this direction von Weizsäcker, Lovins and Lovins (1995) promote an increase in eco-efficiency by a factor of four (this means one quarter of current levels).

Steps have already been taken within industry to increase the average eco-efficiency of production techniques. Most of these efforts focus on *incremental* environmental improvements to existing working methods, products and services at operational level. These options often bring significant progress in the early stages of process and product development because they capitalize on the 'low hanging fruit' (the easy improvements), but performance then levels out as marginal improvements become more difficult and hence more costly (Arthur D. Little 1996).

In order to reach the target of a tenfold increase in the average eco-efficiency mentioned above, *more far-reaching, innovative* improvements are needed in current production techniques. This contribution will focus on how we can bring about the change processes needed to achieve this in industry.

## 2. From Incremental to Far-Reaching Environmental Improvements

We ought not to underestimate the importance of small, incremental environmental improvements. Indeed, the environmental gain that can be achieved by *optimizing the existing production facilities and products* is far from negligible. To start with, in the 1970s, the emphasis lay almost exclusively on curative measures which involved the application of end-of-pipe techniques (such as filters or grease traps). This enabled the diffuse distribution of pollution to be prevented (and collected in filters or grease traps), but it did nothing to remove the cause of the pollution. Since the end of the 1980s, there has been a rise in interest in the optimization of processes and products by means of preventive measures.

The aim of this has been to employ better process management or environmentally-oriented product development to prevent waste and emissions as far as possible and to save raw materials and energy. This prevention-oriented approach has been successful from an environmental point of view.

When added together, the incremental environmental improvements in lots of different companies represent a considerable benefit to the environment. Furthermore, incremental improvements of this kind pave the way for far-reaching environmental improvements. Companies are not usually keen to make more fundamental improvements to processes, products and services from an environmental point of view if they have not yet gained any experience at all in the field of environmental issues. In view of this, the introduction of sustainable development can be seen as a continuous learning process. The challenge now is to stimulate this learning process so that it develops in a more eco-efficient direction - leading to an even lower consumption of energy and raw materials. How do we bring about such radical changes? Generally speaking, there are two possibilities:

a. far-reaching modernisation of *existing* processes, products or services
b. the design of *entirely new* product chains by means of function-oriented innovations.

Some companies have already started to gain practical experience with innovations geared *to far-reaching modernisation* of the current production techniques. The time scale for such innovations lies between 5 and 20 years, depending on the lead time of the product or process. In the case of consumer electronics products, where product innovation is rapid, the time scale is shorter (5 to 7 years) than for innovative transport systems, for example, or large-scale production processes in the chemical or raw metal industry. The time scale is therefore dependent on the period which the relevant company can envisage for their specific product or process.

On the whole, far-reaching modernisation of the current production techniques involves one of three types of modernisation:

- Firstly, a fundamental modernisation of the existing production processes. This focuses on a redesign of the existing production installations so that the eco-efficiency is improved greatly. Examples include modernisation of the process management in energy-intensive sectors, such as the (petro)chemical and raw metal industries.
- Secondly, far-reaching modernisation can mean an increase in the eco-efficiency in product chains. It is particularly those larger companies and (government) organisations which play a key role within the product chain that are often the ones

taking the lead in this change process at the moment (IVA 1995). They analyze the places in the product chain where the greatest burden on the environment is caused and they then try to work together with other producers in that chain to solve these problems. This type of approach is also known as 'integrated chain (or 'life cycle') management' (Cramer 1996). It requires intensive exchange of information about environmental aspects and collaboration between companies and organisations on many different fronts (including co-makership agreements).

- Thirdly, far-reaching modernisation of the current production techniques can be carried out on a regional scale. A relatively simple example of this is the heating of houses via central energy-saving total energy units. It is also possible to develop more complex systems for the exchange of energy, raw materials and (waste) water. A good example of this is the initiative introduced by an electricity company, a nearby oil refinery and a large pharmaceutical company in the Danish town of Kalundborg (Tibbs 1991, Knight 1992). Here, waste heat from the factories is used to provide district heating in the town. Hot water is also supplied to fish farmers for use in heating the fish breeding tanks. Waste materials such as fly ash and gypsum are processed locally by a cement factory and a plasterboard manufacturer. The factories also use each other's waste water and waste gases. This form of regional chain management is also known as industrial symbiosis or industrial ecology.

In addition, we will also have to look further ahead to the development of *function-oriented innovations*. This involves adopting a fundamentally new conceptual approach which necessitates great adjustments in our current production and consumption patterns. Individual companies and organisations tend to be reluctant to take the lead, particularly if such a process of adjustment spans a very long period. It is difficult for them to envisage the contribution that they themselves can make in practice. Some of them are, however, willing to participate in research programmes which work towards achieving this aim. A good example of this is the Dutch programme 'Duurzame Technologische Ontwikkeling' (Sustainable Technological Development) (Jansen, Vergragt). This programme aims to develop innovative ideas about how to find a sustainable way to enable society to fulfil its social needs in the year 2050 (such as food, housing, clothing and mobility). Working on the basis of the period up until the year 2050, this programme endeavours to work out which types of sustainable technological solutions are feasible and can be implemented. The resulting research programmes focus on considerable increases (by approximately a factor of ten) in eco-efficiency. Programmes like these thus generate 'breakthrough' technologies which will form the basis for a society that is organised in a much more eco-efficient way.

If we want to make greater eco-efficient strides in environmental areas, there are therefore two things we need to do: 1. Stimulate research into function-oriented innovations and, 2. Support practical initiatives which lead to far-reaching modernisation of the current production techniques. It takes time to develop and introduce such modernisation.

That is why it is important that we take action now to set up activities in these fields so that in the long term we will be able to harvest the 'high fruits' these provide.

Implementation of these initiatives in practice necessitates not only technical but also economic, socio-organisational and broad social change processes. The more radical the environmental innovation, the *higher the risk* and the *more complex* such change processes prove to be. Naturally, this is a challenge, but at the same time it is also the problem. Why would companies and organisations want to embark upon such an uncertain adventure? If we look at the economic risks that are associated with the different types of environmental innovations, then we see that radical innovations usually require the largest initial investment, but can ultimately also lead to greater benefits (see figure 1). Prevention-oriented incremental environmental improvements do admittedly already save costs in the short term, but in the longer term they bring fewer benefits than far-reaching environmental improvements. Application of 'end-of-pipe' technology generally requires investment (for example, in filters), yet the financial gain is minimal (although there are then lower dumping or pollution costs).

Figure 1: Costs and Benefits Resulting from Different Types of Environmental Innovations

| ➢ Type of environmental measures ➢ | Curative technology | Preventive technology | | | |
|---|---|---|---|---|---|
| | | Optimization of existing production and products | | Far-reaching modernization of the current production techniques | Function-oriented innovations |
| ⮟Economic changes ⮟ | "End-of-pipe" measures | Prevention of waste and emissions | Environmentally-oriented product development | Integrated chain management | Sustainable development |
| costs (-)<br>benefits (+) | - | + | + | from -<br>to ++ | from --<br>to +++ |

- = costs
+ = benefits

It is not only the economic risks, but also the complexity of the change process that will increase as the innovation becomes more radical. More groups in the chain or in society in general become involved as we take increasingly far-reaching environmental measures. For example, in order to bring about regional chain management, all the companies on one industrial site will have to work together and also make agreements with the local authorities about supply of the residual heat to households and/or organisations (for example hospitals or schools). All of the groups that become involved in initiatives of this sort will experience, to a greater or lesser degree, the economic and socio-organisational effects of this. It involves a complex process of weighing up interests and negotiating between the participating groups so that a choice can be made that is acceptable to all parties. Bringing about more fundamental change processes of this sort is thus not an easy task.

The complexity does not only increase in terms of the rise in the number of groups involved. The subject matter itself also becomes more complex. When far-reaching environmental improvements are made, it is no longer sufficient to treat the environment as a separate issue: environmental issues have to be weighed up against all sorts of socio-economic issues and other social aspects. In addition to environmental specialists, more environmental generalists will therefore have to be employed to ensure that environmental issues are integrated into other areas.

Lastly, the complexity increases for other reasons, too. Decisions about far-reaching environmental improvements require more strategic processes for weighing up the pros and cons than is the case for decisions about incremental environmental improvements. This means that the people high up in the organisation will have to be committed to the introduction of far-reaching environmental improvements. If these are to be introduced successfully, then at the same time basic support will be required from all the parties involved. This is, after all, a collective learning process. Far-reaching environmental improvements are thus of both a strategic and a basal nature.

Given the initiatives that have already been taken in relation to far-reaching environmental improvements, it is certainly true to say that there is a potential willingness to change in this direction. The main problem is how to mobilize this willingness to change as effectively as possible. What sort of change processes are required within companies? And what role can the government play in stimulating such change processes?

## 3. The Change Processes Required within Companies

In order to bring about far-reaching modernisation within companies, a fundamental change is required in a company's existing strategy on the environment. Companies need to adopt a more offensive strategic attitude. It is no longer only a matter of following a defensive strategy that is designed to comply with all the relevant environmental legislation and regulations. A cost-reduction strategy which focuses mainly on measures which provide short-term solutions is also inadequate. A company that wants to introduce far-reaching environmental measures must make strategic choices with regard to the environmental issues which it wants to boast in the market.

In practice it is not easy to follow the above-mentioned offensive strategy. To do so, a company must be able to distinguish itself from its competitors by scoring higher on environmental issues. For newcomers to the market this is perhaps still relatively easy; they can bring their product onto the market right from the start as one which is more ecologically sound. Companies which have already gained a certain image in the market will not want to adjust this image without good reason. Companies that have enjoyed a reputation as a supplier of high-quality products for many years, are reluctant to suddenly make explicit statements relating to the environment.

If they launch a given range on to the market and claim that it is more environmentally friendly, this may suggest that their other ranges are manufactured under less stringent environmental conditions. For this reason, an adapted marketing strategy is required, and there is little experience of this within industry as yet. Furthermore, such an adapted marketing strategy is a more obvious choice for manufacturers of finished products than for producers of basis raw materials. Companies in the chemical or raw metal industries, for example, will have to earn back their efforts by making greater advances in environmental efficiency (by making considerable savings on energy and raw materials) and by creating a good eco-image for all their ranges.

On the basis of my own experience within industry, and within Philips Sound & Vision in particular, the implementation of such an offensive strategy requires the selection of promising green opportunities. In order to prepare for this, Philips Sound & Vision has designed a methodology called 'STRETCH' (**S**election of s**TR**ategic **E**nvironmen**T**al **CH**allenges') (Cramer, Stevels 1996). The basic question that needed to be answered was: What opportunities or threats does the environmental issue present for a company such as Philips, particularly the Sound & Vision division? What technological options are available for dealing as adequately as possible with environmental problems? And finally, which environmental opportunities should be selected to enhance the business and express societal responsibility?

In order to address these questions, data was needed on the strategy and future market perspectives of the company itself. Moreover, information was needed about cultural trends and the possible set of environmental issues at stake in the future. On the basis of this information, scenarios can be formulated related to possible (environmental) futures. These scenarios are used to help prioritise, select and finally implement the most promising environmental challenges to be adopted by the company. In sum, the 'STRETCH' methodology consists of the following four phases:

| | |
|---|---|
| Phase 1: | the collection of data on future market perspectives, cultural trends and environmental opportunities/threats |
| Phase 2: | the integration of the available data into scenario analyses |
| Phase 3: | the prioritisation and evaluation of promising environmental strategies |
| Phase 4: | the implementation of those environmental strategies ultimately selected |

The selection of promising environmental strategies, as described above, is one of the two main pillars of strategic environmental product planning. The other pillar concerns the structural embedding of this endeavour within the organisation. In practice, this is an even harder job than identifying and selecting strategic options. It requires a strategic way of thinking about environmental issues within the organisation, especially at senior management level. In fact, it requires environmental issues to become an integral part of the strategy development and marketing of new products. Achieving this involves a process of cultural and organisational change that takes time.

In the case of incremental improvements, it is still possible to introduce the environmental aspects in a later phase, but in the case of far-reaching environmental modernisation, that is no longer true. If, for example, a company wants to bring a product onto the market that consumes four times less energy (and therefore reduces energy consumption to a quarter of the current level of energy consumption) or can be run entirely on sustainable energy, then this represents a strategic choice which must be made by the senior management in a very early phase. Naturally, the senior management will base a strategic choice like this on estimates of the market chances, on what is technically and financially possible as well as on the environmental benefits that will be generated. Such estimates are prepared jointly by a number of different senior staff departments (including marketing, strategy and planning and the environmental department). Once the senior management has selected certain spearheads, the strategic choices that have been made will have to be translated into product requirements and, following this, into project plans which indicate how these product requirements can be fulfilled. It will then often be necessary to run R&D activities for this, and this can give rise to considerable financial costs. The results of these activities can then be used to determine how the proposed product plans, in adapted form if necessary, can be realised and in the end the newly developed products will be marketed.

Instead of only devoting attention to the environment at an operational level, senior managers will also have to make choices relating to the environment at a strategic level. For this purpose, additional rules will have to be drawn up in procedures which have been developed within a company for the purposes of product development. Naturally, it is not just important that these rules are recorded in writing, but also that they are implemented in practice.

This does not mean that only 'top-down' initiatives are important. In each company very useful 'bottom-up' proposals are often made which can improve the performance of a product in environmental terms, sometimes considerably so. Some of these improvements can be carried out at lower levels in the organisation, particularly if they do not involve any fundamental changes to the product. However, if far-reaching environmentally-oriented product improvements are involved, then the support of the management is essential.

In addition to greater involvement of the senior management, far-reaching environmental improvements also require a closer collaboration with the other groups involved in the product chain. This collaboration does not relate exclusively to the environmental issues. After all, the aim is still to bring a high-quality product on to the market, with the only difference being that greater account is taken of the environmental component of the product during negotiations between companies.

In the case of far-reaching process modernization within a company or integrated chain management initiatives, this can mean, for example, that suppliers have to supply products with a modified specification. If suppliers are not prepared to do this, the initiating company has two options: to look for another supplier, or to work with the current supplier to find a solution that is acceptable to both parties. In practice the bottlenecks here often lie in the cooperation. For example: the Dutch company Van Hecke Catering asked its suppliers to supply their products wherever possible in one certain type of plastic (polystyrene). This would have enabled Van Hecke Catering, in collaboration with a waste processing company, to recycle on as large a scale as possible. Most of the large suppliers were not prepared to do this because they had already made other agreements under the Nederlandse Convenant Verpakkingen (Dutch Covenant on Packaging) relating to the use of plastics (van Leenders 1996). For the (in their view) relatively small market made up by the catering companies, these suppliers were not prepared to bring a separate product onto the market. In such a situation, Van Hecke Catering can do little else than look for other solutions itself.

It is clear therefore that needs have to coincide both within the company and outside it if far-reaching environmental improvements are to take place. This is why we cannot just expect large numbers of companies to take initiatives of this sort off their own bat. There is a greater chance of a company taking the initiative if they also have some assurance that they will be able to reap the rewards of doing so. This could be because:

a. after initial investments they become more competitive as a result of a considerable reduction in the (environmental) costs and an improvement in the efficiency of their process management,
b. their market share increases as a result of them being able to distinguish themselves from their competitors with a more ecologically-sound product,
c. the know-how and environmental technology which they have developed can be sold on to third parties,
d. they have secured themselves a position in the market for the future.

There is an even greater chance of success, of course, if the other groups involved in a product chain or regional chain can also cash in on the benefits. In this way, real 'win-win' situations can be created.

# 4. External Stimuli

Change processes which are geared to far-reaching environmental improvements are, as we have seen from the examples above, difficult to get off the ground. These are high-risk and complex processes for which a favourable outcome is not necessarily guaranteed. Companies that are nevertheless prepared to stick their necks out for this, must not be discouraged from doing so by the outside world, indeed they must be encouraged. These front runners do after all play an essential role in the acceleration of change processes. They are the ones who, when they do succeed, manage to drag the others along with them.

So far external parties have not been very creative in stimulating this category of front runners. Many more ways need to be found to reward them, either materially or otherwise. If the front runners are manufacturers of finished products, the obvious course of action is to help create a greater demand for their products from the outside. Government bodies and other organisations can do this by gearing their own product procurement policy accordingly. In Switzerland, in the field of energy for example, there are priority lists of energy-saving electronics products which the organisations mentioned above can use when selecting their products. In a number of American states (including California), lists of this kind are also used. If the front runners are manufacturers of semi-finished products or raw materials, then other incentives will be required, such as the (joint) financing of R&D, for example.

Encouragement of the front runners is certainly not exclusively a task for the government. It is time we dropped our fixation with the 'father state'. By publishing their product tests, consumer bodies and environmental organisations could, for example, single out companies that perform well on the environmental front. They could also advertise these more than they do at present. Initiatives which enable companies to help themselves to produce cleaner products (such as the assignment Greenpeace gave to Swiss designers to develop a very energy-saving car, called 'Smile') even go a step further.

The financial world, too, can support the front runners in their attempts to bring about far-reaching environmental improvements. First of all, if shareholders were to base their preferences more on the long-term solvability of a company (and therefore also on its long-term environmental aims) this would have a great effect. In addition, with regard to the environment, the new, innovative companies in particular would benefit from an extension of, for instance, the 'Green Fund Ruling'.

The 'Green Fund', which has been set up to finance activities which have been 'declared green', is also starting to catch on in the Netherlands. In particular, projects in the field of nature conservation, organic farming and wind energy are emerging in large numbers. So far, however, few projects have been put forward which relate to far-reaching environmental improvements within the industrial sector. Banks could take initiatives in this field.

The question is of course, whether it is enough to encourage only the front runners if, in the long term, we are to achieve the necessary level of eco-efficiency - an increase by a factor of between 4 and 10. We will probably have to do more, particularly in the case of activities which constitute a heavy burden on the environment and where few or no front runners are willing to take the lead. National governments as well as the European Union will then have to take the lead to determine what measures will have to be taken with regard to these activities. They will have to formulate a limited number of spearheads from which they expect a high environmental gain, but which they know will not be achieved in the absence of specific intervention. Our current traffic and transport system would be a good candidate for this, for example.

In these cases, preferably covenants will have to be drawn up in conjunction with the target groups involved, which will indicate what contribution each party can make to these far-reaching environmental improvements. In so doing, the responsibility must be delegated as much as possible to those parties who are in fact the ones with the problem. This requires an entirely different set of policy instruments and an entirely different approach from governments than has hitherto been the case. In addition to monitoring the progress in the environmental sphere, they also have the task of managing change processes and removing conflicts of interest between the various parties.

What I am actually advocating here is a second generation of covenants. In contrast to the first generation of covenants, which have been concluded with various, mainly industrial sectors in the Netherlands and elsewhere, this second generation of covenants does not focus on the incremental, but on the far-reaching environmental improvements. Furthermore, the second generation of covenants is restricted to a number of specific spearheads that have been set by the government. These spearheads are expected to bring a high level of environmental gain, but in many cases there are no initiatives from the actual groups involved. Examples here are spearheads that focus on far-reaching improvement of specific production processes, product groups, regional chain management activities or transport concepts.

If the implementation of these second generation covenants does not produce the required results, the government could then still introduce regulatory measures. It is, however, preferable for solutions to come from within the relevant target groups. Experience gained so far with the 'first generation' covenants that have been used is encouraging in this respect. This applies above all to agreements that are made with sectors in which a limited number of large companies are represented. There are then obvious partners which can be contacted and solutions can often be found in joint consultation. It is important here that the agreements relate to the slightly longer term so that companies have sufficient time and space to prepare for these. In sectors where the small and medium-sized companies or other 'diffuse' target groups are strongly represented, experience with covenants has been less positive. The translation of the agreements that are made at sector level to individual companies or organisations and the control on implementation of these is hard to ensure. For these sectors the traditional instruments of legislation and regulations seem to be more appropriate.

Implementation of this second generation of covenants can have considerable economic and socio-organisational consequences for the companies, organisations and/or local authorities involved. There has to be an incentive to encourage the relevant groups to invest in this, despite the considerable efforts required to achieve far-reaching environmental improvements. The government could introduce various supportive measures here.

*One* possible way of doing this is to remove the bottlenecks which prevent the relevant companies from taking these steps. This means more consultation between the various partners in the change process so that they can discuss the problems which occur in the realisation of these improvements. These problems can be caused by the lack of an infrastructure or a clear market demand, but can also be due to financial hurdles which need to be overcome, or to seemingly insolvable conflicts of interest.

A *second* possibility lies in the field of tax rulings. These can be used to make the repair of products or the investment in R&D or production resources financially more attractive. If the tax system is geared to promoting ecology, a heavier tax burden can also be placed on activities which pollute the environment and there can be a reduced tax burden on other basic factors, such as labour.

A *third* possibility is a considerable expansion of existing incentive rulings in the field of R&D and initial investment. Such programmes would then have to be geared to the spearheads which have been formulated as part of the plan to 'catch the big fish'. Specific technological and even industrial policy can then be linked to these spearheads.

Such initiatives can lead to entirely new economic activities. Consider for example, the creation of an entirely new recycling sector, a sustainable energy sector and sustainable transport systems and the development of 'sustainable technology' centres that can sell their expertise to third parties at home and abroad. Such activities do to some extent lead to replacement of current employment, but at the same time they also create additional employment opportunities.

## 5. Conclusion

If we are to achieve the required increase in eco-efficiency, in the order of a factor 4 to 10, it is going to be essential that we create a social basis for this. This can even lead to shifts in the patterns of standards and values, and these may not necessarily be accepted. For example, a policy geared to recycling and reuse of products will make people more aware of the way they treat their environment (or consumer goods). That is why change processes will have to be shaped in such a way that people feel involved and see the point of what they are doing. Only a collective learning process will lead to more far-reaching steps towards sustainable development.

## References

Arthur D. Little, (1996): Sustainable Industrial Development; Sharing Responsibilities in a Competitive World, The Hague

Cramer, J., (1996): Experiences with Implementing Integrated Chain Management in Dutch Industry, Business Strategy and the Environment, 5, no. 1, p. 38-47

Cramer, J.; A. Stevels, (November 1996): Experiences with Strategic Environmental Product Planning within Philips Sound & Vision, Paper presented at the Greening of Industry Network Conference, Heidelberg

IVA (Royal Swedish Academy of Engineering Sciences), (1995): Environmental Management; From Regulatory Demands to Strategic Business Opportunities, Stockholm, Sweden

Jansen, J.L.A.; Ph. J. Vergragt, Naar Duurzame Ontwikkeling met Technologie: Uitdaging in Programmatisch Perspectief (Heading for sustainable development with technology: A challenge in programme perspective), Milieu, 8, no. 5, p. 179-183

Knight, Peter (1992): Closing the Loop, Tomorrow, p. 40-43

Tibbs, H., (1991): Industrial Ecology; An Environmental Agenda for Industry, Arthur D. Little, Cambridge, U.S.

van Leenders, C., (December 1996): Gevangen in Afval? De Ontwikkeling van Keten-gerichte Milieuverbeteringen bij Van Hecke Catering (Trapped in waste? The development of chain-oriented environmental improvements at Van Hecke Catering), thesis, University of Amsterdam

von Weizsäcker, E.U.; A.B. Lovins; L.H. Lovins, (1995): Faktor Vier, Doppelter Wohlstand - Halbierter Naturverbrauch (Factor four, twice the affluence, half the use of natural resources), Droemer Knaur, München

Weterings, R.A.P.M.; J.B. Opschoor (1992): De Milieugebruiksruimte als Uitdaging voor Technologie-ontwikkeling (Environmental space as a challenge for technological development), RMNO no. 74, Rijswijk

# Business Strategies for a Sustainable Society*

*Walter R. Stahel*

## 1. The Need for a Change in Course in Order to Move Closer to the Vision of Sustainability

The present industrial economy, which has developed over the last 200 years in today's industrialized countries, is based on the optimization of the production process in order to reduce unit costs and thus overcome the scarcity of goods of all kinds, from food to shelter to durable goods, which was the norm 200 years ago. Emphasis is on more efficient process technologies, and a better quality of the goods at the point of sale.

There are indications that the industrial economy is no longer efficiently catering for our needs: (a) the part of goods that go directly from production to disposal (zero-life products in figure 1) has reached 30% in some sectors; (b) the number of goods that are disposed of is comparable to the number of goods sold, for many products, indicating a substitution of wealth rather than an increase in wealth; (c) technological progress is still focused on production, not on utilization; (d) for many goods, increases in efficiency through system break-down are comparable to increases in efficiency through product innovation (e.g. safety generated through traffic jams v. air bags).

And there are indications that the industrial economy itself is incompatible with the aims of a sustainable society:

- **the factor 'time'**: sustainability is a *long-term* societal vision, concerned with the stewardship of natural resources (stock equals wealth) in order to safeguard the opportunities and choices of future generations. The industrial economy is a *short-term* optimization of throughput in monetary terms. Changing course towards a more sustainable society means introducing the indeterministic factor 'time' into economic thinking, which again implies an indeterministic vision of economics.
- **resource productivity**: the linear structure of the industrial economy has as a consequence that its success, both micro and macro, is directly coupled with resource flows, of both matter and energy - it might be called a '*river economy*' (figure 1). But a generalization of the present per capita resource consumption of industrialized countries is not possible without a system collapse. In order to be

---

* first published as Stahel 1997

sustainable, the economy must therefore operate at a much higher level of resource productivity, i.e. be able to produce the same utilization value out of a greatly reduced resource throughput - it might be called a '*lake economy*' (figure 2)[1]. Changing course towards a more sustainable society means to de-couple economic success from resource throughput - one way to do this is to change to a service economy, in which the measure of results refers mainly to stocks and their utilization, instead of flows (Giarini and Stahel 1989/1993).

- **social and cultural ecology**: the industrial economy has been largely *technology*-focused, using *monetarized values* as its main yardstick. A sustainable society is result-focused and based on *social and cultural values (non-monetary assets)*, integrated with economic values. Changing course towards a more sustainable society means to take into account social and cultural factors as peers to economic ones.

Figure 1: The Linear Structure of the Industrial Economy (or 'River' Economy)

▶ zero-life-products ▶
Resources ▶ Base materials ▶ Manufacturing ▶ P.O.S. ▶ Utilization ▶ Waste

**junction 0: product-life or waste**

Source: Stahel and Reday (1976/1981)

A service economy is fundamentally different from the industrial economy in that its main objective is to maintain or increase total wealth and welfare, i.e. the monetary and non-monetary assets of society, over long periods of time. Its focal point is the optimization of utilization, i.e. of the performance and the results achieved with goods, rather than the goods themselves. The central notion of economic value in the service economy is the value of utilization over time, in contrast to the momentary value of exchange at the POS (point of sale) in the industrial economy (the added value system is only a subsystem of a larger economic concept). Similarly, quality in the service economy is defined as long-term optimization of system functioning, not as a momentary quality at the POS.

The invisible hand of the free market prefers junction 2 to the economically more advantageous junction 1 (figure 2), if mandatory recycling legislation is introduced.

---

1 It has been calculated that industrialized countries need to reduce their resource flows by a factor of 10, in order to enable the Less Developed Countries to multiply their per capita resource input within a sustainable level of World resource flows (Carnoules declaration of the Factor 10 club 1994).

The reason for this 'wrong' choice lies in industry's familiarity with throughput optimization, as well as in incomplete legislation. The economic optimization of the loops in figure 2 *only* becomes an objective for manufacturers if legislation imposes closed liability loops (figure 3: product take-back and product stewardship 'from cradle to the next cradle' by manufacturers), in addition to closed material loops. These liability loops are 'invisible' in a techno-economic vision and thus easy to overlook.

Figure 2: Closing the Material Loops: The Loops of a Self-Replenishing, More Sustainable Service Economy (or 'Lake' Economy), and the Junctions Between These Loops and a Linear Economy.

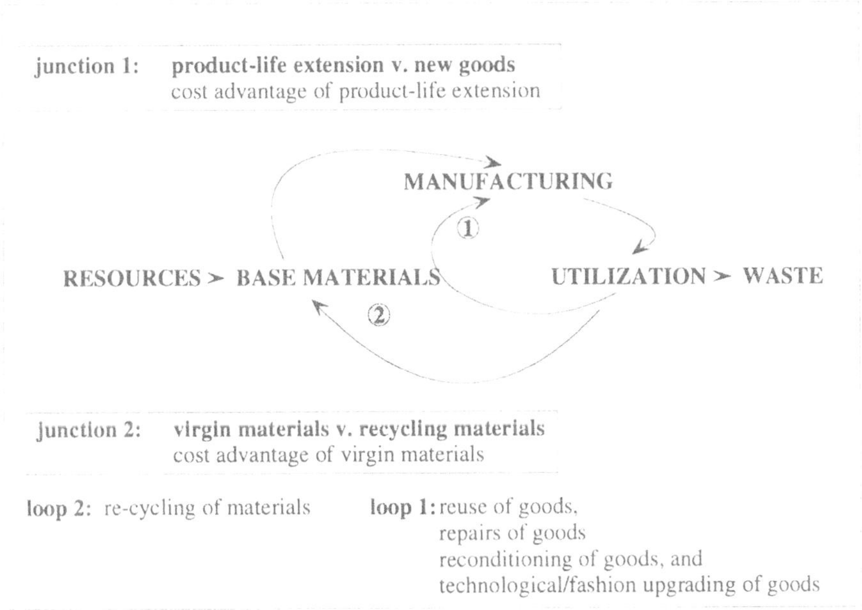


Source: Stahel and Reday (1976/1981)

In the case of the mandatory or voluntary take-back of goods, the new economic objective for industry now becomes to maximize profits through the re-use of components and goods, instead of the old minimization of costs in recycling and disposal of goods. In some cases, manufacturers may need to develop strategies of 'retained ownership' (operational leasing, renting, selling results instead of goods) in order to guarantee the return of their goods after each cycle. Xerox's marketing strategy of selling customer satisfaction in addition to its technological life-cycle design strategy is a brilliant example for asset management (for stock equals wealth).

Figure 3: Closing the Liability Loops: The Economic Optimization of Loops only Becomes an Economic Objective if the (Invisible) Liability Loops are Closed (Take-Back of Unwanted Goods and Materials by Their Manufacturer).

| | |
|---|---|
| **junction 3:** | **asset management v. waste management**<br>profit maximization in re-use v. cost minimization in recycling and disposal |

A transition from a resource-flow-based industrial economy to a wealth-management-based service economy will be greatly facilitated if a majority of people and Nation-States can agree on a common vision of sustainability. Such a vision, however, is almost by definition more cultural than technological; it further needs a clear structure to avoid misinterpretations.

## 2. The Pillars of a Sustainable Society

The concept of sustainability is based on several techno-economic pillars, each of which is essential for the 'survival' of the natural eco-system - of which mankind is part - on Earth. It is of no use to argue on priorities, or speculate on which of these pillars can be lost first; society cannot take the risk of losing any single one of them:

(1) *nature conservation*, or the eco-support system for life on the planet. This pillar contains global aspects (e.g. oceans and atmosphere as global commons, biodiversity), as well as regional ones (e.g. drinking water, the carrying capacity of nature with regard to populations and their lifestyle).

(2) *health and safety* (non-toxicology, qualitative): a danger mainly related to the health of people and animals, resulting increasingly from man's own activities (e.g. (accumulation of) toxic substances in the environment: DDT, mercury, Thalidomide).

(3) *reduced flows of resources,* or higher resource productivity (quantitative, e.g. $CO_2$): a potential of radical change for the planet (towards a re-acidification and/or climate change), and thus a threat to man's life on Earth. Also a factor of disequilibrium between economies in North and South.

The 'Quest for a Sustainable Society', however, must be much broader and include the longevity and sustainability of our non-techno-economic structures:

(4) *social ecology,* the fabric of societal structures: this pillar includes issues such as democracy, peace and human rights, employment and social integration, security and safety.

(5) *cultural ecology* includes education and knowledge, ethics and culture, as well as values of national heritage at the level of the individual, the corporation and the State: 'Show to others that you are able to care, by looking after e.g. your car, your house (instead of buying a new one)'; 'Good engineering and industrial design has always also been ecologically responsible'; 'Only people, not robots, can permanently improve product quality'; 'Waste is inefficient and therefore un-japanese'[2].

Historic examples of sustainability, such as the native Americans' rule of 'everything you do should have positive repercussions on the next seven generations', and the Prussian management rules for sustainable forestry, both at least 200 years old, were based on communities and their traditional values, i.e. a socio-cultural, not technological, ecology. The precautionary principle, one of the key principles agreed upon in the Rio declaration, is also primarily based on socio-cultural values - but it has hardly been put into practice so far. The question therefore arises if modern society, based on legal frameworks and penal systems, can find a recipe for sustainability in areas where precaution is the most efficient (or only) strategy, such as the global commons, without falling victim to 'the prisoners' dilemma' (where each individual fares better than his or her inmates by ruthlessly exploiting his or her personal advantage, but where the prisoners as a whole would be better off by cooperating with each other).

The holistic vision of a sustainable society was already at the base of the movement that coined the English term 'sustainability' in the early '70s: the Woodlands Conferences in Houston, Texas, and the related Mitchell Prize Competition (Coomer 1981). In order to understand the necessity for changing course towards a more sustainable economy, it is vital to keep the wider reference of a sustainable society (including subjects such as full and meaningful employment, quality of life) in mind.

## 3. Sustainable Society as a Common Global Vision

The vision of sustainability should be based on a global consensus, and like the concentric waves in a lake after a stone was thrown into the water, develop from a few abstract key issues or principles towards a multitude of increasingly concrete and regionally adapted applications:

- Vision
- objectives

2 Sources of quotes: John P. Kusz, IDSA, 1995; Siemens PC engineers, 1985; Toyota's president on opening the labour-intensive assembly lines in the RAV4-factory, 1995; MITI report, 1995.

- industrial policy
- business strategies and management tools
- industrial design for ecological solutions (goods and services).

The following structure is a more detailed example of these concentric waves, focused on the objective of a higher resource productivity (i.e. pillar 3 of the preceding section):

| | |
|---|---|
| The Common **Vision:** | sustainability. |
| **Objective:** | to build and improve all pillars of a sustainable society, including a considerably higher resource productivity. |
| **Industrial Policy:** | to promote a self-responsibility of economic actors through e.g. closed liability and material loops, an extended result-focused product responsibility by economic actors, free-market safety-nets[3] (e.g. mandatory insurance cover), and a legal framework (including taxation) fostering sustainable solutions (goods and services). |
| **Business Strategies:** | to develop innovative technical and marketing strategies which identify and optimize sustainable and economically viable solutions "from cradle to the next cradle", with the aim to provide customer satisfaction over long periods of time, interpreting quality as a long-term optimization of system functioning. |
| **Management Tools:** | to optimize asset management, resource productivity and risk management, including relevant controlling instruments; and to define benchmarks and methods to measure improvements towards sustainability. |
| **Design** for eco-solutions, goods and services: | zero-options (sufficiency),<br><br>system solutions, and utilization optimization through a longer and more intensive utilization (efficiency), dematerialized solutions (eco-products).<br><br>Details of business and design strategies which lead towards more sustainable solutions are given in figure 4. |

---

3 'Free-market safety-nets' are economic actors which can give a guarantee that financial losses resulting from innovators' mistakes do not have to be borne by the State: pools such as P&I clubs in shipping, insurance companies (including captive insurers, reinsurers), 'Berufsgenossenschaften' in Germany. These losses can arise from environmental or product liability, workers safety and compensation, etc.

Reality, i.e. short-term business optimization, has led to the opposite trend of creating concentric waves from the outside inwards: first on the market were 'green' products (each with its own reference frame), followed by services for 'greening businesses' promoted by consulting firms (eco-labels and eco-audits) - even before an agreement on a common vision is in sight.

Figure 4: Demand and Supply Strategies for a Higher Resource Productivity

| Increased resource productivity through: | Type of strategies:<br>**closing the material loops**<br>**technical strategies** | <br>**closing the liability loops**<br>**commercial / marketing strategies** |
|---|---|---|
| **sufficiency solutions**<br>(demand side) | near ZERO-OPTIONS<br>ploughing at night<br>loss prevention (vaccination) | ZERO-OPTIONS<br>towels in hotels<br>non-insurance (rearend accidents CA) |
| **system solutions**<br>reducing *volume and speed* of the resource flow<br>(supply side efficiency) | SYSTEM-SOLUTIONS<br>Krauss-Maffei PTS plane transport system,<br>skin solutions, accessibility | SYSTEMIC SOLUTIONS<br>lighthouses,<br>selling results instead of goods<br>selling services instead of goods |
| **more intensive utilization of goods**<br>reducing the *volume* of the resource flow:<br>(supply side efficiency) | ECO-PRODUCTS<br>dematerialized goods,<br>multifunctional goods. | ECO-MARKETING<br>shared utilization of goods<br>selling utilization instead of goods |
| **longer utilization of goods**<br>reducing the *speed* of the resource flow:<br>(supply and demand side efficiency) | RE-MANUFACTURING<br>long-life goods,<br>service-life extension of goods and of components,<br>new products from waste | RE-MARKETING<br>dis-curementservices,<br>away-grading of goods,<br>marketing of fashion upgrades for goods in the market. |

Source: Adapted from: Giarini and Stahel (1989/1993)

# 4. Wealth Without Resource Consumption: Facing New Risks in a Service Economy

The objective of 'wealth without resource consumption' is obviously of little interest to the industrial (river) economy, as it will lead to "economic disaster" (as measured in resource throughput). There is therefore a considerable untapped potential of technical innovation and economic activity ahead for pro-active entrepreneurs that recognize and successfully develop this potential. The key to 'wealth without resource consumption' is the service economy: if customers pay an agreed amount per unit of service (and service equals customer satisfaction), service providers have an economic incentive to reduce resource flows, as this will increase their profits doubly: by reducing procurement costs for materials and energy, and by reducing waste elimination costs (Giarini). Examples for this are the Xerox life-cycle design programme for photocopiers, the retreading of tyres, the elevator business, Speno's railgrinding services, Du Pont's voluntary programme to re-take and recycle nylon carpets, and remanufacturing activities in general.

The main benefits for pro-active entrepreneurs are a higher long-term competitiveness through reduced costs, as well as higher product quality and customer loyalty, in addition to a 'greener' image; the main risk is the increased uncertainty due to the introduction of the factor 'time' into the economic calculation. The latter can, however, be substantially reduced by appropriate design strategies, such as modular system design for interoperability and compatibility between products families, component standardization for ease of re-use, remanufacture and recycling, loss and abuse prevention built into products.

Sufficiency is one strategy for higher sustainability and wealth without resource consumption. Witness a hotel: by offering its guests to 'save the environment' by re-using towels for several days, the hotel does indeed reduce the consumption of water, detergents and washing machines. But it also reduces its laundry costs and extends the useful life of towels and washing machines, thus increasing its profit margin. Zero-options, or sufficiency, are among the most ecologically efficient solutions - and they also offer the highest savings.

Systems solutions and the shared utilization of goods are also very effective efficiency strategies of higher resource consumption. A number of people sharing in the utilization of a pool of goods can draw the same utilization value through a more intensive utilization of a substantially reduced number of goods, thus achieving a higher resource productivity per unit of service. Examples for this are, besides public infrastructures such as lighthouses, roads, concert halls and railways, the Lufthansa car pool for flight crews, the 'Charter Way' concept by Mercedes for trucks, and the textile leasing of e.g. uniforms, towels and hospital linen.

A shared utilization is possible in the (monetarized) economy through rental services and the sale of services instead of goods (laundry and dry cleaning), but also within communities (non-monetary) through lending and sharing. The former takes place within the legal framework of society, the latter's principles of sharing and caring are based on community values (trust and tolerance) which are part of socio-cultural ecology. Some of the issues involved in the sharing of immaterial and material goods are open to misinterpretation because they incorporate values of both society (law) and community (trust). Distrust leads to increased individual consumption, conflict or failure[4]. A shared utilization of *immaterial* goods has two major advantages: a great number of people can profit from the goods simultane-

---

4 This dilemma might partly have been the reason for the failure of the initiatives to develop 'terotechnologies' (tero = caring) in the UK in the '70s.

ously - in contrast to material goods - and: immaterial goods are by definition dematerialized. The technology shift from analog to digital or virtual goods will further enhance shared utilization, even if the main reason for the change to virtual goods is competitiveness, not ecology. Product-life extension services of analog (mechanical) goods lead to a regionalization of the economy, whereas digital and virtual goods enable producers to stay global, by providing solutions (for e.g. the technological upgrading of goods) through do-it-yourself activities. This gives producers direct access to the customer; it also eliminates distributors and distribution costs. The coming change to digital television, accompanied by long-life hardware combined with later technological upgrading through software, is an example of this trend - pushed by the novel German take-back legislation for electronic goods.

Wealth with less resource consumption is further possible by substituting maintenance-free long-life products which deliver high-quality results for disposable products. Modern examples include music CDs (Compact Discs), and supercondensors instead of batteries in electrical goods. CDs are also a point in case for the resulting shift in income from manufacturers to distributors (secondhand sales and rental shops), if the manufacturers themselves do not become service providers (e.g. selling music instead of CDs) - which would have demanded a structural change from global manufacturing to local rental services.

A longer utilization of goods through product-life extension services (loop 1 in figure 2), as well as dematerialized product design, also increases resource productivity, but needs to be promoted as it goes against the logic of the linear economy. Doubling the useful life of goods reduces by half the amount of resource input and waste output, and in addition reduces the resource consumption in all related services (distribution, advertising, waste transport and disposal) by 50 %. Furthermore, product-life extension services are often a substitution of manpower for energy, and of local workshops for (global) factories, thus enhancing social ecology. Economic success comes through an understanding of the logic inherent in a 'lake economy' based on services: to optimize utilization demands a proximity to the customer, and thus a regionalization of the economy. As the stock of goods in the marketplace is the new focus of economic optimization (the assets), these goods become the new 'mines' for resources. They cannot economically be centralized - an efficient service economy has to have a decentralized structure (service centers, remanufacturing workshops and minimills). Service centers ideally are accessible 24 hours a day, such as the emergency department of a major hospital.

## 5. Benefits for the User Cum Consumer

'Service is the ultimate luxury', according to a publicity by the Marriott hotel group. The shift to a service economy (e.g. product rental instead of purchase) encounters few problems of acceptance on the demand side. The consumer turned user gains a high flexibility in the utilization of goods (something ownership can never give him), as well as guaranteed satisfaction at a guaranteed cost per unit of service. And there is no loss of status: the marketing of the industrial economy has wrongly created the idea that status symbol value is linked to ownership - in reality, it has always been linked to leasehold. The driver of a red Ferrari gets the same attention from bystanders if he has bought, rented or stolen the car. Ownership therefore only makes economic sense in cases where durable goods increase in value, normally through an increase in rarity, such as antique furniture, vintage cars, real estate.

And ownership only makes ecologic sense for individuals interested in asset management. In many countries, an increasing part of individuals live mentally in a multioption society: they do not want to commit themselves medium or long-term, neither to goods nor people (Gross 1995). They want new toys all the time - and can afford them. Only a service economy can fulfil their needs without creating an avalanche of waste, by selling them results and services instead of goods, flexibility in utilization instead of bondage by property.

Most of these strategies of a higher resource productivity also offer the customer a reduction in costs. Sufficiency solutions based on a better (scientific) understanding of a problem reduce resource flows and costs: ploughing at night, for instance, reduces weeds and thus herbicide costs by 90%; remanufactured goods cost on average 40% less than equivalent new goods of the same quality; sharing goods also means sharing costs. But sufficiency and efficiency solutions often demand that the users cum customers develop a new relationship with goods and/or people - knowledge and community become substitutes for resource consumption.

## 6. Innovation and an Industrial Policy for Sustainability as the Keys to Higher Resource Productivity

A fundamental change in actors and issues occurs when society evolves down the 'sustainability pillars' from 'health and safety' to 'resource productivity' (figure 5). In the past, biologists and chemists have been the driving force through command and control regulations in order to conserve nature and limit toxicology, in the name of Nation-States. Now, engineers and industrial designers, marketeers and businesspeople will take the lead through innovation, in order to achieve an increase in resource productivity by a factor ten. 'Innovation by enterprises' and 'an industrial policy to promote sustainability' become the future key strategies not only towards a sustainable society, but also towards competitiveness! (Innovation strategies open to economic actors are summarized in figure 4.)

This corresponds to a fundamental change in political thinking, from ecology v. economy (and State v. industry) towards ecology with economy (and State with enterprises). The new industrial policy can best promote sustainability by removing obstacles which hinder, and by creating incentives which foster, innovation towards more sustainable solutions. The State still has to determine the need for safety barriers to protect people and the environment. However, the State should not provide this protection itself, nor carry the costs of accidents, but foster free market safety-nets such as mandatory insurance (e.g. environmental impairment liability, product liability)!

At a time when tax authorities increasingly leave it to the stock exchanges to define valid accounting guidelines (because banks and stock exchanges have a prospectus liability, and therefore a self-interest to verify the figures they are given), the State should define the aim of, but not the strategies to, a higher resource productivity (e.g. eco-products). But the State should make sure that the economic actors which innovate get rewarded and promoted, and that those caught cheating (or their safety-net) will pay up. By doing this, the State could become considerably leaner and more efficient. The principle of 'insurability of risks' would automatically introduce the precautionary principle into the economic mechanisms to chose between possible technologies, present and future.

The fundamental change in actors and issues occuring when society evolves down the 'sustainability pillars', from 'health and safety' to 'resource productivity', is summarized in figure 5.

Some of the key issues of an industrial policy for sustainability can be summarized as follows:

(1) introduce the factor 'time' into the legislation governing the economy
- develop and use methods to measure sustainable competitiveness over long periods of time, e.g. GPI or ISEW instead of GNP[5].
- define and legislate the minimum quality of goods for sale in function of their service-life, by requiring a long-life warranty (e.g. in accordance with the 10 years in the EC safety directives), instead of the present exclusion of the use of used components in new goods.
- focus funding on R&D as well as education and training on prevention and precaution methods instead of process technologies: long-term behaviour of materials, components and goods (wear and tear versus fatigue), technical risk management, industrial design for system thinking, ways to popularize sustainability in terms of socio-cultural ecology.

---

5 GPI General Progress Indicator (U.S.), ISEW Index of Sustainable Economic Welfare (European), GNP Gross National Product; for details of GPI and ISEW please refer to van Dieren (1995).

Figure 5: Key Actors and Issues in Each of the Five Pillars of Sustainability

| pillars of sustainability (values) | define objectives | actors which can identify solutions | deal with abuse | monetary costs and benefits |
|---|---|---|---|---|
| 1 nature conservation (natural assets) | States, preventive legislation (asset management) | nature itself (scientists) | precaution (avoid "non-repairable" damages) | lost opportunity costs |
| 2 safety and health (non-toxicology) | States, legislation to limit damages (after scientific proof) | scientists and M.D.s. | financial compensation to victims, fines and prison sentences | additional costs |
| **3 higher resource productivity** | **consumers** | **sufficiency** | **change supplier** | **savings** |
| | **enterprises** | **better business solutions through innovation** | **free-market financial safety-nets, e.g. insurance** | **savings in procurement and waste disposal** |
| | **States** | **new industrial policy based on incentives for innovation and sustainability** | | **savings through lean administration and risk transfer** |
| 4 social ecology (invisible fabric) | parents, communities, corporations, States | education and knowledge | feed-back loops to peer groups (punishment) | savings in social costs |
| 5 cultural ecology | individuals, corporations, States | education and ethics | ??? | savings in social costs |

(2) increase the self-responsibility of economic actors

- through a product responsibility 'from cradle to the next cradle',
- by replacing mandatory technical standards by mandatory free market safety-nets, thus introducing the insurability of risks as the main criterion for an economic choice between technological options,
- by eliminating subsidies and incentives for economies of scale which often hide diseconomies of risk.

(3) use industrial policy as a locomotive for economic competitiveness: change industrial policy ahead of the economic development in order to increase innovation towards sustainability.

(4) sustainability is a holistic principle; the requirement of 'unity of matter' in legislation has become an obstacle to problem solving (e.g. levying taxes on resource consumption in order to finance old age and unemployment).

(5) introduce self-correcting taxation loops in the economy: tax resource consumption and waste instead of labour, thus rewarding all sufficiency and efficiency solutions (and eliminating the discrimination of 'voluntary work', 'moonlighting' and 'non-productive work' at the same time).

Few incentives and little knowhow have been developed under the present economic or industrial policy to develop and apply strategies of sustainability or a higher resource productivity in practice. A society which 'saves the environment' by replacing ("destroy and produce new") millions of vehicles in working order when a 'cleaner' technology becomes available (e.g. unleaded petrol, lean burning engines, catalytic converters), based on industry's claim that existing engines cannot be upgraded or converted, does not act efficiently, neither with regard to its engineering development nor the environment, and acts on short-term assumptions (the proof for this was delivered by a handful of skilled Swiss mechanics converting the engines of their fleet of vintage Junkers Ju-52 aircraft to unleaded petrol).

## 7. Benchmarks for Sustainability

Experience has shown that the resource efficiency of existing solutions can be improved by up to a factor four (e.g. water use through drip irrigation in Israel, use of herbicides by railways). For an increase in resource productivity well beyond a factor four, however, innovative strategies for new solutions are needed (figure 4), attacking problems on a systems instead of a product level, or departing from a new understanding of the underlying need, or using new technology (Stahel 1995).

The discussion on resource productivity which was started recently by Schmidt-Bleek and others (1994/1996) has shown the need to measure old and new solutions not against alternatives but against optimums. Otherwise, most of the praise might go to the worst actors of the past, whereas existing ecologically optimal solutions will go unnoticed, or even be forced out of the market by aggressive new-green marketing. Many traditional solutions have indeed reached a high degree of sustainability: an Austrian cabinet maker that uses timber from the local forests to produce furniture and toys for the regional market, repairs products when broken and heats his workshop in winter with waste timber, can hardly improve the sustainability of his activity even by a factor 4. The same goes for a local brewery in Wales which buys its raw material from local farmers and sells barrels of beer to the local pubs. The fact that these firms can hardly improve their ecological efficiency does not mean they are working in an unsustainable way - quite the contrary! But it shows the necessity to establish benchmarks in order to define priorities and objectives in the quest for a higher resource productivity.

Benchmarks are easy in domains where people can be used as a yardstick, such as mobility. 'Sustainable mobility' can be defined as any method of mobility which enables a person to move faster and with less energy input than by walking, such as the bicycle for horizontal and the elevator for vertical mobility. The chances, however, that improvements to the motorcar will ever reach the human yardstick are low. In other cases, such as the coffee brewed by different coffee machines, the optimum benchmark is the quality of the result achieved. During the last coffee tasting competition organised by the EU consumer associations, one of the best results was achieved by the Bialetti espresso machine, an early eco-product designed and first produced in 1930 which is still on sale - together with hundreds of other coffee machines, all more expensive, more recent and more material intensive. Benchmarks can therefore also be used to indicate areas of eco-mature solutions.

## Summary

The present economy is not sustainable with regard to its per capita material consumption in the industrialized countries. A dematerialization of the economy of industrialized countries can only be achieved by a change in course, from an industrial economy where success is measured in throughput and its exchange value, to a service economy where success is measured in wealth (stock) and its utilization value. Wealth management, new corporate and industrial design strategies, and different economic policies can lead to a higher sustainability as well as an increased international competitiveness due to a substantially higher resource productivity. The term 'service economy' refers not to the tertiary sector, but to an economy where the majority of value is created by services, and the majority of jobs are in service activities (Giarini and Stahel 1989/1993).

## References


Carnoules Declaration of the Factor 10 Club (1994); available from Prof. Dr. F. Schmidt-Bleek, Vice-President, Wuppertal Institute, D-42103 Wuppertal

Coomer, James C. (ed.) (1981): Quest for a Sustainable Society, New York, Oxford etc. (Pergamon Press, published in cooperation with The Woodlands Conference); ISBN 0-08-027168-5

Giarini, Orio and Stahel, Walter R. (1989/1993): The Limits to Certainty, facing risks in the new Service Economy, 2nd edn; Dordrecht, Boston, London - Kluwer Academic Publishers; ISBN 0-7923-2167-7

Gross (1995): Die Multi-Options-Gesellschaft (the multi-option society), Frankfurt/M., Suhrkamp Verlag

Gruhler, Wolfram (1990): Dienstleistungsbestimmter Strukturwandel in deutschen Industrieunternehmen; Köln, Deutscher Instituts Verlag; ISBN 3-602-24406-7

Schmidt-Bleek, Friedrich (1994/96): Wieviel Umwelt braucht der Mensch? MIPS - Das Mass für ökologisches Wirtschaften; Berlin, Basel, Birkhäuser Verlags AG, ISBN 3-7643-2959-9; published in English: The Fossil Makers - Factor 10 and more

Stahel, Walter and Reday, Geneviève (1976/1981): Jobs for Tomorrow, the potential for substituting manpower for energy; report to the Commission of the European Communities, Brussels/Vantage Press, N.Y.

Stahel, Walter R. (1984): The Product-Life Factor; *in:* Orr, Susan Grinton (ed.): An Inquiry into the Nature of Sustainable Societies: The Role of the Private Sector; HARC, The Woodlands, TX

Stahel, Walter R. (1985): Hidden innovation, R&D in a sustainable society, *in:* Science & Public Policy, Journal of the International Science Policy Foundation, London; Volume 13, Number 4, August 1986: Special Issue: The Hidden Wealth

Stahel, Walter R. (1992): Re-use And Re-cycling, Waste prevention and resource savings in utilization, conference manuscript, Guildford

Stahel, Walter R. (1994): The impact of shortening (or lengthening) of life-time of products and production equipment on industrial competitivenes, sustainability and employment; research report to the European Commission, DG III, Nov 1, 1994

Stahel, Walter R. (1995): Intelligente Produktionsweisen und Nutzungskonzepte - Handbuch Abfall 1 - Allg. Kreislauf- und Rückstandswirtschaft; Band 1 und 2, Karlsruhe, Landesanstalt für Umweltschutz Baden-Württemberg (Hrsg.), [300 examples of higher resource productivity in today's industry and society]

Stahel, Walter R. (1997): The Service Economy - Wealth without Resource Consumption? *in:* Philosophical Transactions of the Royal Society, Series A, London, Feb. 15, 1997

van Dieren, Wouter (1995): Taking Nature into account, Basel, Birkhäuser-Verlag, ISBN 3-7643-5173-X

# Services Instead of Products: Experiences from Energy Markets - Examples from Sweden

*Lars J. Nilsson*

## 1. Introduction

The overall objective of energy systems is to provide energy services, at affordable cost and without socially unacceptable side effects. However, energy related security, development, and environmental problems will continue to worsen if present trends in energy demand and the energy supply mix persist. Therefore, energy was a critical area of debate at the United Nations Conference on Environment and Development (UNCED) in Rio de Janeiro in 1992. In Agenda 21, chapter 9, two directions for the energy system to evolve were identified: (1) more efficient production, transmission and distribution, and end-use of energy, and (2) greater reliance on environmentally sound energy systems, particularly new and renewable sources of energy (UNCED, 1992).

Improving efficiency in the end-use of energy is one of the least expensive ways of improving the situation with respect to energy related environmental and other problems. A saved kWh does not, in most cases, contribute to, for example, climatic change or increased reliance on imported fuels. The energy services we enjoy, e.g. illumination, process heating, comfortable indoor climate, can be delivered at different levels of end-use energy efficiency. For example, a compact fluorescent light uses only 20 to 25 percent of the energy used by an incandescent lightbulb to produce the same amount of light.

The concept of energy services is not a new one. When Thomas A. Edison invented the electric light bulb and developed the power production and distribution system to keep it burning, he envisioned a large electricity industry that would sell various energy services to its customers. His goal was to compete with fuel-based lighting by offering the same service, illumination, at a lower total cost (Hughes, 1985). With this system, the electricity industry would have been able to increase profits by improving the efficiency of light bulbs. However, the electricity industry developed in another direction where profits became coupled to sales of kilowatt-hours rather than services.

The energy industry, in particular gas and electric utilities, has developed as state controlled or regulated monopoly enterprises in most countries. Present electricity systems are based on institution building around fossil fuels and ever larger-scale steam turbines during the last century. Efforts have concentrated on meeting an increasing demand for kilowatt-hours. However, during the last two decades many utilities, notably in the United States and primarily driven by regulation, have increased their efforts to help customers get more energy efficient through what has become known as demand side management (DSM) programmes. This has in most cases been in the best interest of the energy end-users who could get the same amount of energy services at a lower total cost by using more efficient end-use technologies. Least cost planning (LCP) or integrated resources planning (IRP), both of which include DSM programmes as a key element, has been mandated in many parts of the United States. European utilities have also been more or less involved in various DSM activities.

Electricity markets, and to some extent gas markets, are subject to reform in many countries. The reforms aim at introducing competition between suppliers and opening up markets to new entrants. An important argument for such reforms is that they will result in increased economic efficiency, more flexible contracts, and lower electricity prices. Electricity market reforms have also been facilitated by the development of new technologies, e.g. small scale power plants and information technology, which allow for more flexibility and less centralized market structures. However, separating the electricity generation business from the transmission, distribution and retail business, a key measure to introduce competition, fundamentally changes the prospects for utility driven DSM. In this paper the experience from electricity market reforms is reviewed and new approaches to support energy efficiency in competitive electricity markets are explored.

## 2. The Potential for Higher Energy Efficiency

Energy demand is now stable or growing slower than historically in industrialized countries. National energy intensities expressed as energy use per unit of gross domestic product are decreasing in several industrialized countries and in some developing countries (Nilsson L.J., 1993). These trends result from structural changes, i.e., a shift of economic activity to less energy intensive sectors of the economy, and from increasing efficiency in the conversion and end-use of energy. Industrial processes have become more energy efficient, even during long periods with decreasing real prices of energy (Williams et al., 1987). The efficacy in lumens per watt for a modern light source is several times higher than for Thomas A. Edison's original carbon filament lamp, which in turn was more efficient than candles or wick-lamps. Conversion and distribution losses have also been reduced. For example, the average efficiency of thermal power plants has increased by a factor of six since the turn of the century (Williams and Larson, 1989).

Estimates of the potential for saving energy through improving end-use efficiency typically vary from 5-15% up to 75-90% depending on the end-use application and technical and economic assumptions, figure 1. At the lower end are typically estimates of the over-night potential for profitable changes to existing installations. At the higher end are typically estimates of what can be achieved using advanced technology which may not yet be commercially available and for which costs may be uncertain. In between are typically estimates of savings that would result if presently best available technology was introduced at the rate of capital turn-over and expansion, e.g., when energy using equipment must be replaced at the end of its technical life-time.

Figure 1: Energy Efficiency Potential Concept

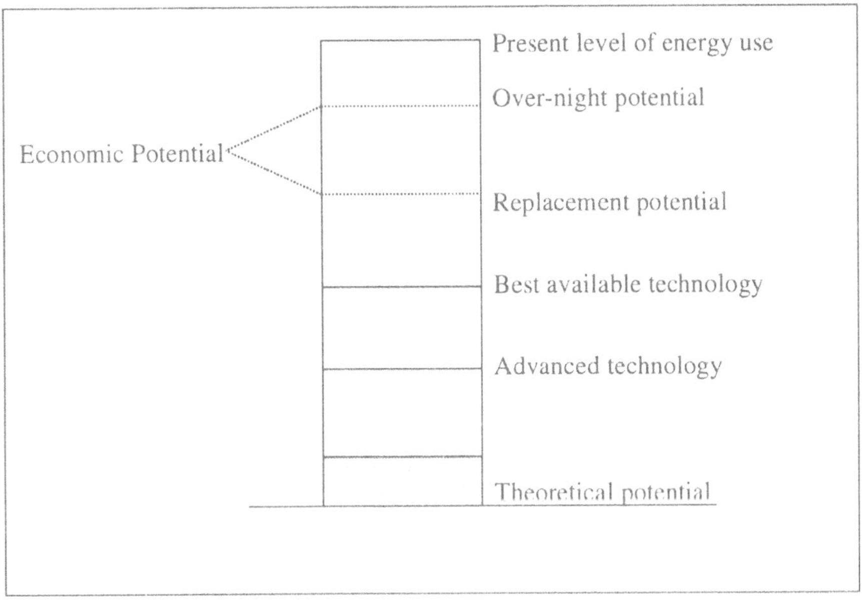


Note: The theoretically minimum energy to perform a specified task is usually a small fraction of what is used today, and it is often zero. Advanced technology, available in prototypes or on the drawing-table, is often considerably more energy efficient than best available technology. What is considered economical is sensitive to what economic criteria are applied and the timing of the efficiency improvements. The over-night potential is less than the potential for efficiency improvements when equipment is replaced at the end of its lifetime or for other reasons than energy efficiency only.

Potential estimates and efforts to improve efficiency sometimes concentrate on reducing energy losses in individual components, for example, air-conditioners or boilers. Greater opportunities for cost-effective energy efficiency improvements are typically identified when using a system-wide approach as illustrated in figure 2. The cost of improving the efficiency of a cooling or heating system of a house may increase up to a level where it becomes uneconomical to continue making further efficiency improvements. However, system-wide efficiency measures through, for example, improved insulation and building design may bring cooling and heating needs down to a level where the conventional cooling or heating system, albeit efficient, can be replaced by a much less expensive system or eliminated.

Figure 2: A System-Wide Approach May Result in Greater Savings at Lower Cost than when Each Component is Viewed in Isolation

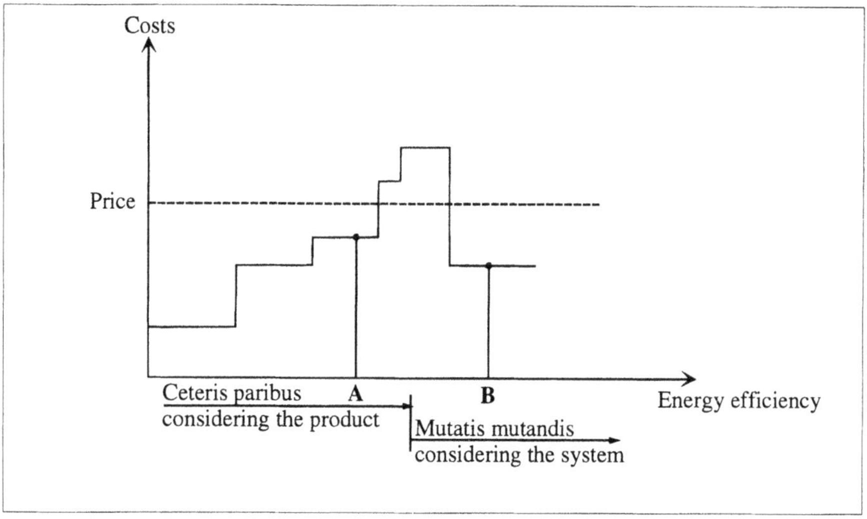


Source: Nilsson H., 1995

A common misconception of energy efficiency is the idea of ever-rising costs which says that energy efficiency is an added value which can be achieved at a higher price (Nilsson H., 1995). One example is that efficient and CFC-free refrigerators would require more expensive insulation materials and compressors. However, this approach does not take into account the dynamics of real markets where factors such as technological breakthroughs and development, learning, volume, and industrial retooling bring costs down. It also ignores that energy efficiency improvements often are introduced in conjunction with other product or process improvements that have a value, e.g., improved quality and productivity.

## 3. Barriers to Efficiency and Policy Options

There are several reasons why apparently economically attractive improvements in energy efficiency are not implemented (see e.g., Jochem and Gruber, 1990). Three general categories of barriers can be identified:

- Relatively low energy prices
- Differences in economic criteria between end-users and suppliers
- Energy is a relatively low priority to most users.

The environmental, security and other external costs associated with energy use are generally not reflected in the price. Even though it is difficult to quantify externalities, such as the cost of future climatic change, risks associated with nuclear power, or the cost of keeping the oil flowing from the Middle East, the decision not to consider them quantifies them implicitly by setting their value at zero. Direct or hidden energy subsidies are common in many countries and prices to end-users usually reflect the average cost of production, or even marginal operating costs, rather than the long-run marginal cost.

Under-investment in energy efficiency on the end-use side as a result of low energy prices is further compounded by the difference in economic criteria between energy users and suppliers. Investements in new power plants are often evaluated using real discount rates of four to six percent. In contrast, end-users often require one to three year payback time on investments in energy efficiency. This difference in economic criteria is partly a result of that end-users do not have the same access to capital as large energy suppliers and that energy is a low priority to most end-users. As a result there is a lack of awareness and information about the opportunities to improve efficiency. The high required rates of return are also in part a reflection of the transaction costs involved in identifying and evaluating investment options and the risk that the investor will not receive the expected benefits.

To overcome these barriers, governments and utility regulators can introduce various policies. One measure is to include external costs in the energy price through taxes. However, taxes are not sufficient to ensure that investments in energy conservation is treated on an equal footing with energy supply since the rest of the barriers remain in place. Partly motivated by the difference in economic criteria, sometimes called the pay-back gap, governments or regulatory agencies in several countries have encouraged or mandated utilities to promote energy efficiency through DSM programmes.

Governments can also work to improve consumer information and institute minimum efficiency standards. Examples of the former are ongoing and planned appliance labelling programmes. Sweden has among the strictest building standards in the world, and as a result Swedish housing is among the most comfortable and energy efficient. Other governmental policy measures to stimulate energy efficiency include market transformation programmes, and voluntary and negotiated agreements. The experiences from these and other approaches to stimulate energy efficiency are discussed below.

# 4. Utility DSM Background and Experience

Most of the experience from utility operated DSM comes from the United States where electric utilities are typically vertically integrated monopolies. These monopolies are regulated by regulatory commissions with the overall goal to promulgate and preserve the public interest. Important objectives have been to ensure reliable power at the lowest price and design rate structures that result in sufficient revenues to attract investments in electricity infrastructure and which encourage the wise use of electricity. During the 1970s and 1980s a number of regulatory commissions started to require utilities to invest in measures to reduce demand for electricity rather than build new power stations. This became known as least cost planning (LCP). Important drivers for this development were a growing recognition of the advantages of energy efficiency, environmental concerns, and high costs associated with new power stations.

LCP involves calculating the comparative costs of making investments in supply and transmission and distribution against investments in measures to reduce load or demand. The concept of LCP has been broadened and refined to incorporate consideration of external costs and methods to value the benefits of a diversity in supply, distributed generation, risk avoidance, etc. Over time, the term integrated resource planning (IRP) has come to replace LCP. DSM is a broad term which encompasses planning, implementation, and evaluation of utility-sponsored programmes to influence the amount or timing of customers' energy use. Load management is one important component of DSM. This is done through reducing peak loads, increasing off-peak loads, and shifting loads through, for example, thermal storage. The other important component of DSM is reducing total load through energy efficiency improvements.

Typical DSM programmes have included: education/information; design assistance, energy audits and equipment replacement; loans and grants; point of sale discounts and rebates on efficient equipment; tailored agreements; and customer bidding (see e.g., Nadel, 1992). The programmes fill different niches. For example, rebate programmes can be effective at promoting basic component technology improvement, such as compact fluorescent lamps. Energy audits coupled with tailored agreements can be effective with larger commercial or industrial customers. With advancements in communication technologies, utilities are also looking at two-way communication allowing real-time DSM, better evaluation, innovative and direct billing, as well as incorporating other services, e.g. building security systems.

To the extent that costly operation of peaking plants or investments in supply expansion are avoided through load management and energy conservation, DSM can result in overall lower electricity prices. In other situations, DSM can lead to higher electricity prices but lower total cost for the energy service with participating customers. Care must be taken in this case to avoid that non-eligible customers end up paying higher rates to fund the DSM programme cost and the utility's lost revenues from lower energy sales. That DSM may result in increased energy costs to non-participating customers has been one of the main criticisms against DSM. Other criticisms are that insufficient attention has been given to free-riders and that programmes have been ineffective and evaluations flawed (see e.g., Anderson, 1995).

While recognizing some of the difficulties, DSM programmes have become better over time and on balance been an overall success. Data for the United States provided by electric utilities indicate that utility operated DSM programmes reduced electricity use by 52 TWh and had the potential to reduce peak demand by 43,000 MW in 1994 (EIA, 1996). In addition to the environmental and social benefits of these savings, a vast body of knowledge about different types of energy efficiency programmes and their implementation has been built up (Owen, 1996). Many utilities in North America are now responding to the prospect of increased competition by cutting what is considered non-essential expenditures, including DSM programmes (Nadel et al., 1995). Nevertheless, the knowledge gained from DSM programmes about the end-use side may prove to be a valuable asset in a more customer-oriented and competitive electricity industry.

DSM programmes are more recent in Europe and have not been as widely implemented in Europe as in the United States. By one estimate, 666 utilities in the United States spent more than 2 billion USD on over 2,300 DSM programmes in 1992 (Levine et al., 1995). The extent of European DSM activities is not as well known and most countries have not developed any comprehensive database on DSM programmes or evaluation results (Vine, 1996). A rough estimate is that about 600 utility operated DSM programmes were carried out in 1994 (Unipede, 1994). For comparison, total electricity consumption in the United States and Europe in 1993 was 3,175 and 4,081 TWh, respectively (UN, 1995).

An evaluation of 13 DSM programmes, including non-utility DSM, in Europe reported by Vine (1996) shows that the total cost of energy saved by these programmes ranged from 0.5 mECU/kWh to 77 mECU/kWh with a weighted average of 14 mECU/kWh, much less than the cost of producing a kWh. A study of early DSM in Europe reported weighted average costs of about 17 mECU/kWh for utility operated lighting programmes to promote compact fluorescent lamps (Mills, 1991).

Probable explanations for the relatively limited spread of utility DSM programmes in Europe are differences in utility culture and regulation compared to the United States, and the low level of vertical integration in many European countries. The organisation, ownership structure, and level and type of government control and regulation is more or less unique for every country. The Swedish electricity system, for example, has a mix of five large (producing 75, 27, 10, 9, and 6 TWh, respectively in 1995) and 200-300 small (producing 2.5 TWh or less in 1995) public and privately owned generators with and without access to end-use customers. Most areas have local distribution companies, owned by municipalities, that may or may not have their own generation. There are about 270 such utilities. Thus, mandating or stimulating DSM through regulation has not been practical and the relatively few utility DSM programmes that have been undertaken to date have mostly been decided on by politicians represented in the boards of publicly owned utilities (see e.g., Olerup (1994) for a review of the implementation process behind the Stockholm Lighting Programme, one of the first DSM programmes in Europe).

## 5. Utility DSM in Markets with Competition

Market reforms may involve corporatization or privatization of utilities and/or competition in generation, wholesale, and retail down to the smallest household customer. In this paper, the term competitive or deregulated electricity markets is used to refer to markets where all electricity customers are free to buy from any generator or distributor (for practical purposes, e.g. the cost of new metering equipment, individual households may find it difficult to change supplier). The transmission and distribution business remain regulated monopolies. In principle, this is how the U.K., Norwegian, and Swedish electricity markets work, although there are various restrictions regarding small consumers' access to the free market (see e.g., Eikeland, 1995 and MIC, 1996).

The case for utility sponsored DSM, discussed above, is strong in electricity markets where generation, transmission and distribution, and retail are vertically integrated into one company. When the overall objective is to provide a reliable supply of least-cost energy services to captive customers, the supplier can weigh the benefits of investments in electricity supply against investments in energy efficiency. However, this tight coupling between the supply side and the demand side disappears when generation, transmission and distribution, and retail is unbundled through market reform. The role of utility DSM changes considerably in a market where customers can shop around for different suppliers and where utility DSM expenditures cannot be recovered through increased rates. How good or how bad electricity market reform is for energy efficiency is debated (see e.g., Prindle, 1996; Hamrin et al., 1994; Haaland and Wilhite, 1994; Swisher, 1994).

The incentives for electric utilities to work with energy efficiency improvements may be very weak in markets with competition where electricity will be traded like any other commodity. An important goal of electricity market reform is to lower electricity prices which in turn requires price competition. Thus, a utility has no incentive to make investments in end-use efficiency improvements which lead to higher kWh-prices, even if it leads to a lower total cost of energy service to society or the individual customer.

A result of deregulation - one that has already been seen in Sweden - is that the share of fixed charges on electricity bills increase. This is motivated by that higher fixed charges better represent the cost structure in supply, and transmission and distribution. Higher share of fixed charges means that the consumer can save less than before on the bill by reducing consumption. The possibility of reducing demand charges by lowering load may be applicable to larger users but not households that usually pay a fixed hook-up charge.

The main motivation for a utility to continue doing DSM in markets with competition is that there may be customer demand for such services and that DSM therefore could be used to retain customers and attract new ones. Whether or not there will be such demand is difficult to predict but historically energy efficiency has been a low priority for most customers, something which has motivated utility and government involvement. In a market with competition, customers who demand energy efficiency will have to pay the full cost. General rebates and other utility payments that tend to drive up rates will essentially cease to exist.

Utilities that operate transmission and distribution systems may be motivated to undertake DSM in limited areas where it could offset area-specific investments to strengthen transmission and distribution capacities. This was a motivation for some DSM programmes in Stockholm before the electricity market reform. However, it is not clear to what extent the regulated transmission and distribution companies will be able to support efficiency improvements. The suppliers of electricity to customers in the specific area may oppose initiatives by a monopolistic enterprise which would effectively reduce their sales.

## 5.1 The Early International Experience

The experience so far does not support the proposition that deregulation will improve the conditions for energy efficiency. A conclusion from a report issued by the National Association of Regulatory Utility Commissioners in the United States based on a review of the situation in the United Kingdom, Norway, and Chile summarizes the experience so far (Hamrin et al. 1994): "The implementation of energy efficiency in all three cases has dropped from previous levels or was not attempted. There are a number of schemes to remedy this situation, but most depend on some type of government energy tax or special fee on the wire system to recover programme cost in addition to programmatic and regulatory changes that might make the programmes more attractive."

In the United Kingdom, price competition has resulted in lower prices for large consumers. The reform in 1989 did not include any incentives for the 12 regional electricity companies (RECs) to promote energy efficiency. As a result of widespread critique, the Office of Electricity Regulation (OFFER) in 1992 set up the Energy

Saving Trust (EST), the goal of which is the efficient use of all forms of energy in the United Kingdom, leading to an overall reduction in total energy consumption and its consequent environmental impact. The British government will provide EST with £25 million in 1996-97, £15 million in 1997-98, and £10 million in 1998-99 (Owen, 1996). The heated and partly ideological debate around the establishment of EST is described in detail by Owen (1995).

During the 1980s, Norwegian government put pressure on all utilities to develop DSM programmes. The Energy Act in 1991 deregulated the electricity industry but at the same time mandated IRP. Soon thereafter, IRP was deemed incompatible with a deregulated electricity market. The requirement for utility IRP was removed in 1994 and the clauses pertaining to DSM weakened (Haaland and Wilhite, 1994). Since 1991, DSM activity in the electric utilities has been drastically reduced, by at least 50%. Customers are mainly shopping for the lowest price, not for energy services. In an effort to remedy the situation Norwegian Government in 1993 called for the creation of semi-private regional energy conservation centers with access to an earmarked transmission tax to finance energy efficiency. However, these funds can only be used for information programmes and not to support activities such as technology demonstrations, energy audits, or investments in efficient end-use equipment.

## 5.2 The Early Swedish Experience

On the first of January 1996 a new Swedish Electricity Act came into force, making it possible for consumers and retailers of electricity to choose between competing suppliers of electricity (MIC, 1996). Producers and other suppliers are free to choose their customers in the same way, with the exception that a company holding the supply concession for an area has an obligation to serve customers who do not wish to change supplier. Transmission and distribution remain regulated monopolies and a special network authority has been set up at the Board for Industrial and Technical Development (NUTEK). Various provisions have also been made to protect small consumers, small producers, rural customers, etc. Buyers and sellers of electricity can enter into bilateral contracts or trade electricity by the hour and in weekly contracts on the joint Norwegian-Swedish electricity exchange, Nord-Pool, located in Oslo.

Before and after January 1996 different actors on the electricity market have positioned themselves by choosing different business strategies. Most utilities, especially smaller ones, have not actively marketed themselves to attract new customers. Among the utilities that actively have worked to attract new customers, only a few have concentrated on low-price bulk sales whereas others, although competing on price, in addition offer a variety of value-added services, one of which may be energy efficiency, as part of the business strategy. Customers that have changed to a new supplier have typically done so through corporate contracts for electricity. Examples of corporations that have turned to one supplier for all their electricity needs include IKEA, Pharmacia-Upjohn, and Tetra-Laval. There are also examples where relatively large buyers have joined forces to become even larger buyers. One example is Telge Kraft AB which is owned jointly by Astra, Scania, Ericsson and the municipal utility Telge Energi AB. Telge Energi AB's traditional service area is Södertälje where both Astra and Scania have large industrial facilities.

In the preparation of this paper, representatives from several utilities were contacted in order to explore their experience from the new electricity market and how they have chosen to include, or not include, energy efficiency and other services in their marketing. The utilities include the three largest generators: Vattenfall AB, Sydkraft AB, and Stockholm Energi AB; and one small (Nacka Energi AB) and one large (Göteborg Energi AB) municipal distributor, essentially without own generation. Brief discussions have also been held with representatives of other utilities.

A generally held view, not surprisingly, is that prices offered must be competitive to retain and attract customers that may change supplier, i.e. primarily large users in industry or the service sector. Perhaps more surprising was that all five utilities considered value-added services, including energy efficiency, as an important part of their business strategy. Through previous DSM efforts and the electricity market reform there is a growing recognition that what used to be treated as "loads" are actually sales to a number of customers with different needs. The inclusion of value-added services in marketing reflects the expectation that those customer needs go beyond contracting for lowest price.

Utilities that have focused more or less exclusively on low-price bulk sales are relatively few. Vattenfall, although offering a range of energy services, served several electricity intensive industries prior to the market reform. Some of these customers are likely to remain with Vattenfall as bulk-buyers with relatively little interest in energy efficiency or other value added services. The company Brukskraft was formed jointly by the municipal distribution companies in Kristinehamn, Filipstad, and Degerfors together with the steel-mill Scana Björneborg. Brukskraft is a registered trader on the electricity exchange for the purpose of buying electricity for its owners at the lowest possible price. Brukskraft has also contracted with several corporations who entered financial contracts for electricity but needed a partner for the physical trade.

The early experience from Sweden is that some customers do request various services in addition to the product - electricity. However, the contacted utilities did not yet have an assessment of the number of customers requesting services, and type of service requested, or did not wish to share any detailed information. One representative estimated that about half of the customers in mainly the service sector were interested in including various services in the contract. Representatives from two utilities noted that adminstrative services, e.g. electronic or otherwise simplified billing and other adminstration, were in greater demand than energy efficiency. Telge Kraft may have gone furthest in this area by offering the service "power support" whereby Telge Kraft monitors and administrates all energy bills for the customer without actually being an energy supplier for that customer.

The larger utilities offer a range of services or packaged products and have experts in energy efficiency and other areas on their staff. One example is Sydkraft which has organised its services to industrial customers in four areas of competence: reliability and power quality, information technology and monitoring, energy efficiency, and new applications for electricity. A number of product-sheets describing what Sydkraft offers in each of these areas are used in marketing. For example, in the energy efficiency area Sydkraft offers electric motor control to identify opportunities for improvements. In all cases where utilities offer value-added services, these services are offered on commercial terms in contrast to, for example, free energy audits in traditional DSM programmes.

Thus, preliminary experiences from Sweden suggest that there is a market for value-added services and there are indications that energy efficiency will be one important component. How important remains to be seen. One utility representative made the point that utilities must educate their customers in the area of energy efficiency and thereby make it sell. In addition to what customers perceive or determine to be their needs, knowledge is an important factor. Who is representing the customer was noted by one utility representative as very important for the outcome of a contract negotiation. For example, reliability and power quality are likely to be important components in a contract if the customer representative is the electricity manager. Energy efficiency and green electricity may be important if the environmental manager is involved or if being environmentally friendly is an important part of the company's marketing strategy. A repesentative from the purchasing department may focus on price only.

Nearly all efforts to market various energy services so far have targetted relatively large customers. Representatives who were asked about the market for energy efficiency for households thought that the consumption and absolute efficiency potential for household customers was too small to carry the cost of efforts in this area. The only initiative that targets households so far was launched jointly by seven utilities in southern Sweden in September 1996. The registered trademark is "Fördel" (Advantage). Against an annual fee of about 45 ECU charged through the electricity bill subscribers get a number of services, e.g. personal energy advice over the phone, quick service against a fixed charge if major appliances need repairing, rebates on electrical appliances, access to metering equipment, and information about energy efficiency opportunities. In addition, a small part of the fee is placed in a green fund for local environmental projects. The goal is to enroll 10-15% of the household customers in this programme.

## 5.3 Information and Communication Needs

One effect of competition in the electricity market is that the need for communication and exchange of information between suppliers and buyers of electricity increases considerably at all levels. Most value-added services require a relatively close and ongoing dialogue with the customer and access to information about the customer's energy use. The costs associated with communication and information exchange must be brought down to a level that small customers can afford. For example, changing supplier presently requires that the customer has metering equipment capable of hourly metering. At present, the investment cost for such equipment in Sweden is about 700-800 ECU. For comparison, the annual energy bill for an electrically heated single family house may be 1,500-2,000 ECU, only a few percent of which can be saved by changing supplier. It has been proposed, however, that the hourly metering requirement for households should be removed and replaced by billing according to a typical household load curve.

Energy information services and communication needs include real-time pricing, on-line electronic billing, outage-detection, consumption benchmarking, and intelligent equipment/appliance control and submetering. At present, automated meter reading is increasingly replacing manual reading. The number of installations in the United States, for example, are expected to increase from about 6 million in 1995 to 20 million units by the year 2000. This increase is reportedly much due to the recognition of the broader benefits of energy information services, including the possibility of retaining existing customers and to win new ones (Rufo, 1996). Future two-way communication systems are likely to include several services in addition to automated meter reading. This development creates a demand for innovations and cost reductions in the area of information and communication technologies.

Several Swedish utilities are involved in using and developing information technology for communicating with customers. Vattenfall, for example, has entered into an agreement with Microsoft, Pacific Gas & Electric (a major American utility) and TCI (the biggest American cable network company) to develop an interactive electronic system to communicate with household customers and for energy control. Sydkraft, for example, is offering larger customers a system for monitoring energy use and for two-way communication between Sydkraft and the customer. The system requires, in addition to energy use data, a personal computer and a modem.

## 5.4 Discussion

It is still too early to draw any conclusions regarding the market for energy efficiency and other value-added services in the Swedish electricity market. However, the relatively widespread inclusion of value-added services in marketing in Sweden and the proprietory results of market surveys that have been undertaken by utilities in recent years show that there is a market for value-added services, at least in the commercial and industrial sectors. The early reported experience from utility representatives also supports this thesis.

The relative absence of a market for value-added services in the United Kingdom and Norway may be a poor predictor of Swedish market behaviour due to differences in, for example, past and present national energy policy and utility culture. For comparison, reported results from a market survey in the United States indicate that there would be a market for value-added services in the United States (Prindle, 1996). It should also be noted that there are signs that the market in the United Kingdom is beginning to mature. Customers are beginning to request value-added services after a few years of shopping around for lowest electricity price (Owen, 1996).

Competition in the Swedish electricity market could, in principle, lead to higher rates of improvement in end-use efficiency than prior to the market reform. The effect of the reform on end-use efficiency may not be possible to measure and discern, but the future level of activity of utilities in this area should give an indication. Traditional DSM, although very attractive in theory and relatively successful in the United States, has not been easily applicable and never really attempted in Sweden, much due to the fragmented structure of the Swedish electricity market and surplus electricity supply.

The notion that utilities would want to sell less by helping their customers to use their product wisely is not as strange as it may sound (Nelson, 1996). In the steel industry, for example, a significant amount of effort goes into helping the automotive companies find ways to use less steel. This approach is considered good customer relations, and a good strategy for keeping their firm as the number one supplier, and for keeping steel competitively positioned versus plastic and aluminum.

The extent to which households will be offered value-added services and be willing to pay for these services, including energy efficiency, is an open question. Prindle (1996) concludes for the United States market that some market segments, including low-income households and small businesses will not be served in competitive markets and will need various forms of regulatory and programmatic involvement to achieve their efficiency potential. The low level of utility activity in this area so far indicates that the same conclusion may be true for Sweden.

# 6. Green Electricity

The development of green pricing and environmental labelling of electricity to accelerate the development of renewable sources of electricity is closely related to the introduction of competition in the market. As is the case for energy efficiency, customers' willingness to pay will largely determine the success. Consumer interest in energy efficiency and other services will in many cases be linked to a general environmental awareness. This is reflected, for example, in the "Fördel" initiative, see above, where a fraction of the fee is put in a green fund.

The Swedish Society for Nature Conservation has developed a system for environmental labelling of electricity which in essence says that a large fraction of the existing hydro power and other renewable sources of electricity qualifies for labelling whereas nuclear power and fossil fuel based power generation does not qualify. Labelling started in March 1996 and reportedly about 15% of the potentially qualifying power production is already labelled under this scheme (Hedman, 1996). Several applications for labelling are waiting to be evaluated according to the criteria developed.

Some utilities have resisted the Society's labelling scheme and prefer to use the concept "product-specified" electricity by which the customer is guaranteed that the electricity purchased is produced in a certain way. For example, Stockholm Energi AB has offered household customers in Stockholm to buy electricity exclusively from hydropower or, alternatively, nuclear power plants against an annual administrative charge of about 30 ECU. Other utilities have established green foundations or funds, similar to that included in the "Fördel" offer. One example is Vattenfall's foundation Elvira, to which customers and others can contribute through the electricity bill or otherwise. Vattenfall has pledged to contribute the same amount as the public does to the foundation. A few hundred thousand customers were informed but so far, only a few hundred customers have signed up. Similarly, customers with Göteborg Energi can opt to contribute a small fraction of the electricity bill to a green fund.

Several utilities have, however, adopted the Society's labelling as a result of direct customer demand or as a tool for marketing. Customers' willingness to buy green electricity may also go further than demanding electricity that has been labelled according to the Association's criteria. For example, Swedish State Railways when electrifying the trains between Malmö and Ystad, a 70 km stretch in southern Sweden, demanded that the electricity supplier, Sydkraft, erected a wind turbine that would roughly meet the annual energy needed to operate the train (in addition, the wind turbine should be visible from the train). Such customer demands would hardly have been met in a monopoly market.

# 7. Combined Heat and Power Production

The electricity market reform may strengthen the position of district heating and combined heat and power (CHP) production. In a scenario where electricity prices increase due to increasing electricity demand, closing of nuclear reactors, or increased electricity exports, there is a great potential for energy efficient CHP production. Opening the electricity market to competition should, in principle, make it easier for CHP producers to get fair prices for electricity produced, although the commercial risk may increase.

The heat delivered in Swedish district heating systems in 1995 was 41 TWh and the electricity produced in district heating CHP was 4 TWh (Fjärrvärmeföreningen, 1995). For comparison, corresponding numbers for Finland in 1994 were 25 TWh of heat and 11 TWh of electricity (Statistics Finland, 1995). The potential electricity production in existing Swedish plants is estimated to 8-10 TWh. The capacity has not been used to its full potential in recent years due to relatively low electricity prices. Essentially all district heating is owned and operated by the same municipal utilities that also distribute electricity. However, district heating customers remain captive customers, unless they switch to fuel or electricity, since district heating remains local monopolies.

The potential market in 1995 for district heating, i.e. if all buildings that would be economical to connect were connected, has been estimated to 56.5 TWh (Fjärrvärmeföreningen, 1995). By this measure, the 41 TWh of delivered heat in 1995 results in a market share of 73% for district heat. Low electricity prices during the last 25 years, as a result of inexpensive hydropower and surplus nuclear capacity with low operating costs, is the main reason why the potential for CHP production in district heating systems has not been exploited. One estimate is that 29 TWh of the 41 TWh delivered could be used as a heat load for CHP production. The corresponding potential electricity production is 14-29 TWh assuming electricity-to-heat ratios of 0.5-1. There is also a potential to increase CHP production in industry although the size of it is less well known than the potential in district heating systems. About 4 TWh of electricity was produced in industrial CHP plants in 1995 (SPA, 1996). For comparison, process heat demand in the pulp and paper industry alone is probably on the order of 25-30 TWh (ÅF-IPK, 1995).

## 8. Outsourcing of Heating and Electricity

Outsourcing of energy supply and other non-core activities in industry has become more common in recent years. The operation of energy equipment may be farmed-out to independent companies or utilities, and in some cases such assets have been sold outright to free up capital and allow industries to concentrate on their core-business. There are several examples of this in the pulp and paper industry in the United States (Nilsson et al., 1995) and some examples in Finland (IVO Group, 1996). Swedish pulp and paper companies have such outsourcing agreements for several of their facilities outside Sweden but it has been less common so far at their facilities in Sweden.

Many utilities in Sweden are now offering industrial and other customers to outsource heating and electricity. For example, Vattenfall recently signed a contract to deliver its product "ready-to-use" electricity at an industrial plant. In this case, Vattenfall owns and operates transformers and other high voltage equipment at one of the automobile maker SAAB's plants. Entering outsourcing agreements or other types of partnerships is an important strategy for utilities to build long-term business relationships with important customers.

More common than industry applications, however, is that utilities and other actors are offering end-users to outsource in the area of space heating. The basic idea is that the utility takes over the operation and maintenance, and in many cases ownership, of furnaces and boilers for space heating. The concept is marketed under many different names, e.g., local heat, ready-to-use heat, total heat, etc. Through such contracts the utility guarantees the delivery of heat and the end-user does not have to worry about fuel-choice, repairs, future investments, etc. In the case of Stockholm Energi, this outsourcing agreement specifically targets customers who in the longer term may become connected to the district heating system.

Utilities have been willing to operate, or own and operate, equipment in order to provide customers with heat and hot water at the right temperature or electricity at the right voltage. However, this is where most of the utilities draw the line. One exception is Göteborg Energi which on customer demand in isolated cases has become an energy service company in a true sense, i.e., responsible for heating, ventilation, and other services. Utilities otherwise prefer not to get involved in building management or industrial processes due to the difficultiy of defining energy services, for example good indoor climate.

# 9. Innovative Government Approaches to Energy Efficiency

Deregulation per se does not remove any of the barriers to energy efficiency that were discussed in section 3. The early experience from Sweden, supported by the experience from Norway and the United Kingdom, also shows that energy efficiency cannot be left to the market. In some customer segments there may be a market for energy efficiency, as indicated above, but for most customers and in particular for small customers, energy efficiency remains a low priority.

The policy measures taken by governments to promote energy efficiency and, for that matter, renewable energy must be adapted to the new market situation. Traditional command and control regulation, e.g. mandating energy efficiency programs or forcing purchases of wind electricity, may distort competition between utilities and, at worst, present considerable adminstrative costs to the regulator. Policies to promote energy efficiency should be non-discriminatory and able to adapt to changing market conditions. Governments must get better at influencing the market forces and thereby contribute to transforming the market for energy efficiency.

To get rid of the worst performing products on the market, standards prescribing the lowest acceptable performance level is a well known and tested method. RD&D and technology procurement programmes can be used to promote the market introduction and diffusion of new energy efficient technologies (cf. figure 3). For example, governments can make skilful use of their own demand for products, or assist in organizing buyer groups, to stimulate the preintroduction and acceleration of improved technologies in procurement programmes. The term in vogue to denote such programmes and make a distinction between these programmes and traditional DSM is market transformation (MT).

Figure 3: Prevalence of Products on the Market as a Function of their Performance Characteristics

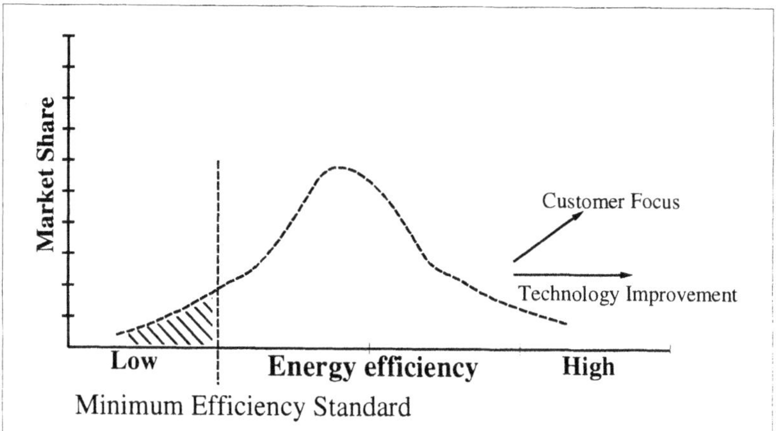


Note: Standards define a minimum performance level. Technology procurement programmes can be used to stimulate the early introduction of improved technology. Various policies with customer focus may be needed to ensure that the curve is shifted or tilted to the right.

Source: Adapted from Nilsson H., 1995

There is yet no widely accepted definition of market transformation (MT) programmes. One approach is that these are programmes which encourage wide-spread adoption of advanced energy efficiency technologies that were either not available, or were so narrowly distributed as to be practically unavailable, prior to the programme. MT programmes are different from traditional DSM programmes in that they focus on the producer of energy using equipment. DSM programmes for most end-uses focus on the consumer as the decision maker and provides incentives to induce the consumer to make different decisions. MT programmes may also include incentives to consumers but the effort is made only to the extent that it is necessary to induce technology changes at the producer level (Goldstein, 1994).

A technology procurement programme organized in 1990/91 by the Swedish Board for Industrial and Technical Development (NUTEK) together with some of the major building companies, owning large stocks of flats, was perhaps the world's first procurement programme directly aimed at improving end-use efficiency. The performance requirements in the tender documents for combined refrigerator-freezers were tailored to improve the performance by 25% compared to the best product on the market, 35% compared to the average sold, and 55% compared to the average in use. The winner, who received a cash prize and a guaranteed delivery of a certain number of units, presented a refrigerator-freezer that actually used 35% less compared to the best product on the market. The specific electricity use of the ten best refrigerator-freezers on the market decreased from an average of 1.15 kWh/liter-year in 1991 to 0.88 kWh/liter-year in 1994. The average price of the top-ten increased by only 7% in nominal terms (Nilsson H., 1995), equivalent to a decrease by about 10% in real terms. Energy efficient models accounted for 5% of the sales in 1995 which is less than the 10% forecasted by NUTEK in 1991. NUTEK has since organized procurement programmes for several other products, including clothes washers and dryers, office equipment, lighting, fans, automated factory doors.

Another European example is Deutsche Bundespost's procurement, on a life-cycle cost basis, of one thousand air-handling units for switchboard stations in 1991/92. When this procurement was first announced, the electricity use of a typical unit for the specified task was about 50,000 kWh per year. This consumption was later cut to about half in various bids to deliver the equipment (Nilsson L.J., 1995). Several market transformation programmes, sometimes organized as contests under the name "Golden Carrot" programmes, similar to that for refrigerator-freezers in Sweden, have also been done in the United States (Nadel and Geller, 1994).

## Voluntary Agreements and Environmental Management Systems

Voluntary or negotiated agreements between governments and industry to achieve various environmental goals are relatively novel in environmental policy and their use is increasing in many OECD countries. Typically, such agreements involve industry committments to reduce emissions or energy use at some specified rate in exchange for government committments to meet some industry demands, e.g., lower environmental and energy taxes. The agreements can be between government and individual companies, a group of companies, industrial branches, or industry as a whole. A widely cited example is German Industry's offer in 1995 to undertake, on a voluntary basis, special efforts to reduce their specific $CO_2$ emissions. In return, industry expected the federal government to refrain from imposing emission- and energy-based taxes. Some European governments, e.g. in Netherlands and Denmark, have started to enter such agreements.

A Swedish example, specifically targetted to improve energy efficiency, is the Eco-Energy programme launched by NUTEK. Under this programme individual companies undertake to establish a long-term energy and environmental policy, to analyse their present patterns of energy use, to establish specific objectives for energy efficiency improvements, and to apply purchasing procedures based on life-cycle cost in accordance with a protocol developed by NUTEK and the Association of Swedish Engineering Industries. NUTEK undertakes to carry out energy surveys and analyses, draw up proposals for purchasing procedures and to carry out other activities aimed at improving acceptance and motivation for energy efficiency in the company (NUTEK, 1996).

The Eco-Energy programme has been inspired by government operated United States programmes, e.g. Energy Star and Green Lights. For example, participants in the United States Environmental Protection Agency's Energy Star Buildings programme agree to improve the overall efficiency of their facilities through the implementation of a comprehensive set of profitable upgrades. The Environmental Protection Agency assists participants by providing technical and administrative assistance to ensure maximum energy savings while satisfying criteria for cost-effectiveness (EPA, 1996).

Voluntary agreements can include the introduction of environmental management systems, e.g. the European Union's Ecomanagement and Audit Scheme (EMAS) or the standard ISO 14000. Interest in environmental management systems is growing rapidly in Sweden and several other European countries. In Germany, 220 facilities were EMAS registered as of summer 1996 out of a total of 281 facilities in Europe. In Sweden, six industrial facilities were EMAS registered as of August 1996 and many more were planning or waiting to be registered (Österberg, 1996).

Environmental management involves planning, organizing, and leading the business towards specified goals, analogous to, for example, quality management. One aspect of environmental management systems is that their introduction requires decisions at high levels of management and thus sends a clear message to the organization about this being a corporate committment. Environmental management systems may also become an important instrument for companies in their relations with customers, the public, the capital market, insurance companies, government agencies, etc.

The growing interest in environmental management systems as such is not related to the electricity market reform. However, increasing environmental awareness and a willingness to take an increased environmental responsibility can have an impact on the rate of energy efficiency improvements and how green electricity will be valued on the market. Energy, if applicable, is one of many components that should be incorporated in an environmental management system. For example, according to EMAS, energy conservation shall be considered in the certified company's environmental policy, programme, and revisions.

There is a risk, however, that environmental management systems become relatively weak instruments since the formulation of policy and goals is left to the company. Although the introduction of an environmental management system does not automatically result in any stringent demands for improved environmental performance it does mean that energy use and environmental issues get a more prominent role in the business. Experience so far indicates that in particular energy, water, and waste handling costs can be reduced considerably by working with environmental management systems.The U.K. company NOR Systems estimates that it has cut its energy consumption by 10-15% over one year and made significant reductions in water usage - largely because staff awareness of these issues has increased (Anonymous, 1995).

## 10. The Need for Technical and Organisational Innovation

Reductions of energy related emissions of pollutants by 50-90%, or more, are necessary in order to meet long term goals for the environment in terms of, for example, critical load levels for sulfur or stabilization of atmospheric $CO_2$ concentrations (Nilsson and Johansson, 1994). Far reaching improvements in the energy efficiency of technologies that produce energy services is a key component in a least cost strategy to meet such goals. However, energy efficient technologies per se are not enough. Organisational, financial, and policy innovations are also necessary to facilitate both the development and the widespread use of energy efficient technologies. Market transformation efforts involving, for example, technology procurement programmes, is one example of such innovative policies. Environmental management systems, if applied successfully, can contribute to making energy efficiency an integrated part of industrial day-to-day operations and decision making. Partnerships, such as Eco-Energy in Sweden and Green Lights in the United States, exemplify policy innovations aimed at accelerating the rate of energy efficiency improvements in participating companies.

The need to realise substantial efficiency improvements in the end-use of energy comes at a time when growth in demand for fuels and electricity in many industrialized countries is already slowing or even negative. In response to slow or negative market growth, many utilities and other energy industries are exploring new business areas. For example, several utilities in the United States and Western Europe are expanding their operations in third-world markets and in Eastern Europe where they can use their experience in building new energy supply. The way they do business in their home markets must also change and perhaps the best way to describe this is a need for profound change in utility industry culture.

Many businesses outside the energy industry have gone from being strongly product oriented to focusing increasingly on customer utility, comfort, function, etc. One example is the auto industry where the inclusion of extensive service warranties with purchases of new cars have become commonplace during the last 10-20 years. Swedish appliance manufacturer Electrolux, for example, is increasingly speaking in terms of utility and function rather than product - clean laundry instead of washing machines, food storage rather than refrigerators. A simultaneous trend is increasing producer responsibility for products at the end of their lifetime. A first step along this dematerialization path is to recycle materials. A second step is to recycle and replace components in products that have been designed to facilitate disassembly and reassembly. A third step is that the company never actually sells the product but instead sells the utility or service, e.g. food storage, through a leasing system or the like.

Companies in monopoly markets, such as electric utilities, have to some extent been immune to market trends such as those descibed. Competition in electricity markets will certainly increase the pressure on utilities to change. An optimistic view, perhaps, is that they will change in the direction of becoming more service oriented. Although the idea that utilities would strive to sell less of their main product in already stagnant markets may seem paradoxical at first, the carrying concept should be to grow by selling more *services*. If this actually means pushing less of the *product*, e.g. electricity, then becomes less important.

# 11. Summary and Conclusions

More efficient use of fuels and electricity is a key strategy in a transition to more sustainable energy systems. The challenge to society is finding ways of accelerating the development of energy efficient technologies and in particular their market introduction and widespread use. Historically, end-use energy efficiency and other value-added services has not been a high priority with many consumers and suppliers of fuels and electricity. Governments and publicly owned utilities have attempted to improve the situation through taxes, regulation, DSM programmes, R&D support, and other policy measures. Increased competition in electricity markets does not remove any of the traditional barriers to energy efficiency. However, policy measures to promote energy efficiency in deregulated markets must be adapted to the new situation. Governments must learn to influence the market forces and thereby contribute to transforming the market for energy efficiency. There are some indications from Sweden that the electricity market reform has induced utilities to become more customer and service oriented. Deregulated energy markets, in combination with appropriate government intervention and increasing environmental awareness among consumers, may prove to be better suited than monopoly markets to achive many of the goals set up by society for the development of energy systems.

## References

ÅF-IPK (1995): Energiförbrukning i massa- och pappersindustrin 1994, (Energy Use in the Pulp and Paper Industry 1994), Report to the Swedish Forestry Industries from Ångpanneföreningen-IPK, Stockholm

Anderson D. (1995): Roundtable on Energy Efficiency and the Economists - Six Perspectives and An Assessment, *Annual Review of Energy and the Environment*, Vol. 20, pp. 493-573. (Includes seven chapters by (1) Anderson D., "Energy Efficiency and the Economists: The Case for a Policy Based on Economic Principles" (2) Cicchetti C.J., "Four Misconceptions About Demand Side Management" (3) Cavanagh R., "Energy Efficiency Solutions: What Commodity Prices Can't Deliver" (4) Joskow P.L., "Utility Subsidized Energy Efficiency Programs" (5) Levine M.D., Koomey J.G., McMahon J.E., Sanstad A.H., and Hirst E., "Energy Efficiency Policy and Market Failures" (6) Nichols A.L., "Demand Side Management: An Nth-Best Solution" (7) Anderson D., "Roundtable on Energy Efficiency and the Economists-An Assessment")

Anonymous (1995): Benefits and Shortcomings of EMAS Revealed as First Five Sites Win Registration, *ENDS Report 247 (Environmental Auditing No. 5)*, August

EIA (1996): Profile: U.S. Electric Utility Demand Side Management, Executive Summary, U.S. Energy Information Agency, Department of Energy, Washington, DC, (http://www.eia.doe.gov/cneaf/electricity/pub_summaries/dsm_sum.html), visited 960924

Eikeland, P.O. (1995): Norway and the UK: A Comparative Institutional Analysis of Competitive Reforms in the Electricity Supply Industries, EED Report 1995/3, The Fridtjof Nansen Institute, Lysaker, Norway

EPA (1996): U.S. EPA Energy Star Buildings Program, US Environmental Protection Agency, Washington, DC, (http://www.epa.gov/docs/GCDOAR/esbhome.html), visited 960814

Fjärrvärmeföreningen (1995): Prognos 1995, (Forecast 1995), Swedish District Heating Association, Stockholm. (in Swedish)

Goldstein, D.B. (1994): Market Transformation to Super Efficient Products: The Emergence of Partnership Approaches, *Proceedings from the ACEEE 1994 Summer Study on Energy Efficiency in Buildings*, 6:92-99, American Council for an Energy Efficient Economy, Washington, DC

Haaland, H.O. and Wilhite, H. (1994): DSM and Deregulation: Experiences from Norway, *Proceedings from the ACEEE 1994 Summer Study on Energy Efficiency in Buildings*, 6:101-110, American Council for an Energy Efficient Economy, Washington, DC

Hamrin, J.; Marcus, W.; Morse, F. and Weinberg, C. (1994): Affected with the Public Interest, Electric Utility Restructuring in an Era of Competition, National Association of Regulatory Utility Commissioners (NARUC), Washington, DC

Hedman, G. (1996): Swedish Association for the Conservation of Nature (personal communication, October 1996)

Hughes, T.B. (1985) Edison and Electric Light, *in:* MacKenzie D. and Wajcman J. (eds.): *The Social Shaping of Technology*, Open University Press, Milton Keynes, UK

IVO Group (1996): Kraftvärme och 'outsourcing' lönsamt energialternativ, (Cogeneration and Outsourcing Profitable Energy Alternatives," Energimagasinet, No. 4, pp. 36-40. (in Swedish)

Jochem, E. and Gruber, E. (1990): Obstacles to Rational Electricity Use and Measures to Alleviate Them," *Energy Policy*, Vol. 18, No. 4, pp. 340-350

Levine, M.D.; Koomey, J.G.; Price, L.; Geller, H. and Nadel, S. (1995): Electricity End-Use Efficiency: Experience with Technologies, Markets, and Policies Throughout the World, *Energy - The International Journal*, Vol. 20, No. 1, pp. 37-62

MIC (1996): The New Swedish Electricity Market, A Summary of the Reform, Minstry of Industry and Commerce, The Printing Works of the Cabinet Office and Ministries, Stockholm, Sweden

Mills, E. (1991): Evaluation of European Lighting Programmes, *Energy Policy*, Vol. 19, No l, pp. 266-278

Nadel, S. (1992): Utility Demand-Side Management Experience and Potential - a Critical Review, *Annual Review of Energy and the Environment*, Vol. 17, pp. 507-536

Nadel, S. and Geller, H. (1994): Market Transformation Programs: Past Results, Future Directions, American Council for an Energy Efficient Economy (ACEEE), Washington, DC

Nadel, S.; Geller, H. and Pye, M. (1995): DSM Under Attack: Are Utilities Overreacting to the Threat of Retail Wheeling?", American Council for an Energy Efficient Economy (ACEEE), Washington, DC

Nelson, D. J. (1996): Expanding the Customer Service Toolkit: Mixing Electrotechnologies with Strategic Conservation, *Proceedings from the ACEEE 1996 Summer Study on Energy Efficiency in Buildings*, 7:115-119, American Council for an Energy Efficient Economy, Washington, DC

Nilsson, H. (1995): Market Transformation: An Essential Condition for Sustainability, *Energy for Sustainable Development*, Vol. 1, No. 6, pp. 20-29. Published by International Energy Initiative, Bangalore, India

Nilsson, L.J. (1993): Energy Intensity Trends in 31 Industrial and Developing Countries 1950-1988, *Energy - The International Journal*, Vol. 18., No. 4, pp. 309-322

Nilsson, L.J (1995): Air-Handling Energy Efficiency and Design Practices, *Energy and Buildings*, Vol. 22, No. 1, pp. 1-13

Nilsson, L.J. and Johansson, T.B. (1994): Environmental Challenges to the Energy Industries, *in:* N. Steen (ed.): *Sustainable Development and the Energy Industries: Implications and Impacts of Environmental Legislation*, Royal Institute of International Affairs/Earthscan, London.

Nilsson, L.J.; Larson, E.D.; Gilbreath, K.R. and Gupta, A. (1995): Background Paper on Energy Efficiency and the Pulp and Paper Industry, *Proceedings from ACEEE Summer Study on Energy Efficiency in Industry: "Partnerships, Productivity, and Environment"*, American Council for an Energy Efficient Economy, Washington, DC. Also published as an independent ACEEE report and Report #294 from the Center for Energy and Environmental Studies, Princeton University

NUTEK (1996): Resultat och möjligheter, (Results and Possibilities), Swedish Board for Industrial and Technical Development (NUTEK), Stockholm

Olerup, B. (1994): The Stockholm Lighting Programme, *Utilities Policy*, Vol. 4, No. 4, pp. 273-284

Österberg, K. (1996): Mölnlyckes miljömål klarar EU-kraven, (Mölnlyckes Environmental Targets Meet EU Requirements), *Ny Teknik*, No. 37, p. 43. (in Swedish)

Owen, G. (1995): Energy Policy, the Government and the Energy Regulators: A Case Study of the Energy Saving Trust, CSERGE Working Paper GEC 95-35, Centre for Social and Economic Research on the Global Environment (CSERGE), University of East Anglia, Norwich, UK

Owen, G. (1996): A Market in Efficiency, Promoting Energy Savings through Competition, Institute for Public Policy Research, London

Prindle, W.R. (1996): Can Efficiency Keep the Rustlers Out? Energy Efficiency as a Customer Retention Tool, *Proceedings from the ACEEE 1996 Summer Study on Energy Efficiency in Buildings*, 7:135-143, American Council for an Energy Efficient Economy, Washington, DC

Rufo, M.W. (1996): Energy Information Services, *Energy*, Vol. 21, No. 2 (April), pp. 16-19

SPA (1996): Kraftåret 1995, (Power Year 1995), Swedish Power Association, Stockholm. (in Swedish)

Statistics Finland (1995): Energy Statistics 1994, Tilastokeskus/Statistics Finland, Helsinki

Swisher, J.N. (1994): Barriers and Incentives for Utility Energy Efficiency Programs in Deregulated Markets, *Proceedings from the ACEEE 1996 Summer Study on Energy Efficiency in Buildings*, 6:201-211, American Council for an Energy Efficient Economy, Washington, DC

UN (1995): 1993 Energy Statistics Yearbook, United Nations, New York

UNCED (1992): Agenda 21, United Nations Conference on Environment and Development, Rio de Janeiro

UNIPEDE (1994): Integrated Resource Planning and Demand Side Management in Europe: Present Status and Potential Role, Economics and Tariffs Study Committee, 60.04.TAROPT, Union Internationale des Producteurs et Distributeurs d'Energie Electrique (UNIPEDE), Paris

Vine, E. (1996): International DSM and DSM Program Evaluation: An INDEEP Assessment, *Energy - The International Journal*, Vol. 21, No. 10, pp. 983-996

Williams, R.H. and Larson, E.D. (1989): Expanding Roles for Gas Turbines in Power Generation, *in:* Johansson T.B., Bodlund B., and Williams R.H. (eds.): *Electricity - Efficient End-Use and New Generation Technologies, and Their Planning Implications*, Lund University Press, Lund, Sweden

Williams, R.H.; Larson, E.D. and Ross, M.H. (1987): Materials, Affluence, and Industrial Energy Use, *Annual Review of Energy*, Vol. 12, pp. 99-144

# 3. Policy Issues: Requirements and Consequences

# The Policy Concept Behind the Dutch National Environmental Policy Plans

*Paul E. de Jongh*

## 1. The Origins of the Environmental Planning Approach

The Dutch Cabinet Lubbers-1 (Christian Democrats and Liberals, 1982-1986) focussed on balancing the budgets after the economic decline in the second oil crisis (1979), on deregulation and general improvement of economic conditions in the country.

The Cabinet decided to shift the Department for Environment from the Ministry of Health and Environment to the Ministry of Housing and Landuse Planning. A programme for deregulation for environmental and landuse regulations was set up.

In the meantime the follow-up of the discovery of toxic waste dumping (in newly built residential areas, e.g. the Lekkerkerk village) and some scandals of non compliance by important industrial firms (Uniser-affaire) played an important role in keeping the environment on the political agenda.

In the discussions between the Department of Environment with representatives of industry (including more progressive CEO's) a not officially outspoken but more and more clear sort of agreement was developed, being:

- Industry would take environmental protection serious, i.a. by the introduction of internal environmental management schemes (environmental care), whereas
- Government would provide a more long term and comprehensible insight in the developments of environmental policies, to avoid surprises and to promote the smooth introduction of adaptions to environmental standards in industry.

Until the early eighties environmental policy was based on a compartment-by-compartment and an issue-by-issue approach. To give a comprehensible insight to people outside the government, it was necessary to seek for ways of integration of all the different issues, regulations, problems etc.

Another reason for integration of environmental policies was the scattered way responsibilities were divided in the central government. Although the Department of Environment had responsibilities for coordination, and for some major areas as air pollution and waste management, the responsibility for water quantity and quality was in the Ministry of Transport and Waterworks, the responsibility for nature protection was in the Ministry of Agriculture, Nature Protection and Fisheries, and the responsibility for all kinds of resources (energy, mining etc) was in the Ministry of Economic Affairs.

The Cabinet formation of 1982 had made clear that there would be no way of getting all those responsibilities into one "big" Department of Environment (as was hoped for in the seventies by some policy makers). By working jointly on a common plan for environmental protection, the cooperation between the different Ministries and Departments could be improved, and the coordinating role of the Department of Environment would be strengthened.

The insight that environmental policy making would be more than just writing regulations, promoted the introduction of all kinds of new skills in the Department of Environment: project-management, strategic choice approach[1], handling uncertainties, negotiation training, consensus building skills and the like. This promoted the professionalisation of the management of environmental policy making and improved the status of the Department of Environment in the Central government.

A training was set up to deal with so-called risky decisions in which principles and tools for the management of politically risky situations and for the proper advising of the Minister were introduced.[2]

## An Integrated Approach for Environmental Policies

The structure for integrated environmental policy was found in two complementary ways:

- Themes, being areas of environmental problems which should be analysed and solved in an integrated way; five themes were defined in 1985:
  - Acidification
  - Eutrophication
  - Waste generation
  - Dispersion/toxication
  - Disturbance (local hindrance, noise etc)[3].

  For each theme a theme-coordinator on a senior level was nominated, who had to manage a process towards integrated analysis of the problem, answering the following questions:

---

1 Introduced by Allen Hickling and Arnold de Jong, who - as facilitating consultants - played an important role in several policy developments.

2 Cooperation with Prof. Lawrence Susskind, MIT, Boston. The cooperation was later institutionalized in the Sustainability Challenge Foundation.

3 Later climate change, dehydration and "squandering" were added to the themes (NEPP, 1989).

(1) What is the nature of the problem in terms of causes and effects? (To be described as quantitatively as possible); what is the level of (un)certainty by which the causes and effects relate to each other?
(2) What would be the environmental quality standard by which the problem could be considered as being solved?
(3) Which economic sectors are biggest contributors to the causes of the problem; what is their share in the causes; which possible measures could be taken by them to reduce their contribution to the problem; what are the costs of those possible measures?
(4) Which reductions in terms of the causes (discharges, emissions etc.) are necessary, when the environmental quality standard as defined under 2 had to be achieved?
(5) Which measures as defined under 3 could contribute most cost-effectively to the reductions as defined under 4; what would be the time-frame to introduce these measures?

The problem of uncertainty (see question 1) was of great importance in the policy debates. As Minister Winsemius put it for acidification: "If the level of certainty about causes and effects is more than 80%, we should not hesitate to take action, because that is a level of certainty which far exceeds the level of certainty in any kind of (commercial) investment."

- Target-groups, being the economic sectors which contribute most to the causes of the themes and which presumably will be affected most by policies in the years ahead. Four priority target-groups were defined in 1985:

  - Agriculture
  - Transport
  - Energy generation
  - Refinaries[4].

  For each (priority) target-group a so-called target-group manager was nominated on a senior level in the Department of Environment, who was assigned to build up and to maintain working relationships with that specific target-group and to coordinate all the policies and negotiations which might affect that specific target-group. In a later stage (1992) the organizational structure of the Department of Environment was changed, so as to offer a recognizable set-up for the target-groups.

---

4 Note that the focus shifted from manufactoring industry to other sectors, which was a form of priority setting asked for by industry. Later in the NEPP the list of target-groups was "completed" and included: chemical industry, other sectors of industry, the building trade, the waste management sector, the water supply sector, households, small business etc. The completion was necessary to get an involvement in Dutch society as big as possible for the farreaching policies proposed in the NEPP (1989).

Each target-group manager had to analyse his target-group according to the following scheme:

(1) What are the contributions to the causes of the different themes of the target-group at hand?
(2) What are the "desired" reductions in terms of causes (discharges, emissions) possibly asked by the theme-coordinators to the target-group at hand?
(3) What are the possible measures the target-group could take to meet the reductions as mentioned under 2; what are the costs and what are the time-frames for those measures to be taken?
(4) What is the economic and social structure of the target-group; who are key persons; which are the key organizations; which are the more progressive corporations and institutions in that network? Which role play other government organisations in influencing developments in the target-group at hand?
(5) Which are the (national and international) economic perspectives for the target-group at hand? Which technological developments might take place, resp. will take place in the (near) future? Which developments are of relevance to the environment?
(6) Which government actions could be most effective for the target-group at hand to promote the reductions of emissions and discharges?

These analyses were discussed in the Department of Environment, but also with the departments usually dealing with the target-groups for economic reasons (mainly Department of Energy, Department of Agriculture, Department of Transport, Department of Industry) and with the target-group-representatives. This approach enhanced the knowledge of environmental policy makers about the feasibility of measures and broadened the network within which environmental policy making took place. Note that in the analyses the policy-instruments (like licensing, agreements, subsidies and levies) had only a minor place (nr. 6), the focus was more directed on the (physical) measures to be taken and on the costs of those measures.

These analyses and network-building activities lasted for at least half a decennium (second half of the eighties). The above mentioned questions were developed in the course of the process rather than designed at one moment in time.

## 2. The National Environmental Policy Plan

The first NEPP (1989) was more of a "societal contract" than just a government actionplan. There are three reasons for this:

- the analysis made by the State Institute for Health and Environment showed the necessity of drastic emission reductions[5];
- the plan was based on the notion of sustainable development, as worked out in the so-called Brundtland-report[6] (leading to a longer time perspective than the originally foreseen four years);
- the attention in the preparation of the plan shifted from government institutions to economic sectors as target groups of environmental policies.

In 1986 the RIVM was asked to analyse the current environmental quality standards and notions, and to compare those with the economic and technological developments in the 25 years ahead (1985 - 2010), taking into account international developments affecting the Netherlands' environment.
The analysis was based on two scenario's:

(1) a scenario of "business as usual" (no new policies, the current policies and regulations just being implemented in the near future); and
(2) a scenario in which all known environmental technologies to reduce emissions would be applied in due time.

The idea behind the two scenario's was that these would provide a continuum of environmental measures which could be compared with the desired environmental quality, whereby then the most cost-effective measures would be chosen as basis for government policies and regulations.

**Scientists Message to the Government**

Early 1988 a draft of their findings was presented to the Department of Environment, the main conclusions being:

- To achieve a sustainable environmental quality in The Netherlands, given the economic developments, emission reductions of 70 to 90 % were necessary for almost all environmental themes;
- The known environmental technologies, mainly add-on technology and clean-up technology, are not sufficient to achieve 70 to 90 % emission reductions; therefore
- Environmental policies should also aim for structural changes in production and consumption processes.

---

[5] State Institute for Health and Environment (RIVM): "Concern for tomorrow, a national environmental survey 1985 - 2010", Bilthoven, 1988.

[6] World Commission on Environment and Development: "Our Common Future", 1987.

These conclusions were beyond the expected conclusions (of about necessary emission reductions of 20 to 30%). This led to a more general strategic approach to promote the involvement of all stakeholding economic sectors and a drift away from the original idea of a more prescriptive strategic plan.

The notion of sustainable development was chosen as main motive for environmental policies. Three reasons for environmental policies were given in the NEPP:

- the (traditional) health reason;
- the ecological reason; and
- the economic reason.

For this last reason the argument was that spoiled and polluted areas would not provide the proper physical conditions for modern economic developments (for example to attract new electronic industries, the country should provide clean and attractive areas for the high skilled and demanding labourers in those industries).

The notion of sustainable development bridged the contrast between environmental policies and economic policies, at least on an abstract level. This provided a common ground with the Ministry of Economic Affairs and with representatives of industry.

## Redefining Sustainable Development

The definition of sustainable development as introduced in the Brundtland report turned out not to be very useful for policy making[7]. A discussion about the needs of current and future generations would take a long (and may be everlasting) philosophical discussion, which would not lead to emission reductions as were considered to be necessary.

Therefore, in the NEPP sustainable development is defined as a development by which every generation solved their own environmental problems, so to hand over a clean environment to the next generation.

As the environmental problems were known from the RIVM analysis, and one generation would last for about 25 years time, this definition led to the conclusion that the necessary emission reductions of 70 to 90 % had to be achieved in a timeframe of 25 years.

---

[7] According to the Brundtland report Sustainable Development is defined as "A development which satisfies the needs of the present generation without compromising the possibilities of future generations for satisfying their needs".

This new notion of sustainable development turned out to be a strong appeal to all sectors in society. 25 Years is long enough to imagine drastic changes in the economy and in society, and it is short enough to relate the changes to your children. Also, the notion of 25 years time took away the threat of overnight government actions of which industry was most afraid.

To oversee the impacts of policies leading to changes in production and consumption patterns (in order to achieve the emission reductions in 25 years time) and to shift away from just cleaning up the environment to a more preventive policy, a third scenario was developed.

The third scenario was based on the notion of taking away the general causes of environmental deterioration. These general causes were indicated as follows:
"Environmental problems are not isolated problems; they are interconnected and they share common causes:
- the opening or changing of substance cycles (for example, in eutrophication or with the waste problem);
- the more intensive use of energy (for example, in acidification, dehydration, climate change); and
- the neglect of quality aspects in production processes and products (for example, in diffusion of dangerous substances and in nuisance and disturbance)."[8]

The third scenario consisted of a number of physical measures (on top of the scenario 2 measures) on the basis of:

- integrated life cycle management (recycling schemes);
- energy extensification (improving efficiency, use of renewable energy sources and energy saving);
- quality improvement of products, production processes, raw materials, waste and the natural environment.

## Economic Analyses and Cost-Figures

The outcomes of the economic analyses of the different scenarios were backing the notion that structural changes in production and consumption were at the long run the best way to avoid environmental problems and to meet the targets of emission reductions.

Under the condition that other neighbouring countries would follow the same policies, the third scenario could eventually lead to more GDP-growth than the standard economic policies foresaw in the longer run! The conclusion was drawn, that - on a

[8] NEPP, page 9.

macro level - strict environmental policies, without big surprises for industry and in cooperation with the countries of the European Union, were not harmful for the economy as a whole. This conclusion bridged the contrast between environmental and economic policies on a somewhat more concrete level than the notion of sustainable development did.

An important element in the preparation of the plan was the availability of cost-figures of possible measures. This made it possible to make the mentioned macro economic analyses and also to have discussions with representatives of economic sectors and in the Cabinet.

Part of the costs should be paid for by the government (clean-up operations, improvement of support and enforcement by government agencies, some subsidies, investments in infrastructure). Therefore, the Cabinet started a preliminary discussion about the plan. The Cabinet discussion was not about the environmental long term targets as such, but about the necessary budget for the first four years.

## Setting Targets

According to the findings of the RIVM, long term targets were set for each of the environmental themes. Most of the targets were described as emission reductions rather than as environmental qualities. Environmental qualities to be achieved were described in a more qualitative form. The emission reduction targets were described in a quantitative way and were the main focus for debate. This was a tactical choice: a policy debate about environmental quality as such would be meaningless as is a debate about the desirability of nice weather, whereas emission reductions relate much more to real economic life (via physical measures and their costs).

From the long term (2010) targets, intermediate targets for 1994 and 2000 were derived. The 1994 targets related most directly to short term measures to be introduced by implementing the plan.

In the plan, reference was made to almost all government departments to make changes in their policies towards sustainable development. The re-introduction of energy saving programmes (after a period in which the Ministry of Economic Affairs had skipped all these programmes) was of crucial importance in this process of integration environmental issues in other policy-areas.

As the plan got more and more the character of a "social contract" which would promote actions from all stakeholders in society, the idea of explicit priority setting in terms of environmental issues was skipped. The priority setting had to take place when target groups would draw their plans upon the NEPP. Furthermore, of course, priority setting took place in the discussions about the funding of government actions. So, priorities were not set on the level of environmental issues or themes, but on the level of measures to be taken: not solely on the basis of environmental risk, but on the basis of cost-effectiveness in the implementation stage.

The original plan was not decisive about the policy instruments to be used for implementation. The option of covenants was mentioned, as were options of financial mechanisms (some of which were introduced by the plan, like the reduction of commuter tax relief) and regulations. Most of the plan as far as industry would be involved, would be implemented finally by the licensing procedures of the provinces and municipalities.

## Regulations or Negotiations?

After the elections of 1989 the new Cabinet, a coalition between Christian Democrats and Social Democrats, an addition to the plan was made (NEPP-plus) in which more discussion was devoted to the question as to whether the implementation would take place via regulations or via other instruments as negotiated agreements/covenants.

The distinction between regulations and negotiated agreements were seen at that time as absolute: regulations would give all power to the Cabinet and finally to Parliament, whereas in negotiations Parliament could only "wait and see" what the Cabinet had achieved in the negotiations with industry. For a number of reasons and with some conditions negotiated agreements were the overall mechanism of implementation of the plan in industry, the reasons being:

- the plan was so comprehensive, that the amount of specific regulations would have been almost overwhelming;
- the plan focussed on targets 20 years ahead; regulations cannot go beyond the practical options of the time when they are written; so they tend to be conservative;
- for many regulations for industry, the Dutch government has no competence: these would be regulations on the European Union level, which meant even more delay than the preparation of national regulation;
- regulations are not a direct tool for the management of change within the corporations; they don't "hit" the management of corporations, and all the time of preparation of regulations would be perceived as "silence" by industry.

The conditions for negotiated agreements were:

- agreements should be signed by key corporations in a specific economic sector, not only by the associations;

- agreements should consist not only of targets and measures to be introduced including time frames, but also of monitoring programmes and contingency plans (not excluding regulations at the end of the day);
- draft agreements should be sent to Parliament so to give Parliament the option to block an agreement before the minister would sign in;
- agreements should also consist of international actions to promote other (European) countries to follow the same path of emission reductions. (This was an important condition for industry).

As the cost-calculations of the possible measures to meet the targets were rather rough and uncertain (it was the first time that such calculations were made), representatives of industry were hesitant to sign in on the plan as a whole. For that reason a joint monitoring committee was set up by the Government and industry. This committee played a crucial role in the implementation of the plan by way of negotiated agreements in a later stage.

**The Plan as a Policy Package for a Social Contract**

In retrospection, the plan can be seen as a form of an overall policy package forming a "social contract" consisting of:

- a vision (sustainable development)
- an analysis (the findings of RIVM)
- objectives (which effects should be changed)
- targets (which causes should be changed)
- measures (as strategies: the changes in real life)
- costs (making priority setting possible)
- implementation (conditions for implementation)
- monitoring (checking the outcomes, feedback).

In this retrospection the policy instruments can be seen as part of the implementation conditions.

Reports do not change the world, people do, when they are determined, and when they have the possibility to make changes. Therefore, the social process of policy development, including the process of drafting a plan like the NEPP, is of utmost importance for the success of the policies. It was recognized in an early stage of preparation of the plan that the social process, which would lead to the plan, would need a lot of emphasis and attention.

The preparation of the plan went through different crises, each of them can be analyzed as periods in which the process was "not in a good shape".

## A Plan is just a Step in a Process

The preparation of the NEPP can be seen as only a small step in a bigger series of steps together forming a social process on the scale of a country towards sustainable development. The final steps being the change in practical terms on the workplace in a specific factory or facility, in a specific household, by a specific individual. The ways leading to these changes are only tools. In many discussions in the government, however, these tools (for example some kind of regulation) are seen as the final steps, quod non.

A policy process takes time. The steps in the process can be seen as part of one process of preparing (integrated) policies, implementing them, getting (first) feedback on the implementation and readjust the plan in a second (or third) generation. The total introduction of these overall, integrated policies lasted effectively for ten years.

The continuity of the process is an important element in its success. Changes in the coalition of the government did affect the emphasis on specific elements, but did not affect the overall process.

In this kind of processes, different people play different roles. In retrospective some of these roles can be distinguished (cf. figure 1):

- *The Sponsor*
  Each policy process needs some-one at a certain distance of the real day-to-day work, who defends the fact that the process exists (against the ones who try to frustrate the whole process), who for example by mentioning the process in speeches, advocates the process (but not taking a personal standpoint in the process) and who is a caring person for the people involved in the process. Such a person has normally a senior position, has a helicopter view of things, and can relate the specific process to other policy developments. Mostly those persons are hardly visible in the process and do not fullfill specific tasks in the process.
- *The Process Manager*
  This person really has an overview of what is going on and who is able to direct the different interactions between the different players. This person is not necessarily heavily involved in the content of the developments, although he or she is well informed about the content and about the different positions and interests of the different players. First of all, this person feels responsible for the process as such, not necessarily for the outcome in terms of the content of policies. Usually,

the process manager is a senior official, but this role can be played by others as well.

- *The Driving Force*
  This person's focus is on the content of the developments, is very much interested in results, preferably of a specific nature, and tries to give input to the process again and again by providing the other players new options, revised drafts of documents, new ideas etc. In terms of the content of the policy issues, this person is the most creative one in the process.

Figure 1: The Roles in Process Management

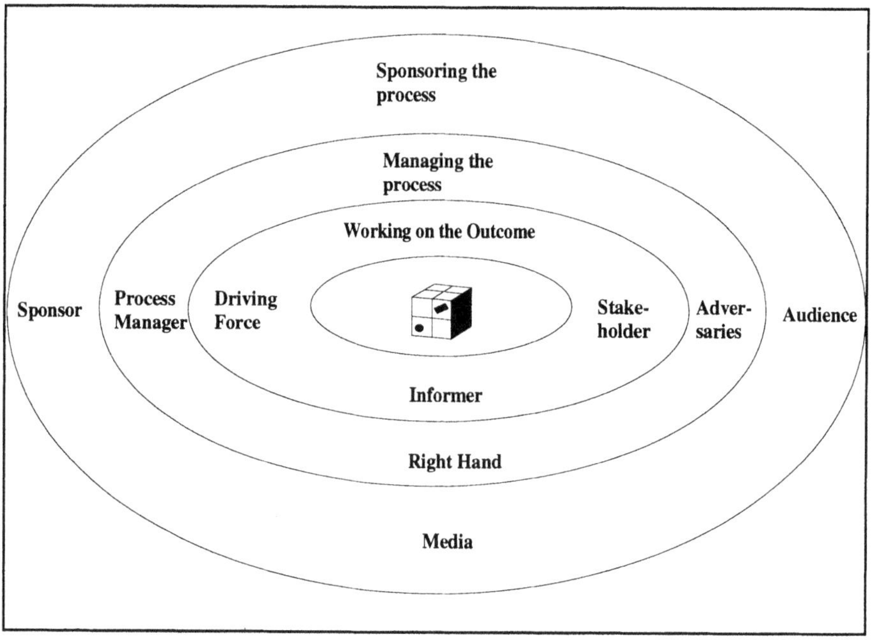


- *The Informer*
  This person's focus is on delivering information to the process players; mostly this person has a scientific background, plays a critical role when decisions tend to be made too quickly, when they are not well funded with proper insights, while he might not be interested in the outcomes as such, rather in the sound way scientific or other information has been handled.

- *The Adversary*
  This person sees the process as something that might negatively affect his interests and so he is opposed against the process as such, no matter the outcomes of the process in terms of the content. Many adversaries stay outside the process

and just wait for the moment to stop it. Luckily, not all processes have adversaries, but adversaries may turn up at any unexpected moment.

- *The Stakeholder*
  These persons (there are always more stakeholders than one) are not adversarial to the process as such, though much of their interests might be affected by the outcomes of the process, and so they want to play an influential role in the process. Sometimes, they represent policy fields with interests which are directly under "attack" by the process at hand, sometimes they are interested because they represent organisations which have to implement the possible outcomes of the process.

- *The Right Hand*
  This person is the one who cares for the process in a very practical way: sending documents out, informing everybody in the process about meetings and other events, caring for involvement of all stakeholders, helping the process manager. Usually this person has a more junior status, and is often forgotten as one of the main players, but I can assure that this kind of person is crucial for the success of the process.

- *The Audience*
  There might be a broader audience: media, general public, but also the neighbour of the process manager, the family of the stakeholders, the friend with whom the adversary has his happy-hour drink. The audience is also often forgotten, but plays sometimes a crucial role. (A good example of that is the role played by grandchildren of CEO's to convince them that sustainable development is something which relates to the caring character of the grandfather - grandchildren relation.)

- *The Media*
  The media play an important role in any substantial policy making process; first, by setting political agendas; second, by "translating" the sometimes difficult policy language into ordinary speech; and third, by posing questions on behalf of a broader audience.

Retrospectively, some lessons from the process can be drawn:

(1) It is important in drafting a process to realize who could play the role of sponsor, process manager and driving-force, being the three roles necessary for even the start of a process. In some early stages in the Dutch process a sponsor was missing and that immediately affected the process: in that case adversaries and stakeholders do not take the process seriously.

(2) The distinction between process manager and driving force is crucial. The driving force needs protection of the process manager to develop ideas and to be as innovative as possible; the process manager needs to defend the ideas of the driving force, as "options" for a possible outcome, not as "the" outcome (in the latter case he becomes driving force him/herself).

(3) The distinction between adversaries and stakeholders is evenso important; many policy makers mistake stakeholders for adversaries (and then making them being adversaries). The process manager can play an important role in converting adversaries into stakeholders with whom negotiations can be started about the content of the policies and implementation strategies.
(4) It is not necessary that the roles are played by the same persons during the whole process; in processes like this it is even impossible to have that kind of continuity. However, when personnel changes take place (as for example the introduction of a new minister), it is important to realize that the newcomer may play a different role than the person he or she replaces officially. For example, Minister Nijpels (minister for environment from 1986 though 1989) played first of all a role as sponsor of the process (from 1988 onwards), but his successor Minister Alders (minister from 1989 through 1994) played the driving-force role himself; therefore senior civil servants had to play a sponsoring role during this period.
(5) Never neglect adversaries or possible adversaries: as environmental policies will affect so many people in the shorter or longer run, it is important to get "everybody on board". The big challenge is to seek for possible adversaries and to turn them to stakeholders (which is something else than to turn them to environmentalists).
(6) The "helper's" roles (informer, right hand, media) need attention right from the beginning. The informer's role is not just a scientist to send in a report, but is somebody who is daily involved in the negotiation process and seeks for ways to provide information in such a way that this can be used in negotiations. The way the different measures with their costs and the options for financing were set up in a spreadsheet was crucial for the final discussions about the NEPP in the Cabinet.

## Departments Involved

The Ministry of Transport and Waterworks, responsable for water quantity- and quality-policies, traditionally played a role as driving force in the environmental debate. Its department of waterworks was not in favour of an environmental quality approach rather than an emission reduction approach at all times, but that discussion faded away after the findings of the RIVM. The department of transport was aware of the importance of more environmentally friendly transportation for economic reasons (fight against traffic-jams) and needed the help of the Department of Environment for shifting policies.[9]

[9] It is said that the Minister of Transport and Waterworks Mrs. Kroes (minister 1982 - 1989) was converted to more environmental policies after visiting one of the bigger natural areas which developed in the new polders in the former Zuyderzee.

The Ministry of Agriculture, Nature Protection and Fisheries was an ally concerning nature protection, although the focus of nature protection policies was mainly on effect-oriented measures (so to avoid source oriented discussions about agricultural policies). The department of agriculture played a stakeholder's role right from the beginning, realizing that changes in agricultural development would take place in any case. By doing so they took away the direct stakeholder's position for the representatives of agricultural businesses themselves. Although many local initiatives in agriculture have been taken, the agricultural sectors as such remain one of the most difficult towards a more sustainable development.[10]

The Ministry of Economic Affairs played the role of adversary, although some of the senior representatives saw the importance of being stakeholder in the process (for example to get funding for the re-start of energy-saving programs). Overall, there was reluctance to set up policies which affect free market ideology[11]. This attitude made it possible to have more direct relations between the Department of Environment and the representatives of industry and to use the information about the forerunners of industry. As the Ministry of Economic Affairs had no precisely defined interests (only more ideological statements) it was difficult to make "deals"; discussions with Economic Affairs tended towards yes-no discussions.

The Ministry of Finance/Treasury played an important role in the last stages of the preparation of the NEPP, because of the proposed funding of several measures. Because their strong and well defined interest (no growth of direct government spending and of the so-called collective financial burden for the private sectors) it was possible to work together at finding innovative ways for funding. After the NEPP-plus the Ministry of Finance set up a sector for environmental taxes, which was important for the introduction of an energy-tax and other forms of new taxes.

### Provinces and Municipalities Involved

The provinces and municipalities had a direct stake in the outcome of the NEPP-process: the NEPP would play a role in their excercizing their responsibility in i.a. licensing procedures. However, in the course of the process they realized that the NEPP would not be useful directly for them, but could be used as source of inspiration to work on joint implementation schemes both for the 12 provinces and for the municipalities (united in an association). One of the outcomes of the NEPP-

[10] The import of fodder for cattle and pig-raising is one of the most important technical elements causing a severe manure problem in the country. Part of the developments in agriculture have been under heavy influence of the Common Agricultural Policy of the European Union; economically, agriculture is still a strong sector.

[11] The trauma of subsidizing old style industries (like the ship-building industries) as was the policy in the seventies and which turned out to be a waste of money, overshadowed many of the reactions of the Ministry of Economic Affairs during the late eighties.

process, however, was the enhancement of central government funding for environmental activities of provinces and municipalities. This funding was given under the condition that at least the licenses would be made up-to-date; also the money was used for strengthening the environmental sectors in comparison to the landuse sectors and the development sectors in municipalities.

**Private Sectors Involved**

The private sectors, especially industry, played a decisive role in the preparation of the plan. The forerunners saw the importance of being stakeholder rather than adversary. The overall commitment of industry to the draft-NEPP[12] (not the NEPP-plus), the Cabinet needed not to bother at that time (early 1989) about the support from the main economic sectors. Later, when the NEPP plus was announced by the new Cabinet, this caused a major shock: the government had lost part of the credibility by going further than the NEPP. By proper consultation during the NEPP-plus preparatory process this feeling could have been taken away for the bigger part. Later, a sudden proposal for an energy tax shocked industry again and trust had to be restored by talks facilitated by the Prime Minister.

The environmental groups played an important role in two ways: first, agenda setting long before the proper preparatory process began, and second, delivery of ideas for alternative measures. The third scenario was funded on all kinds of studies previously made by environmental groups about i.a. transport, agriculture, industry, and energy. Once the NEPP was issued, the role of the environmental groups became less important for the process. The environmental groups shifted their strategies from government orientation to a focus on households, on small businesses, on international items (timber) etc. Big controverses (like nuclear energy in the early eighties) are not on the agenda; in the nineties it is about "quick or quicker" (see low energy car of Greenpeace).

## 3. The Implementation Process

Of course, a piece of paper, even with the commitment of many involved people, remains still a piece of paper: the way towards implementation is still ahead. The problem of implemention for a bureaucracy is to get the policies "out of the bureaucracy", because bureaucracies are by nature not the right institution for application in real life.

---

[12] This commitment was worked out in the joint committee on the monitoring of costs and implementation.

Explicitly, a decision was made not to establish one "big" implementation organization for the NEPP; the main institutions to apply the NEPP would remain the provinces and the municipalities and besides these, it was important to involve the other ministries in the implemention of environmental policies, so to enlarge the support and to spread political risk.

This meant that the Department of Environment had to play a coordinating and stimulating role in the implementation process apart from many policy actions to be performed by the Department itself.

Within the Department of Environment all the policy actions were divided among the different directorates. More-over the policy actions were combined in policy programmes for the implementation of which senior officials were made responsible. Although all directorates had been involved in the preparation of the NEPP, it took about a year (until the fall of 1990) to integrate the different policy actions in the workprogrammes of the directorates.

A training programme was set up (together with Prof. Lawrence Susskind, M.I.T.), called the "Implementation Challenge" to train all the 400 officers who were somehow involved in the implementation of the NEPP. Trainers were recruited from the senior staff in the Department itself. In the training simulation games were played which related to possible future developments in the implementation phase of the NEPP.[13]

Figure 2: The Implementation Process

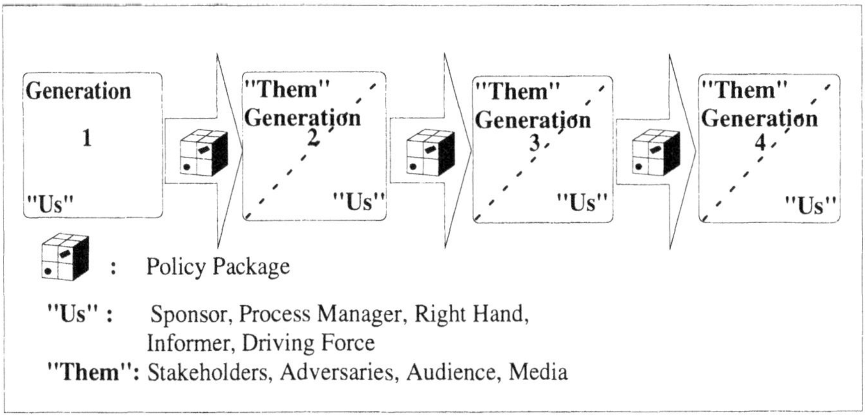


[13] See: Lawrence Susskind and Jeffrey Cruikshank: "Breaking the impasse, Consensual Approaches to Resolving Public Disputes", The M.I.T.-Harvard Public Disputes Programme, Basic Books, New York, 1987; Roger Fisher and Danny Ertel: "Getting ready to negotiate, the getting to yes workbook", Penguin Book, New York, 1995.

### The Plan Gives Birth to Other Plans

In the first stages of the implementation of the NEPP an unforeseen development occured: many public and private institutions started to make their own Environmental Policy Plan, often being a kind of translation of the NEPP into the setting of that specific institution.

In the central government the NEPP coincides with a number of strategic policy documents from different departments[14], some of them being rewritten after the publication of the NEPP by decision of the then new Cabinet (1989).

The NEPP should be seen in relation to these policy documents as overall government policy. In the early nineties the following government documents were approved by Parliament, all relating to the NEPP:

- Fourth Whitepaper on Landuse planning
- Third Programme on Watermanagement
- Nature protection plan
- Agriculture restructuring plan
- Energy saving programme
- Sustainable housing programme
- Second transportation scheme.

Also, the provinces made a joint implementation plan for the NEPP. Some of the policy actions in the NEPP, for example those relating to specific areas, were taken care of explicitly by the provinces. All provinces made environmental policy plans in the early nineties, sometimes updates of older plans, in most cases new plans. The association of municipalities made an implementation plan which was related to the extra funding for municipalities from the central government. Almost all bigger cities made environmental policy plans on a voluntary basis. In some of those plans (Amsterdam, Rotterdam) innovative approaches for balancing the different interests in the inner cities were developed.

In the NEPP and in the Fourth Whitepaper on Landuse planning ten areas were defined where special attention was necessary either to solve severe environmental problems, or to protect the still existing natural values. Among these areas were the Amsterdam Airport Area (Schiphol), The Rotterdam Harbour Area, and the Green Heart of Holland Area. For all those areas steering groups on a high level were set up consisting of representatives of public and private sectors. In most cases the

---

[14] The Cabinet Lubbers-2 (1986 - 1989) worked on the so-called "Agenda for the future"; somehow this had affected almost all departments in looking ahead some decades.

provinces took the lead in the processes which had to lead to some kind of joint plan for those areas. In many cases it was the first time that a combined focus on environment, landuse and economic development took place with many stakeholders.

The Amsterdam Airport Area has become a "cause celebre" in that for the first time discussions were directed towards restrictions for the extension of the airport. The Schiphol airport is of utmost importance for the transport sector and for economic development in the Amsterdam area; at the same time the airport is located in one of the most densely populated areas in the Netherlands. In 1995 Parliament approved the "deal" being an extension of the airport, a new airstrip (to avoid extra noise nuisance) and a maximum of 40 million passengers per year.

## Implementation by Industry

The implementation of the NEPP by industry got the most attention being an innovation in policy implementation. The NEPP was clear about involvement of target-groups in the implementation of the NEPP; the NEPP also indicated that covenants might be a good way of implementing the plan.

Figure 3: Dutch Industry Sectors Covered by Environmental Covenants

Basic Metal Industry
Chemical Industry
Dairy Industry
Paper Industry
Printing Industry
Metal Working And Electrical Engineering Industry
Textile Industry
Meat Processing Industry
Bricks And Roof Tiles Industry
Rubber And Plastics Industry
Oil And Gas Production

Besides these overall covenants to implement the NEPP, some 30 covenants have been signed between industry and the department of energy to improve energy efficiency with 20% before the year 2000.

Covenants did exist already; the oldest being just a piece of paper signed by some CEO's and by the Minister saying that phosphates should be phased out as detergents. Covenants developed rather than being invented as new policy tool. In the programme to screen all waste streams (which was set up before the preparation of the NEPP) the Department of Environment worked together with all relevant stakeholders and they came up with covenant-like agreements. One of the more politically sensitive was about packaging reductions, finally signed in 1991. For the representatives of industry, notably the employer's organization VNO/NCW, the commitment to the implementation of the NEPP was related to direct involvement in the implementation strategies, because the main reason for cooperation from their side was to "buy certainty" (or at least to reduce uncertainty) about government's actions.

Realistically, implementation of the NEPP solely by regulation would have been almost impossible, in any case very time consuming and the implementation would not get "out of the bureaucracy" in that way (at least not for a period of more than five years).

Figure 4: The Direct Involvement of CEO's in Negotiated Agreements

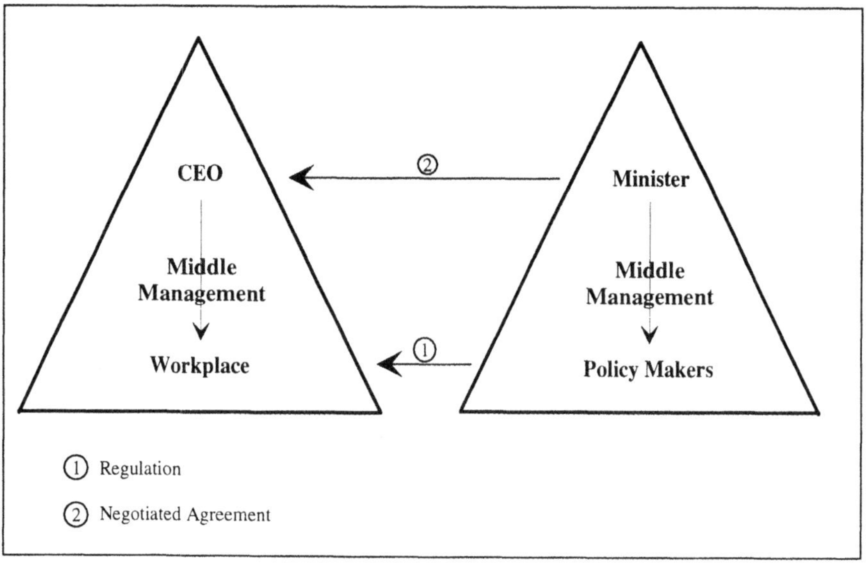


In retrospective, the main advantages of the "translation" of the NEPP to different sectors of industry were:

- involvement of CEO's directly in signing up;
- feedback from industry to the central government;
- maintaining a multimedia, integral approach;
- long term targets remain the focus of policies;
- industry gets flexibility;
- strong relation to internal environmental management schemes in corporations.

At the other hand, doubts remain until results are shown. Environmental groups and members of Parliament were very skeptical in the beginning of the process. The covenants don't replace the licensing procedures, but are management tools on top of the "normal" licensing. As the Environmental Management Act asks for update of licenses every four to five years, and as the covenants are worked out by corporations in corporate and facility improvement plans, these plans fit in the licensing procedures for updating. Joint monitoring is an important element in the overall process of implementation.

The skepticism about negotiated agreements among environmental groups has lately been changed in some actions towards negotiated agreements between industry and environmental groups directly, without government influence: a covenant was signed between the potato growing industry and Friends of the Earth about changes of the use of pesticides in due time in exchange for upholding consumer actions by the environmental groups (which can be very effective, as was shown in the case of PVC in packaging materials and in the case of the Brent Spar).

## Learning Points, Different Concerns at Different Times

Once adversaries are turned to stakeholders (and that is what happens in the process towards e.g. a covenant) four types of concerns of stakeholders can be categorized, which form together the kind of development in the relation between the stakeholder and the government.

The first concern is to get a "credible story" why actions are necessary. In the words of the employers' organisation VNO-NCW "targets must have a solid foundation and must not be subject to constant change". The approach via environmental themes helped developing such credible stories, also by the constant emphasis on scientific consensus about the analysis of causes and effects. The credible story should be such that the government's counterpart is able to tell the same story in his or her own constituency. This is of utmost importance to trigger the sequence of implementation steps.

The second concern is the classical attitude: "This is a problem for the government; if I have to do something, it should be the government to tell me what exactly to do". Bureaucracies tend to be eager to stick to this stage of concern of stakeholders: they start preparing prescriptive regulations. And by doing so they block the involvement of stakeholders and keep the solutions "in the bureaucracy".

Although in some cases it might be necessary to fix the relation with stakeholders to this concern, in most cases it is better to try to reach the touch upon the next concern, because sooner or later that concern will be of crucial importance for implementation.

Figure 5: Stages in the Concerns of Stakeholders

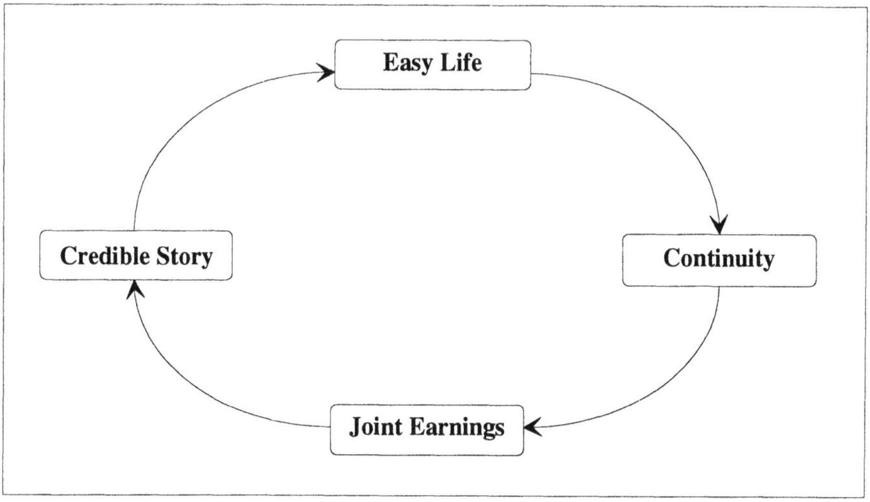


The third concern is about the continuity of the activities of the stakeholder: Can the corporation bear the costs of the proposed policies? Is the municipality well organized to meet the targets? Are the skills available necessary for the application of certain techniques? Those kind of questions reflect the concerns of the stakeholders and should be in the mind of every policy maker. The answers can only be found via communication with stakeholders. The joint cost-calculations and monitoring by the Department of Environment and the Dutch industry can be seen as a good example to answer these concerns on a central level.

A good example of the concern for continuity is the succesful introduction of the certification of environmental care systems in corporations. Certification is a well-known management tool in the better companies and environmental elements can more or less easily be taken up without threatening the continuity in these management approaches.

The fourth concern might lead to a sort of "win-win" situation (rather a joint earning): stakeholders see new opportunities in their markets or they see quality improvements because of changes in the production originally for environmental reasons etc. On a macro level, the economic analysis of the third scenario in the NEPP showed that in principle joint earnings are possible. Many environmentalists "see" joint earnings right away (because of saving of energy and raw materials for example), but they make sometimes the mistake to expect stakeholders to shift from a "credible story" directly towards a "win-win" situation. The experience in the Netherlands has shown that the whole cycle has to be passed and short cuts are not very likely to occur.

## The Audience and the Media Involved

One of the elements of the NEPP was the recognition that production and consumption patterns had to be changed. Therefore, it was of utmost importance to get the message (the credible story) across to the general public (converting the public from audience to stakeholders). An extensive public campaign was set up with the motive: "A better environment begins at home". The campaign started in 1990 after approval of the NEPP by Parliament. The campaign used the same symbol and slogan throughout; other departments (like the Department of Energy) used the same symbol and slogan for their "commercials".

The campaign provided TV-spots, advertisements in magazines and papers, sometimes especially designed for a specific target group (like teachers, youth, sportsfishermen, photographers etc.). The first stage consisted of "commercials" in which well known Dutch persons (sportsmen, TV personalities etc) told why environment was important for them. It was the "credible story" phase. The second stage focussed on what people could do and combined campaigns with policy actions in the stage of proper application, for example the policy to separate waste in the households to promote recycling (paper, glass, green waste). This second stage is still underway; discussions are held how to step towards a next stage.

Looking at the implementation of the NEPP in general terms it strikes that in almost all Dutch institutions the NEPP has had some influence: environment has been taken up in many corporate and institutional strategies, provisions for implementation have been set up, skills have been developed, many practical changes have been made in production and consumption patterns as well as in the application of environmental technologies. The implementation process is a continuous process of "translation" from the beginning (mostly the central top-level) to the practical end (the workplace, the household, the street).

Between "a piece of paper" (like the NEPP) and the practical change in the workplace one can easily define 30 to 50 steps of "translation": within the bureaucracy of the Departments, between the government and the private sectors, in the bureaucracies of corporations, in the management processes directed to the workplace. Each of these steps involve people, each of them going through a cycle as described above. All the processes need the different process roles to be played. The stakeholder in a previous step will be process manager or sponsor in the next step; the audience in one step will be stakeholder in a next step; etc. This is why at least some four to five years are needed to step from "a piece of paper" to real-life changes, provided that the process is in a continuous pace and disruptions do not take place.

**Real-Life Changes**

Real-life changes relevant for the environment as measured in the yearly analysis of the RIVM cannot be attributed solely to the NEPP; they are the result of all the elements of the process and of all the efforts of people involved in the different stages of implementation.

Some real-life changes:

- Except for $CO_2$ and NOx, all types of emissions and discharges have been disconnected from GDP-growth and are on a track towards achieving the 2000 and 2010 targets;
- The ozone-depletion substances have been phased out in industry (leading to a relative good record for the overall Climate change theme);
- The disposal of waste from industry has been reduced by 60% between 1985 and 1995, recycling is booming;
- Cogeneration (industry/electicity production) was so succesful, that these developments had to be slowed down so not to cause serious overcapacity;
- The use of energy in the households (except transport) is almost constant between 1985 and 1995 despite a growht of the number of households;
- $SO_2$ emissions from powerplants have been reduced by 70% between 1985 and 1995, NOx emissions in the same period by about 30%;
- Deposition of acid substances on Dutch soils has been reduced from 7000 acid equivalents in 1985 to 4000 acid equivalents in 1994 (meeting the target);
- Recycling of waste has been improved from 50% of the total waste production in 1985 to more than 70% in 1995;
- The total disposal of waste on disposal sites has been reduced from 16 billion tonnes in 1985 to 6 billion tonnes in 1995.

The above mentioned indications of being on the right track do not mean that all environmental problems are solved, by no means:

- The higher GDP growth (than was foreseen in the NEPP) causes extra growth of energy consumption, especially in the transport sector. The opening of the Berlin Wall in 1989 caused a boom in the transport sector, unforeseen in the NEPP (and elsewhere);
- The rare open space in the Western part of the country is under constant attack for housing, industrial developments, etc.
- The saturation of soils with phosphates and nitrates from agriculture/dairy farming in certain areas is such, that it will last for more than a century until im-

provements in the soil quality can be measured, even if discharges were stopped today.

At the same time the spending for environmental protection is "on track" according to the forecasts in the NEPP: Total costs for environmental protection in the Netherlands went up from 7 billion guilders in 1985 to 17 billion guilders in 1995[15], which is about 2.7% of the GDP.

## 4. Conclusions

What is sometimes referred to as the Dutch approach (an integrated environmental planning system based on long term analyses and implemented via negotiations with stakeholders), can be seen as a management mechanism on top of other environmental policy-actions. The plans does not replace the legal fundaments of environmental policies. The covenants do not replace regulations (are rather precursors for sensible regulation). Negotiations do not replace the findings of scientists about the cause-effect relations in the natural environment.

As in all management processes different roles have to be played; in the Dutch situation the Department of Environment and the government in general played the process-management role. It is not necessarily the government who has to play these roles. Especially on local levels other institutions could take the lead and play process management roles (for example a Chamber of Commerce or a Young Farmer Organization).

Essential for the Dutch approach is the focus on environmental problems and the physical solutions (measures to be taken) and the costs of solutions, and not on policy instruments as such. Policy instruments are seen as to be adapted according to the type of target-group, to the stage of implementation of policies, and to the restrictions in national and international political contexts. Also essential is the focus on integration of measures in relation to stakeholders' interests; the continuity of the stakeholders' business is never questioned, the way this continuity is achieved is in discussion[16]. A mere discussion about policy tools without reference to the environmental problems to be solved, often leads to a breakdown of trust between the government and the stakeholders.

---

15 One Dutch guilder equals about .6 US dollars

16 Of course, in the seventies there were many environmentalists, also in the government, who just wanted to stop some industries or ways of transport. That attitude did not provide the right basis for a societal agreement.

In Dutch environmental policies the direct communication between the Department of Environment and the stakeholders is of utmost importance for the following reasons:

- it promotes the direct influence of stakeholders on policy development, so building up trust;
- it gives direct feed-back from people who have some practical experience;
- it prevents the Department of Environment to become an assembly of "ecological fundamentalists" (with clean hands);
- it promotes the societal coherence by building up networks.

In the consensus building process scientific information is of crucial importance. Scientific information should be as politically and ideologically neutral as possible (focussing on causes and effects, including economic effects of proposed measures) and as much based on consensus in the scientific community as possible. Scientific information always consists of an amount of uncertainty; this should not be hidden away for policy makers, but should play an explicit role in the design of policies. The constant monitoring of costs, emissions and environmental qualities is a way to deal with uncertainties; contingency plans are another way to answer uncertainties in a sensible way[17].

It was recognized in the Netherlands that every player in the area of environmental policy development had his or her own function in this development. Although environmental groups always will argue for stricter and quicker solutions for environmental problems, they are not adversaries in the political process. The direct contact between environmental groups and adversaries from the public and private sectors can be an important management tool to change adversaries towards stakeholders.

## References

Fisher, Roger; Ertel, Danny: Getting ready to Negotiate, the "Getting to yes" workbook, Penguin Books, 1995

[17] The philosophical basis for this approach can be found i.a. in the work of Richard Rorty. See for example Richard Rorty: "Contingency, irony, and solidarity", Cambridge University Press, 1989. In this work Rorty defends the statement that seeking consensus should replace the classical standpoint of seeking the "truth". Many environmental scientists and policy makers still base their actions on finding the "truth" (the "best" policy instrument for solving "all" environmental problems), rather than finding a basis for societal consensus (about the concrete steps in changing our physical relation with the environment).

Friend, John; Hickling, Allen: Planning under pressure, the Strategic Choice Approach, Pergamon Press, 1987

Gardner, Gerald T.; Stern, Paul C.: Environmental Problems and Human Behavior, Allyn and Bacon, Boston, MA, 1996

MacNeill, Jim; Winsemius, Pieter; Yakushiji, Taizo: Beyond interdependence, the Meshing of the World's Economy and the Earth's ecology, Oxford University Press, 1991

National Environmental Policy Plan: To choose or to loose, Second Chamber, session 1988-1989, 21137, nos. 1-2, State Publishing Firm, The Netherlands (English edition)

National Environmental Policy Plan - Plus, Second Chamber, session 1989-1990, State Publishing Firm, The Netherlands (English edition)

National Environmental Policy Plan - 2: The environment: today's touchstone, Second Chamber, session 1993-1994, State Publishing Firm, The Netherlands (English edition)

National Institute of Public Health and Environmental Protection (RIVM), Concern for tomorrow, a national environmental survey 1985 - 2010, Bilthoven, The Netherlands, 1988 (editor: F. Langeweg)

National Institute of Public Health and Environmental Protection (RIVM): Milieubalans 96, het nederlandse milieu verklaard, Bilthoven, The Netherlands, 1996

Organization for Economic Co-operation and Development: Environmental Performance Reviews, Netherlands, OECD, Paris, France, 1995

Osborne, David; Gaebler, Ted: Re-inventing Government, How the entrepreneurial spirit is transforming the public sector, Plume books, 1993

Rorty, Richard: Contingency, Irony, and Solidarity, Cambridge University Press, 1989

Susskind, Lawrence; Cruikshank, Jeffrey: Breaking the impasse, Consensual Approaches to Resolving Public Disputes, Basic Books, New York, 1987

Winsemius, Pieter: Guests in Our Own Home, Thoughts on Environmental Management, McKinsey & Company, Amsterdam, 1990

# The Role of RTD Policy and the Adequate Policy Mix - Comprehensive Policy Approaches and Problems of Implementation

*Erkki Ormala*

## 1. The Evolving Scope of RTD Policies

RTD policies were traditionally oriented towards creating scientific results - strengthening the national (or global) science base. The increasing understanding of the importance of knowledge for economic and social development oriented the focus of the RTD policies more towards the problems of dissemination and utilization of knowledge in the 1980's. New concepts such as the systems model of innovation, national systems of innovation, the distribution power of innovation systems etc. together with a better understanding of knowledge, i.e. the distinction between tacit and codified knowledge, expanded the scope of RTD policies further in the 1990's. Networking and absorptive capacity of firms became important issues in the RTD policies. A new concept of innovation policy was developed to complement the traditional RTD policy.

This development led to the adoption of new types of national programmes, which were aimed at enhancing networking, knowledge circulation and innovation. These national efforts were complemented by developments in the EU activities. The two EU-programmes VALUE II and SPRINT aimed at knowledge diffusion and innovation; they were amalgamated and given a more ambitious mandate and more resources in the 4th RTD Framework Programme in 1994.

The gradual shift in the orientation of the RTD policies towards innovation drew attention to the other conditions of innovation. Innovation activities are dependent on learning, financing, regulations and standards, market conditions etc. which are beyond the scope of RTD and innovation policies. The conditions for innovation are determined by other policies such as industrial policies, education policies, financial policies etc. These issues were discussed extensively in the Commission's Green Paper on Innovation (EC 1995). The Green Paper addressed the important links of innovation to macroeconomic policy, economic growth and employment, education, information society, industry and business, financing, SME policy, service sector and cohesion and regional policy. RTD policies will have to learn to interact with these other policies.

One of the first examples of interaction was based on the observation that proximity is a key concept in providing innovation services to companies. The regional actors and infrastructures play a significant role in this. On the other hand, it was understood that knowledge and innovation are in a number of cases contributing significantly to the economic and social development at the regional level. Regional policies and RTD policies have been able to develop mutually reinforcing elements in a number of regions both in Europe and the US. At the EU level innovation activities are developing new common instruments and effective interaction with structural policies.

## 2. RTD and Innovation Policies in Other Policy Domains

With the increasing importance of knowledge for economic and social progress innovation has become a driving force of development in many policy areas. The interactions and causal links between innovation and relevant policy concerns are often complex and indirect. They are not clearly understood. In particular, it has turned out to be difficult to assess how innovation and RTD policies could contribute to the solution of the problems in some other policy domains. Research on these issues is multidisciplinary and, consequently, not very well suited to the traditional way of organizing research. Despite these difficulties interest to cooperate with the RTD and innovation policies has increased in many policy areas.

One example of a major effort to clarify the complex relationships between innovation policy and a problem of significant social concern was the OECD study on technology, productivity and job creation (OECD 1996b). This study was an attempt to explore the relationships from different perspectives in a balanced way. One of the main findings was that a comprehensive strategy to increase employment should involve a balanced mix of policies that would yield a stable macroeconomic environment, sufficiently responsive and flexible labour and product markets and a continuous flow of new innovations to allow structural adjustment in the economy. The macroeconomic policies, labour and product market policies and innovation policies should work together reinforcing each other. It remains to be seen to what extent this substantial evidence and the recommendations based on it will lead to adjustments in employment policies in different countries.

Employment policy is only one example of the many policy areas where RTD and innovation have been found to play a decisive role in the development. Information society, knowledge based economies, future health care systems, energy systems etc. require a substantial body of new knowledge to be able to develop.

A number of recent studies on industrial clusters carried out in different countries have given new insight into these interactions (see e.g. Hernesniemi et al 1996, Jacobs et al 1990).

## 3. Interaction Between RTD and Innovation Policies and Other Policies

Successful RTD and innovation policies require complementary actions in a number of other policies. In that sense RTD and innovation policies are horizontal policies. On the other hand, many policies are dependent on contributions from RTD and innovation. In these conditions the development of the interaction between RTD and innovation policies and other policy sectors is one of the main challenges for the future.

In Finland we have been able to proceed quite well in our efforts to increase the interaction between RTD and innovation policies and other relevant policy areas. The policy areas in which this interaction was created are economic and fiscal policy, industrial policy, education policy, regional policy, energy policy, health policy and the measures for the development of the Finnish information society.

Effective interaction between innovation policy and other relevant policies requires active contribution from both sides. Experience suggests that some measures - we might call them bridging instruments - can significantly facilitate the emergence and growth of such a contribution. Firstly, there must be a mutual understanding of the various interlinkages between the policies and benefits that can be achieved by both parties from the cooperation. This requires research to clarify these issues. The OECD study on the relationships between technology, productivity and job creation is a good example of the studies needed.

Secondly, a proper institutional framework must be available to facilitate the interaction. National as well as international administrations are usually organized strictly according to the main policy domains. Organizational structures for horizontal interaction are not at place. They have to be created separately. These arrangements should also involve mechanisms which improve an administration's capability to utilize and 'take on board' relevant research results for policy purposes. Finally, common responsibilities and activities, e.g. joint research projects, have turned out to be very helpful both in creating mutual understanding and establishing proper organizational arrangements.

## 4. Innovation Policy and Sustainable Development

One of the policy areas of great relevance to innovation policy is environmental policy. Environmental goods and services is of one the most rapidly growing industries globally. Environmental norms and regulations shape the markets for environmental products and services. Sustainable development has become an equally important issue of public concern as employment. On the other hand, technological progress has a pervasive impact on the conditions of sustainable development. Technology creates new solutions to environmental problems but may also create new problems to be solved. Innovation policy is aimed at enhancing innovation by creating and disseminating new knowledge, improving access to the sources of new knowledge, developing financing for innovation and providing firms with high-quality intermediary services. All these measures will also support the development and dissemination of cleaner technologies. In this section some of the most relevant interactions between RTD and innovation policies and sustainable development are briefly discussed.

The relationships between innovation policy and environmental policy have become an important issue in the US. The issue is extensively debated both among researchers and political actors (see e.g. OTA 1994, Banks and Heaton 1995). At the EU-level these issues have not been discussed very widely.

**Environmental research**

Environmental research which increases knowledge of basic ecological processes and systems, causal interlinkages and the state of the environment, is an essential part of the national research effort in all industrialized countries. The 4th RTD Framework Programme of the EU involves a specific programme on Environment and Climate. The quality and relevance of this research is evaluated in the same way as other national or international research. The critical questions to which extent this research in general is being utilized in the policy formulation processes and how well it takes into account the issues of innovation policy are usually not assessed.

**Promoting cleaner technologies**

A number of the OECD countries have specific financing programmes to promote the development and diffusion of cleaner technologies. According to OECD estimates about $US 1.5 billion were invested by the OECD countries in these programmes in 1993 (OECD 1994). These funds have been increased rapidly. The OECD survey of these programmes concluded that the current government efforts focus almost exclusively on cleaner technology supply side policies and activities. Overall the managers of these programmes considered that the financial and technical support had a positive impact on the quantity and quality of cleaner technologies being developed. There was a clear trend to move support from the RTD activities towards financing the demonstration phase.

This policy approach has been considered too narrow (see e.g. OECD 1994, Banks and Heaton, 1995). In fact, it reflects the old 'technology push' view of RTD and innovation policy. Firstly, it excludes all the important issues of demand which ultimately create the conditions for the implementation and diffusion of cleaner technologies. Wide adoption is, however, a necessary step to achieve the expected environmental impact. The OECD report (1994) suggested that the government policies should proceed to measures which shape the markets and create demand for cleaner technologies. The following is a list of some of the possible approaches highlighted in the OECD workshop:

- Regulations (e.g. designed to be technology stimulating not stifling);
- Government procurement practices;
- Voluntary agreements;
- Clear policy priorities;
- Public education;
- Product labelling (eco-labels)
- Standards and product specifications;
- Eco-taxes;
- Region specific codes;
- Strong tax levied against those technologies contrary to sustainable development;
- Subsidies for the adoption of cleaner technologies.

Secondly, a strong orientation towards supply side policies tends to select technologies which have a direct - but often marginal - impact on the environment leaving aside technologies which may have a significant - but indirect - impact. Good examples of such indirectly but highly significant technologies are e.g. new communication technologies, which may decrease the need to travel and nanotechnologies which may reduce significantly the demand for material or energy.

The OECD report (1994) also discovered that some governments send confusing messages about their policy objectives for cleaner production and products. Conflicting goals, programmes and financial assistance schemes were categorized by the private sector as altogether confusing. In fact, sometimes one Ministry was not sure what another Ministry was doing, but knew that some sort of programme existed. The OECD workshop suggested that to avoid this kind of a situation, governments may wish to coordinate goals to create a cohesive and cooperative programme with clearly stated objectives by consolidating programmes and pooling resources.

**RTD Projects**

Some recent evaluations of RTD projects reflect their environmental effects. The evaluation of EUREKA Industrial and Economic effects (EUREKA 1993) discovered that environmental effects were the most frequent of the broader effects of the projects. Some projects were directly concerned with environmental protection.

The implementation of their results was heavily dependent on the regulatory framework. Another group of environmentally beneficial projects were a broader category of clean technologies which offered more environmentally-friendly substitutes for polluting technologies. However, the most numerous category of environmentally beneficial projects were those, which, though driven by economic motivation, nonetheless resulted in a more efficient use of materials or the incidental elimination of polluting substance.

As an overall conclusion it was discovered that the broader effects - including the environmental effects - were mainly created by projects which were commercially viable. If and when environmental concern has developed to be a relevant feature markets seem to provide an effective mechanism for the implementation and diffusion of environmentally beneficial technologies. Accordingly, a number of environmentally beneficial projects, which anticipated regulatory changes failed to achieve an impact when those changes did not materialise as expected. Similar results have been achieved in some national project evaluations.

## Environmental Markets

The environment industry is one of the most rapidly growing sectors in the global economy. Environmental investments are growing much more rapidly than the GDP in a number of industrialized countries (OECD 1996a). The environment industry is estimated to reach the volume of the pharmaceutical industry or the aerospace industry by the year 2000. Table 1 presents the OECD forecast of the market trends for the global environment industry (OECD 1996a).

Table 1: Forecast of Market Trends for the Global Environment Industry (US$ billion)

| | 1990 | 2000 | Annual growth (%) |
|---|---|---|---|
| Equipment | 152 | 220 | 5,0 |
| Water and effluent treatment | 60 | 83 | 4,0 |
| Air pollution control | 30 | 42 | 4,4 |
| Other | 22 | 32 | 5,1 |
| Services | 48 | 80 | 7,4 |
| **Total** | 200 | 300 | 5,5 |

Source: OECD (1996 a)

The employment effects of the growth of the environment industry are high. Available estimates suggest that employment growth is expected to be strong over the next few years, ranging from around 3% in Canada and Japan to 10% in the US (OECD 1996a).

The market of environmental goods and services is, however, highly fragmented and regulated. Public expenditure and public procurement have been a major part of the total expenditure for pollution abatement and control equipment in all OECD countries. In all countries except the US and the Netherlands, public investment expenditures have outweighed business sector expenditures. The business sector has, however, been increasing expenditures for environmental goods and services, not only to respect environmental regulation, but also to gain the economic benefits from process modifications which reduce consumption of raw materials and energy, and reduce waste and pollution (OECD 1996a). The question to which extent companies are increasing their environmental investment to improve their image on the markets remains open, though.

Innovation has a crucial role to play in the efforts to exploit fully the potential provided by these markets and to meet the underlying environmental objectives. It has been estimated that 50% of the environmental goods which will be used in 15 years' time do not currently exist (OECD 1996a).

Public procurement is an essential part of the demand for environmental goods and services. In the debate on innovation policy the active role of public procurement has been a topical issue since the 1960's. The conclusions drawn from this debate are that public procurement can in certain conditions promote innovation by providing industry with opportunities for reference deliveries, experimentation, joint development etc. All these conclusions are highly relevant for the environment industry.

In addition to public procurement and regulation the public sector can also influence the market behaviour through other types of public interventions. In some recent discussions on the conditions of innovation the public policies are seen crucial in shaping the market and stimulating demand. These measures will have far-reaching effects in many areas including environment (OECD 1996b).

**Regulatory Framework**

National and international regulations have been an engine driving the development of the environment industry. Those countries with tight environmental regulations have larger and more competitive environmental markets. On the other hand, regulations can also impede growth.

The environmental regulatory framework has a great impact on innovation. These regulations shape the markets and have an indirect impact on innovation by stimulating or decreasing demand. This role of regulation is critical, in particular in those areas where the demand can not emerge without public intervention. These issues were discussed briefly above. Regulations may, however, have also a more pervasive role in promoting or impeding innovation. Endeavours to expand the scope of environmental regulation to cover all industrial investments may have a profound effect on the conditions of innovation.

The role of regulation has become a key issue of innovation policy during the last few years. The OECD has launched a major study on the need for regulatory reform in innovation and industrial policy.

In the discussion of the current regulatory framework some problems have been identified (see e.g. OTA 1994, Banks and Heaton 1995, OECD 1996c).

- The requirement to apply specific established technologies may inhibit the spread of new innovative approaches to environmental problems. The regulatory regimes have mainly been oriented towards the adoption of the 'best available technologies' type of approach, which encourages the adoption of existing technologies and incremental improvements and 'end-of-pipe' pollution control technologies. The regulatory regimes should rather be 'performance-based' than 'technology based' and they should encourage a new technology or systems approach instead of 'end-of pipe' solutions.
  This issue is extremely topical at the moment in Europe. The EU is currently introducing a comprehensive regulatory system based on the 'best available technologies' approach for supporting environmental authorities' assessment of new industrial investment. Whether the impacts of this system on the innovative capacity of Europe was ever assessed is an open question.
- Current regulatory regimes tend to apply stricter standards on new investments than old facilities or equipment thus creating an incentive to modify old existing technologies and discouraging the adoption of radically new technological solutions.
- Too short adaptation periods together with unexpected changes in the regulatory frameworks create instability which reduces firms' interest in long term intangible and tangible investment necessary for both the development and diffusion of new and cleaner technologies.

The gradual shift from regulations and standards as the main instrument of environmental policy towards complementary economic instruments (taxes and charges) can have a positive effect on innovation, particularly when the shift towards economic instruments is coupled with clear definitions of expected outcomes and performance which are both realistic and linked with required revisions of the relevant regulations.

Industry has not been actively involved in the shaping and influencing of regulation (OECD 1996a). Only recently in few countries (the Netherlands, some Scandinavian countries) has industry in general been involved in the process of developing regulation.

### Public Awareness

Public awareness is one of the cornerstones of environmental policy. It influences consumers' behaviour thus stimulating demand for environmental goods and services. A predictable development of public awareness would create stability in the markets and could encourage innovation in the long term.

The attitudes of industry have changed during the last few years. Sustainable development is seen throughout the OECD area as an opportunity not as a threat to the development of business in the long term. A good example of this attitude is the European forestry industry which is exploring in joint projects new business opportunities arising from sustainable development. It has also conducted an independent study on the sustainability of the pulp and paper industry (IIED 1996) and made a joint initiative to the European Commission to launch a Task Force on industrial use of renewable resources.

The environmental awareness remains, however, to be a major issue in the future, in particular in some areas such as e.g. agriculture and tourism.

## 5. Some Concluding Remarks

RTD and innovation policies and environmental policies are highly interrelated through a number of links at various levels. Innovation policy can make significant contributions to sustainable development and environmental policy shapes in many different ways the conditions for innovation.

The scope of RTD and innovation policies has been expanding towards diffusion and absorption of new knowledge and towards interaction with other relevant policies. Sustainable development is one of the most relevant policy areas where the progress in interaction has, however, been quite modest, in particular in Europe. A major effort is required to improve the interaction between RTD and innovation policies and environmental policies.

Environmental policies have focused almost exclusively on environmental research and the development of cleaner technologies. In the future these supply side policies need to be developed as part of a larger, systemic, approach to promoting technological transformation towards cleaner products and processes. Without clear market demand new technologies will not be developed nor disseminated. *Thus the natural next step for government environmental policies would be to develop by means of appropriate interventions a strong demand for new clean technologies and relevant innovation.* This would also involve a close interaction with the RTD and innovation policies.

*The scientific base for sustainable development needs to be strengthened.* In particular, the interaction between technological change and sustainable development is not yet sufficiently understood. This understanding is an important element of the integration of innovation and sustainable development and is needed for the development of complementary, mutually reinforcing policy measures in both of these policy areas. *A sufficiently comprehensive and ambitious international programme might be considered to respond to these requirements.*

The current administrative arrangements at the national level or in the international organizations do not seem to facilitate a natural development of the interaction between innovation policy and environmental policy. *New arrangements both nationally and internationally are needed to create fora for dialogue and interaction at the policy level.*

*The organizational rearrangements should be complemented by joint ventures.* RTD projects and programmes, expert committees and other joint efforts can provide important bridging instruments and facilitate significantly the development of interaction and mutual understanding.

RTD and innovation policies while having their main emphases on knowledge creation and diffusion are intrinsically facilitating sustainable development by creating new technologies and providing mechanisms for their diffusion and absorption. However, the question to what extent environmental objectives should influence the innovative activities and technological change remains. It seems reasonable to assume that some guidance is needed to see to it that technological change will not take a direction which is detrimental for environment. On the other hand, it is reasonable to accept that not all technological development must directly contribute to sustainable development. *A balance between environmental objectives and the other objectives of innovation policy must be found.*

*It is important to take better into account the needs of innovation in all planning and preparation of policies and policy instruments aimed at sustainable development.* This is urgent in the regulatory reforms. In addition to this it might be appropriate to reassess all the existing environmental regulations to explore their impact on innovation.

*Environmental regulations should be developed from technology-based regulations and end-of-pipe solutions towards more performance-based regulations and comprehensive systems solutions.* Regulations should also encourage completely new solutions and innovations rather than modifications of existing technologies. The regulatory framework should also be sufficiently predictable and stable.

## References

Banks R. D. & G. R. Heaton (1995): An Innovation driven environmental policy. Issues in Science and Technology Policy; Environmental Policy, pp. 43-51

Eureka (1993): Evaluation of Eureka Industrial and Economic Effects. Brussels.

European Commission (1995): Green Paper on Innovation. Luxemburg.

Hernesniemi H., M. Lammi & P. Yl-Anttila (1996): Advantage Finland - The Future of Finnish Industries. Helsinki.

IIED (International Institute for Environment and Development) (1996): Towards a Sustainable Paper Cycle. London.

Jacobs D., P. Boekholt & W. Zegveld (1990): De economische kracht van Nederland. The Hague.

OECD 1994: Supply side policies to augment government support for promoting cleaner technologies. OECD. Paris.

OECD 1996a: The global environmental goods and services industry. Paris.

OECD 1996b: Technology, productivity and job creation. Paris.

OECD 1996c: Regulatory Reform and Innovation. Paris.

OTA 1994: Industry, Technology and the Environment. Washington.

# 4. Annex

# Research and Technology Policies and Sustainable Development - The Situation in the USA, Japan, Sweden and The Netherlands*

*Uwe Kuntze*

## 1. Introduction

For this study research and technology (R&T) policy was defined in analogy to the delimination of the political sector as resulting from the nature of the departments of the German Federal Ministry for Education, Science, Research and Technology (BMBF). Other fields of governmental action with sustained effect on technological development and diffusion as e.g. public purchasing or the factual intervention, e.g. in the field of infrastructure technologies (traffic infrastructure amongst others things) were only taken into consideration when strong indications as to their systematical use with regard to the paradigm resulted. Government regulations are dealt with accordingly.

As basic parts, research and technology policies with regard to the paradigm of sustainable development comprise particularly the R&T areas of energy, especially the increase of energy efficiency, and the development of additive as well as integrated environmental technologies ("clean(er) technologies"). This concerns R&T areas which have been part of government R&T policies in all countries dealt with (as well as in Germany) for about two decades, and may therefore already be called "traditional". Since the factual point of main emphasis of the research and technology policies with regard to sustainable development is the development of energy and environmental technologies in the countries dealt with these are given priority in the following account.

* This paper is an abridged version of the final report "International Comparison of Research and Technology Policies with Regard to the Paradigm of Sustainable Development", by Uwe Kuntze and Marisa Diana Pfister (1996)

In fact, the paradigm of sustainable development concerns the much more comprehensive approach of social and economic development within the framework of global and inter-generational equity at simultaneous conservation of nature. A reduction of this paradigm to ecological criteria or protection of resources would fall much too short.

For a short deduction of criteria for a sustainable research and technology policies as well as for the judgement of the policies executed in the countries dealt with, this report adopts the definitions of the commission of inquiry ("Enquête-Kommission") "Protection of Man and Environment - Valuation Criteria for Ecologically Harmless Product Cycles in the Industrial Society" of the Deutscher Bundestag (German Federal Parliament, see: BT-Drs. 12/8260, 1994, particularly p. 37 ff.).

Following their arguments, there still are considerable problems concerning the operationalisation of sustainable development and there still is no consensus for ensuing criteria for corresponding research and technology policies. The following, however, should rank among the core contents:

- Environmental and social compatibility, sustainment of the economic utilisation of environmental potentials, defect tolerance and the interference with nature shall be criteria for the support of research and development projects.
- Questions of the natural and engineering sciences shall be examined in combination with economic, social and legal questions; in order to work out societal action options, interdisciplinary problem and solution oriented research is necessary.
- Needed is basic knowledge of ecological systems and precautional research, as well as research into the definition and operationalisation of the fundamental rules of the sustainable development approach.
- The working out of cross-system, integral problem analyses and problem solutions including technology; furthermore for the coping with short and medium-term problems curative resp. preferably integrated environmental technology is needed.
- Exploration of the social frame conditions (e.g. moral concepts, lifestyles) for the enforcement of a sustained way of life and economy.

The research and technology policies of the USA, Japan, Sweden, and the Netherlands have been investigated for this study whether elements of these core contents for a research and technology policy towards sustainable development have been realised. The study only analysed written, open to the public material (official one as well as grey literature) concerning the policies pursued by the governments. It had not been subject matter of this project to establish the actual realisation, the backgrounds and the latent tendencies of policies in this field by personal interviews, so that certain reservations have to be made in the face of the assessment of the particular policies. The state of information is early 1996.

## 2. Short Characteristics of the Policies in the Countries Dealt With

### United States of America

With President Clinton's coming into office in 1993 a change of paradigms to a more application-oriented R&D policy took place; over and above that research and development for the protection of the environment received a higher status. Under the heading "Bridge to a Sustainable Future" (US Government 1995) the results of a wide social dialogue were summarised in long-term vision for the coming 25 years in April 1995. The main items of this "National Environmental Technology Strategy" concern all social levels:

- Change from curative and additive to integrated resource saving ("clean(er)") technologies with higher environment-technological efficiency,
- Introduction of supporting measures for a speedy diffusion,
- Transition to flexible economic policy (e.g. integrated ecological management),
- Support of more efficient local infrastructures, and
- Improvement of the social education in environmental problems.

In the respective official papers of the US government, the term "sustainable development" is not used, although the association is constantly suggested. On the whole, however, they rather start from a limited approach concentrating on a national view and the criteria of more efficient technologies, and understanding development primarily as economic growth. For 2020, only few quantitative targets are named. Actually, they mainly concern the use of more efficient technology for the purpose of environmental protection with the point of main emphasis on "clean(er)" technologies, and the strengthening of the international competitiveness of the American industry through environmental technology. The proceeding report "Technology for a Sustainable Future" (US Government 1994) indicated clearly: A sustainable development should be initiated with the assistance of active industrial policy, particularly by direct project support. Economic growth should create jobs, protect human health and the environment, and support the conservation of natural resources for present and future generations.

The *President's Council on Sustainable Development* was appointed in 1993 to develop a national campaign strategy for sustainable development. Its recent report (PCDS, 1996), too, remains relatively vague regarding an operationalisation of sustainable development. The broad definition of sustainable development used in the

President's decree of appointment as "economic growth, useful for present and future generations without having harmful influence on the biological systems of the planet" is vividly translated and shortened to "pollution is waste, waste is inefficient and inefficiency is expensive" (PCSD 1996). The report does not contain any quantitative (reduction) targets and does not mention any time frame for the "targets to be reached collectively". The problem of international distribution is only dealt with cursorily and - from an American point of view - rather described as an economic chance. Under the heading "economic prosperity and growth", the distribution problems ensuing from the paradigm of sustainable development were discussed only sparingly. The social inequalities in the USA shall be solved by additional growth. Above that the target of sustainable development is defined as creating "more jobs". Alternatives - e.g.: "sufficient supply" - are not discussed as a dimension of value, though a discussion on social values is explicitly denoted as necessary to put the programme of sustainable development in concrete terms. A theme that runs all through the report is *product stewardship*, elsewhere expanded into *corporate stewardship* or generally as *stewardship*. Wherever possible, this shall be carried on voluntarily. However, the report remains without commitment in so far as it does not make a priorisation of the discussed instruments, and does also not explain on which factors of the system of production and consumption the realisation should be started.

There are, however, two components of the national environmental technology programme strategy which constitutively belong to a research and technology policies for sustainable development: in the main theme of ecology systems research the socio-economic dimensions of the development of the environment are dealt with, too, and within the *National Environment Partnership System* of the co-operation of the federal government and the federal states the responsibility of the states shall be strengthened by the determination of national and mutually agreed regional targets for environmental protection.

With regard to a sustainable development a revised version of the energy policy followed in July 1995: "Sustainable Energy Strategy - Clean and Secure Energy for a Competitive Economy" (US Department of Energy 1995). In future the use of energy shall increase international competitiveness, protect the environment and protect the safety of the nation (i.e. reduce the dependability from energy imports).

The fate of the President's environment-oriented R&T policy is essentially connected with the results of the budget debates. As long as the way and the means towards a sustainable development are disputed in the field of home affairs, the realisation of the long-term visions will stay in the dark. For the time being (early 1996) continuity can mainly be expected for the export promotion of environmental technologies. In view of the international growth forecasts there is widespread consensus on the target to take the lead of the global market in environmental technologies.

**Japan**

The Japanese economy is particularly dependent from energy imports. The considerate use of energy resources in short supply has therefore been an important target of the R&D policy since 1966. The paradigm of "Sustainable Growth" shall connect a high economic growth with an energy input as low as possible. The starting point for this paradigm are the conditions of economic shortages, and less an altered environmental awareness. To reduce the energy dependency, the extension of the use of nuclear energy is traditionally supported.

The Japanese government sees its role primarily in the control and co-ordination of private R&D activities, and less in the direct support of projects. Long-term visions of social development potentials supply the basis. They are worked out in a dialogue with the economic sector. The development of R&D "in harmony with mankind and nature" is one of the targets for the 1990s. Competition policy assists the co-operative dialogue of the economy by establishing elbow room in antitrust rules.

Already in the run-up to the 1992 Rio conference the Japanese government had intensified its policy regarding the global targets of environment conservation. In 1989 a Council of Ministers for Global Environmental Protection was constituted which submitted inter alia in 1990 a "Comprehensive Promotion Programme for Global Environment Research, Monitoring and Technology Development for Fiscal 1990" (Government of Japan 1994 a).

After Rio a new "Basic Environment Law", took effect in November 1993. It is regarded as the central element of the Japanese environmental policy. Here, for the first time, the target of sustainable development was put into words: "...sustainable development is ensured by fostering sound economic development with reduced environmental load...". Here the global perspectives are taken up and the interests of future generations are considered as well as national and international measures defined. The law also provides for the government to establish a "Basic Environment Plan" (Government of Japan 1994b). New measures are scheduled in the following fields: appraisal of environmental effects, general economic settings, support of institutions and projects for environmental preservation, support of the use of environmentally friendly products, environmental instruction, support of voluntary private activities, support of science and R&D, international co-operation including technology transfer to the developing countries.

Though the Japanese government emphasises the contribution of R&D as a link for the harmonisation of economic growth and protection of the environment, a long-term environmental strategy corresponding to a "Green Plan" does not exist. Particularly there is no unambiguous definition of sustainable development, and the R&T policy is not aligned coherently to this target. Factually, by sustainable development the Japanese R&T policy considers the use of nuclear energy, saving of energy, and environmental technology; the global aspect of the programme of sustainable development, however, is hardly picked out as a central theme.

**Sweden**

The Swedish environmental policy started early by putting the main emphasis on the traffic and energy fields. In both fields the state intervenes directly or indirectly in the market in order to stimulate the innovation process for environmentally favourable solutions. The focal point is the reduction of the emission of pollutants.

In favour of renewable resources, e.g. projects in the energy management field and in the fields of bio-fuels, wind energy and solar energy are supported. In the traffic sector R&D programmes on the subject of alternative fuels and on the subject of the development of electric cars have been initiated.

Already the research law of 1990 (Swedish Government 1990) set the goal to initiate a sustainable development and emphasised the importance of interdisciplinary research for sustainable development. In view of the complexity of environmental subjects a systems-oriented approach is recommended. Interdisciplinary technical research projects and the integration of technical, social, medical and legal questions are named as key elements for a sustainable development. New technologies and changes in the life styles are therefore seen as factors of equal importance for a sustainable development.

In the beginning of 1994 a Foundation for Strategic Environmental Research (MISTRA) was set up which was to appropriate 250 mill. SEK p.a. for research in sustainable development from the end of 1995, among them for socio-economic questions, too.

In order to realise sustainable development the Swedish government applies specific reduction and recycling targets, a broad social dialogue, government demand *("green procurement policy")* and market-conforming control mechanisms, covenants (the voluntary engagement of the industry), eco-labelling and eco-audits, and the system of taxes and duties for the reduction of emissions from the energy and traffic fields (Swedish Ministry of the Environment 1994a).

The ecocycle law of 1993 extended the manufacturer's liability to the total product life; it is directed at returning waste and scrap to nature in such way as to make them absorbable by the natural cycle ("ecocycle") (Swedish Ministry of the Environment 1994b). Correspondingly the industry will have to improve its resources management considerably. First of all, this concerns the choice of the "correct" raw materials, the increase of the resource efficiency and the share of recycling as well as the recovery of raw materials. The exploration of the complex system of materials cycles is defined as precondition for an efficient resource management and the closure of the material flows.

In compliance with the global co-responsability in a concept of sustainable development the Swedish government has taken initiative, too, in order to finance assistance in the Baltic and Eastern European States as well as in Africa for a further reduction of the $CO_2$ emission, especially in the field of renewable resources and energy management.

Within the framework of an extensive tax reform Sweden introduced environment ("Pigou") taxes for the traffic and energy sectors in 1991. Within a short time only the levying of these excise taxes resulted in a significant decrease of the emission of pollutants. Environmental-conscious consumer behaviour and the development of non pollutant products by the industry mark the success of the "environment taxes". It must be considered, though, that this development was supported by the simultaneous introduction of further actions of environmental policy (inter alia information, advice, teaching actions, investment subsidies).

**The Netherlands**

The Netherlands early recognised the necessity for a long-term environmental policy and translated it into the National Environmental Policy Plan (NEPP) in 1989, cf. the contribution of Paul de Jongh in this volume. Sustainable development is declared to be the main target. The closure of materials cycles, the saving of energy and improvements of the product cycle management and of the production process are named as key elements and quantitative targets are fixed. They underline the general view of the Netherlands government in the pursuance of a sustainable development.

Important parts of NEPP are consultations and negotiations to mobilise society for the changes. Above that, a system of incentives was created to tune the behaviour of all social groups in to the target of a sustainable development. Success was achieved primarily with the introduction of duties and taxes. Subsidies, however, were less successful.

The contribution of technology for the targets of environmental policy is explicitly analysed. A positive contribution is above all expected for the solution of short-term environmental problems. Here direct and indirect measures for the support of environmental technologies are favoured. The government programmes for an extensive life-cycle management and a cascade approach shall provide knowledge for the medium-term instruments in R&D policy. In the longer term technology would not be able to contribute significantly, states the Dutch Commission on Longer-Term Environmental Policy (CLTM, cf. Vergragt, Jansen 1993).

In the Sustainable Technology Development Programme (STD; Netherlands' Government 1994; Jansen, Vergragt 1992) this question was taken up. Based on the definition of a desired state of sustainability in 50 year's time the requirements for a decrease of emissions and the level of resource use were determined, and with the aid of an approach called *"back-casting"* the necessary technological developments are defined for a number of fields of social needs. For selected technologies a process of appraisal and discussion (*"illustrative process"*) is then carried out that serves the demonstration of conceivable technologies with a positive contribution to the target. In this way a long-term orientation of private R&D activities shall be started without a direct government support of the technological development having to follow.

All in all technology and therefore R&D policy are above all ascribed to play a supporting part on the way to a sustainable development. The most important contribution, though, is expected from cultural and structural changes.

## 3. Summary

While the term "sustainable development" had only come into widespread political discussion since the submission of the Brundtland report in 1987, particularly the World Conference on Environment and Development in Rio de Janeiro 1992 and its preparation acted as a catalyst which enormously speeded the development of national policies. This is clearly recognisable in the instance of Japan with the passage of a "Basic Environment Law", and of the USA with the appointment of the President's Council on Sustainable Development.

Nevertheless it has realistically to be stated that the sometimes almost inflationary use of the term "sustainable development" does not always go along with a real alteration of the policy, leave alone that the policy exhausts the approach in full. Above all an intensification of the earlier followed research and technology lines can be noted, particularly in the fields of:

- development of "environmentally friendly" energy forms (including nuclear energy) and increase of the energy efficiency
- development of additive and rehabilitating and integrated environmental technologies.

Although technological modernisation can contribute considerably to the saving of resources, it can be inferred from existing analyses on the other hand that an overly optimistic expectation in a virtually independent dynamism of a saving of resources by new technologies needs a warning for there are varied overlapping trends and specific saving effects are often overcompensated for by economic growth. Furthermore, in many fields only a hesitant use of resource-saving technologies can be noted. In these areas a shifting of the attention of research policy to socio-economic research into the conditions of conversion is needed which identifies the impediments to the use of these technologies and suggests steps to their surmounting. To make producers and consumers prepare for this the research and technology policies have to act considering longer-term perspectives: technical solutions for future problems will increasingly become more complex and therefore will require a considerable temporal precourse since they have to be embedded in *optimised systemic solutions*.

Over and above that the paradigm of sustainable development concerns the much more comprehensive approach of social and economic equity with a simultaneous preservation of nature, so that a reduction of the paradigm to ecological criteria or saving of resources falls much to short.

For a short deduction of criteria for sustainable research and technology policies as well as for the judgement of the policies executed in the countries dealt with, this report adopts the definitions of the commission of inquiry ("Enquête-Kommission") "Protection of Man and Environment - Valuation Criteria for Ecologically Harmless Product Cycles in the Industrial Society" of the Deutscher Bundestag (German Federal Parliament), cf. the introduction of this paper.

Following their arguments, there still are considerable problems concerning the operationalisation of sustainable development and there still is no consensus for ensuing criteria for corresponding research and technology policies. In detail, however, the following should rank among the core contents:

- The working out of basic ecological knowledge and of a scientific basis for the determination of the effect of human action, for an improved early-warning system for ecological problems, and as a basis for regulations and environmental economic instruments.
- The development of technical solutions for the prevention, reduction and rehabilitation of ecological damage.
- The increase of the resource efficiency, including the closing of materials cycles.
- The substitution of non-renewable resources.
- The exploration of the social, economic and political conditions causing ecological problems, as well as specifying their solutions, and of the social frame conditions of the transition to a sustainable way of life and economy.
- The consideration of the international dimension including the development of appropriate technologies and measures of technology transfer.

- The definition of sustainability targets as criterion for the support of research and development projects.

Considering the inclusion of these elements of sustainable development in the research and technology policies of the USA, Japan, Sweden and The Netherlands, the following can be summarised:

- Eco-systems research is spread through all countries, i.e. the acquisition of basic ecological knowledge, serving as well as a scientific basis for the determination of effects of human action and for improved early-warning systems against environmental problems.

- The development of technical solutions to avoid, reduce and rehabilitate damages to the environment has been a central field of the research and technology policies of the countries dealt with for two decades or more. Developments for an integrated environmental technology have been intensified or started in the beginning of the 1990s, particularly emphasised by the USA in its *Environmental Technology Initiative.*

- The increase of the resource efficiency (including energy) in diverse facets has also been part of the standard repertoire of the research and technology policies for some time because it is often combined with economic advantages. It can be characterised as an element of sustainable research and technology policies when it is combined with defined sustainability targets, like in Sweden or the Netherlands.
  In particular the closing of materials cycles helps to increase the efficiency, consequently this target is part of the instruments of research and technology policies in all countries dealt with. However, also with this subject, the binding character of the political statements in the Swedish and Dutch documents is greatest; here are also the clearest plans for a closing of materials cycles at the highest possible level (re-use, cascade use) which may contribute more to a sustainable development than a recycling on a purely material level.

- The approach to substitute non-renewable materials is prominent in the energy sector in all countries where a replacement for fossil fuels is searched for particularly. In other fields of technology there are no indications toward this strategy, but this picture may result from the insufficient level of specification of the available material.

- The differences between the individual countries become clearer in the subject field of research for social, economic and political conditions which cause environmental problems and determine their solutions, and the general social framework of the transition to a sustainable way of life and economy. Here the Netherlands stand out with their approach to the analysis of the fields of social needs within the framework of the programme *Sustainable Technology Development*, while the actual reach of the programmatic statements would have to be checked for the other countries.

- Belonging to the global dimension of the paradigm of sustainable development is the observing of a country's international responsibility which could show itself e.g. in the development of appropriate technologies and measures of technology transfer. This dimension, too, is mentioned in all programmatic documents, even if in some cases obviously only with marginal activities resp. exploited in view of resulting marketing opportunities.

- The definition of sustainability targets as a criterion for the support of research and development projects cannot be found in the strategic documents. Concerning this topic, too, it might be found that with a more detailed material this image should be made more discriminating.

- Quantitative reduction targets with a definite time frame are used particularly in Sweden and the Netherlands, and in the Netherlands they are derived from an operationalised definition of the paradigm of sustainable development.

It had been agreed upon to analyse in this project written, open to the public material exclusively (official one as well as grey literature). It had not been subject matter of this project to establish the actual realisation, the backgrounds and the latent tendencies of policies in this field by personal interviews, so that certain reservations have to be made in the face of the assessment of the particular policies. The details of the national plans and regulations, often essential for a judgement, may stay hidden thereby.

Keeping this memento in mind, the Dutch *Sustainable Technology Development* programme in connection with the national environmental policy plan (NEPP) appears to be a particularly productive and innovative step towards a development of research and technology policies for a sustainable development. This programme reflects all requirements drawn up by the German parliamentary Commission of Inquiry (cf. section 1) regarding the inclusion of elements of sustainable development into the research and technology policies, viz. orientation towards social needs, orientation of action towards the processes of R&D and innovation, and interdisciplinarity. The transferability of such a strongly corporatist programme into the context of the German research and technology policies or those of other countries would have to be examined.

# References

BT-Drs. 12/8260 (1994): Deutscher Bundestag, 12. Wahlperiode, Drucksache 12/8260: Bericht der Enquete-Kommission "Schutz des Menschen und der Umwelt - Bewertungskriterien und Perspektiven für umweltverträgliche Stoffkreisläufe in der Industriegesellschaft": Die Industriegesellschaft gestalten - Perspektiven für einen nachhaltigen Umgang mit Stoff- und Materialströmen, Bonn, 12.07.1994

Government of Japan (1994a): Japan's Action Report on Climate Change, Tokyo 1994.

Government of Japan (1994b): Basic Environment Plan, Translation in English, Tokyo, December 16, 1994.

Jansen, J.L.A.; Vergragt, Ph.J. (1992): Sustainable Development: A Challenge to Technology!, Proposal for the interdepartmental research programme 'Sustainable technological development', June 1992

Kuntze, U.; Pfister, M.D. (1996): Internationaler Vergleich der Forschungs- und Technologiepolitik im Hinblick auf das Leitbild nachhaltig zukunftsverträglicher Entwicklung, Endbericht des Fraunhofer-Instituts für Systemtechnik und Innovationsforschung (ISI) an das Büro für Technikfolgenabschätzung beim Deutschen Bundestag, Karlsruhe, Juli 1996.

NEPP (1989): National Environmental Policy Plan, "To choose or to loose", Second Chamber, session 1988 - 1989, 21137, nos. 1-2, State Publishing Company, den Haag (The Netherlands), English edition

Netherlands' Government (1994): Looking Back from the Future, Dutch Governmental Programme for Sustainable Technology Development (STD), den Haag, February 1994.

PCSD (1996): Report of the President's Council on Sustainable Development [USA], in: http://www1.whitehouse. gov/WH/EOP/pcsd/

Swedish Government (1990): The Swedish Government's Research Bill, Prop. 1989/90, Stockholm 1990.

Swedish Ministry of the Environment and Natural Ressources (1994a): Sweden's National Report Under The United Nations Framework Convention on Climate Change, Stockholm 1994.

Swedish Ministry of the Environment and Natural Ressources (1994b): The Ecocycle - The New View of the Environment, A Summary of the Swedish Government's Ecocycle Bill (1992/93:180), Stockholm 1994; Swedish Environmental Protection Agency, Towards an Ecocycle Society, Stockholm 1994.

U.N. World Commission on Environment and Development (1987): Our Common Future (Brundtland Commission Report), Geneve 1987.

U.S. Department of Energy (1995): Sustainable Energy Strategy - Clean and Secure Energy for a Competitive Economy, Washington, D.C., July 1995.

U.S. Government (1994): Technology for a Sustainable Future, Washington, D.C. 1994.

U.S. Government (1995): Bridge to a Sustainable Future, Washington D.C. 1995.

Vergragt, P. J.; Jansen, L. (1993) Sustainable Technology Development: The Making of a Dutch Long-Term oriented Technology Programme, *in:* Project Appraisal, Vol. 8, No. 3, September 1993.

# The Authors

**Jacqueline Cramer**

Prof. Dr. Jacqueline Cramer was born in 1951, and studied biology at the University of Amsterdam from 1970 till 1976; scientific staffmember of the Department of Biology and Society (1976-1980), and associate professor of the Department of Science Dynamics (1980-1989). Since March 1989 she worked as a senior researcher at the Centre for Technology and Policy Studies of the Netherlands Organisation for Applied Scientific Research (TNO). Her research related to the question of how government, industry and social organizations can stimulate the development and use of cleaner technology.

From April 1995 - February 1997 Jacqueline Cramer worked at Philips Consumer Electronics as a senior consultant, detached from the Centre for Technology and Policy Studies (TNO). Since then she is working with AKZO Nobel in a similar position.

Jacqueline Cramer published many articles, reports and books, under which recently "Theory and practice of integrated chain management" (1993) (with others); "Towards a sustainable city" (1994), and "Development and Implementation of STRETCH (Selection of sTrategic EnvironMental CHallenges)" (1997). She is a member of various advisory bodies of the Dutch government and industry. From 1/11/1990 - 1/9/1996 she was also professor, occupying an endowed chair in Environmental Science at the Department of Environmental Science of the University of Amsterdam. Since September 1996 she works as a parttime professor in environmental management at the Tilburg University.

**Paul Ekins**

Paul Ekins has degrees from Imperial College, London [BSc (Eng)], Birkbeck College, London [MSc (Econ), Ph.D. (Econ)], and University of Bradford [MPhil (Peace Studies)]. From 1990 to 1995 he was a Research Fellow at the Department of Economics, Birkbeck College, London, analysing the relationship between environmental sustainability and economic growth. He is now Senior Lecturer in Environmental Policy at Keele University, and is a Research Associate at the Department of Applied Economics at the University of Cambridge. Paul Ekins is also Senior Consultant to Cambridge Econometrics and joint editor of its publication *UK Energy and Environment* and is a Director of the sustainable development charity Forum for the Future, directing its Sustainable Economy Unit. Paul Ekins' academic work focuses on the conditions and policies for achieving an environmentally sustainable economy. In addition to numerous papers and articles, he is the author of *A New World Order* (Routledge, 1992), co-author of *Wealth Beyond Measure* (Gaia Books, London) and co-editor of *Real-Life Economics* (Routledge, 1992) and *Global Warming and Energy Demand* (Routledge, 1995). In 1994 he received the UNEP Global 500 Award "for outstanding environmental achievement".

**Paul E. de Jongh**

Paul E. de Jongh was born in 1950; he studied environmental biology and got his Masters degree from the University of Leyden in 1976. From 1977 to 1996 he was member of the Dutch Ministry of Housing, Spatial Planning and Environment; in this function he was project leader of the first Dutch National Environmental Policy Plan and later served as deputy director-general for the environment. After an assignment as interim director for Strategy and Coordination at the Dutch Ministry of Transport and Waterworks, since 1997 he serves as director for Nature Management in the Dutch Ministry for Agriculture, Nature Management and Fisheries. Between 1991 and 1996 he was a member of the Environmental Policy Committee of the OECD and in 1996/1997 he was vice chairman and member of the bureau of the United Nations Commission for Sustainable Development. He is a board member of the Sustainability Challenge Foundation and initiator and chairman of the International Network of Greenplanners.

**Uwe Kuntze**

Uwe Kuntze, born in 1945; after economic studies (business administration) he joined the Fraunhofer Institute for Systems and Innovation Research (ISI), Karlsruhe in 1973; he worked on numerous research projects in the fields of industrial innovation strategies, innovative behaviour of small and medium-sized enterprises, national and international technology and innovation policy, evaluation of technology and innovation programmes, environmental economics; additionally, he is scientific assistant to the director of ISI.

**Frieder Meyer-Krahmer**

Frieder Meyer-Krahmer was born in 1949, and studied economics, mathematics and political science at the universities of Heidelberg and Bonn. In 1982 he was visiting research fellow at the Yale University, New Haven. Habilitation Stuttgart 1989. He is the director of the Fraunhofer Institute for Systems and Innovation Research (ISI), Karlsruhe, and professor of innovation economics at the University Louis Pasteur, Strasbourg. His research subjects are technology and innovation policy, evaluation of governmental R&D programmes, barriers to innovation in industry, innovation in small and medium-sized firms, innovation and regional development, structural change and industrial policy, innovation and environment. He is member of the Scientific Board of the Maastricht Economic Research Institute on Innovation and Technology (MERIT) and of the Advisory Board of the Science Policy Research Unit (SPRU), University of Sussex, and one of the main editors of "*Research Policy. Journal devoted to Research Policy, Research Management and Planning*".

**Lars J. Nilsson**

Lars J. Nilsson was born on August 12, 1963. He has a MSc (1987) in Engineering Physics and a PhD (1993) in Environmental and Energy Systems Studies from the Institute of Technology, University of Lund, Sweden. He was a Visiting Research Fellow at the Center for Energy and Environmental Studies at Princeton University 1994-95 and is the acting Professor of the Department for Environmental and Energy Systems Studies since June 1995.
He has primarily worked in the field of energy policy and end-use oriented energy analysis, and with assessments of energy efficient end-use and renewable energy technologies. He has also studied long-term trends in national energy intensities, nuclear proliferation issues, and regulatory and institutional aspects on the integration of intermittent sources of electricity.

**Erkki Ormala**

Erkki Ormala was born 1950. He has his M.Eng. degree in 1974 and his Dr.Tech. degree in 1986 from the Helsinki University of Technology.
He worked as a research engineer at the Technical Research Centre of Finland 1974-1987. In 1976 he was a visiting scholar at Stanford University in the USA and in 1982 at the International Institute of Applied Systems Analysis in Austria. Since 1987 he has been the secretary of the Science and Technology Policy Council of Finland. The Council is chaired by the Prime Minister with the task to give advice to the Government and administration in issues related to science, technology and innovation policies.
He has published over fourty papers on evaluation and innovation policies. He has been a consultant to industrial companies and worked as an expert for international organisations and for a number of European governments. In 1992-1993 he chaired the international expert group which carried out the evaluation of EUREKA. Since 1994 he has been a member of a number of EC R&D Programme evaluation panels. He is currently the chairman of the OECD Working Group for Technology and Innovation Policy.

**Walter R. Stahel**

Walter R. Stahel works today as a consultant in the field of business management and industrial analysis. An alumnus of the Swiss Federal Institute of Technology (ETH) in Zürich, where he received a diploma in architecture and town planning in 1971, he worked for several years as a private architect in the UK and Switzerland; in 1973, he joined the Battelle Geneva Research Centres as project manager in the

Centre for applied economics, working mainly in the fields of business strategy and feasibility studies; in 1980 he became personal assistant to the CEO of a holding company with worldwide activities in railway maintenance, shipping and real estate, with special responsibility as a financial controller.

Since 1984, Stahel has worked as an independent business consultant mainly in the field of:

- research into utilization-related technologies such as the re-use, repair, reconditioning and technological upgrading of components, goods and systems, from points of view of technical and commercial strategies as well as industrial design,
- risk management and insurance, in terms of an industrial and a service economy,
- regional economic development,

in most European countries, the U.S. and Middle and Far Eastern countries.

Since 1982, Stahel has been one of the founder-directors of the Product-Life Institute, Geneva. He is associate editor of the Geneva Papers on Risk and Insurance - Issues and Practice; editor of the Risk Management Newsletter of the Geneva Association; member of the editorial board of The Journal of Industrial Ecology, Yale/USA (MIT Press), and the International Journal for Disaster Prevention and Management, Bradford/UK.

**Rainer Walz**

Rainer Walz was born in 1960, and studied economics and political sciences at the universities of Freiburg and Brock University, Canada. In 1987/88 he was research fellow at the University of Wisconsin, Madison. PhD Freiburg 1992. He is Deputy Head of the Department Environmental Technology and Environmental Economics of the Fraunhofer-Institute for Systems and Innovation Research (ISI), Karlsruhe, and lecturer for applied environmental economics at the University of Karlsruhe. His main research areas are macroeconomic effects of environmental policies, environmental indicators, valuation of environmental problems, and policies for sustainable development and climate protection. He is a member of various national and international committees in the field of environmental economics. In 1993 he received the Friedrich-August-von-Hayek-Award.

# TECHNOLOGY, INNOVATION and POLICY

Series of the Fraunhofer Institute
for Systems and Innovation Research (ISI)

---

Volume 1:
Kerstin Cuhls, Terutaka Kuwahara
**Outlook for Japanese and German Future Technology**
1994. ISBN 3-7908-0800-8

Volume 2:
Guido Reger, Stefan Kuhlmann
**European Technology Policy in Germany**
1995. ISBN 3-7908-0826-1

Volume 3:
Guido Reger, Ulrich Schmoch (Eds.)
**Organisation of Science and Technology at the Watershed**
1996. ISBN 3-7908-0910-1

Volume 4:
Oliver Pfirrmann, Udo Wupperfeld and Joshua Lerner
**Venture Capital and New Technology Based Firms**
1997. ISBN 3-7908-0968-3

Volume 5:
Knut Koschatzky (Ed.)
**Technology - Based Firms in the Innovation Process**
1997. ISBN 3-7908-1021-5

GPSR Compliance

*The European Union's (EU) General Product Safety Regulation (GPSR) is a set of rules that requires consumer products to be safe and our obligations to ensure this.*

*If you have any concerns about our products, you can contact us on ProductSafety@springernature.com*

In case Publisher is established outside the EU, the EU authorized representative is:

Springer Nature Customer Service Center GmbH
Europaplatz 3
69115 Heidelberg, Germany

**Batch number: 10725973**

Printed by Printforce, the Netherlands